THE
TALIBAN PHENOMENON

Afghanistan 1994–1997

THE
TALIBAN PHENOMENON

Afghanistan 1994–1997

With an Afterword covering
major events since 1997

Kamal Matinuddin

OXFORD
UNIVERSITY PRESS

OXFORD

UNIVERSITY PRESS

Great Clarendon Street, Oxford OX2 6DP

Oxford University Press is a department of the University of Oxford.
It furthers the University's objective of excellence in research, scholarship,
and education by publishing worldwide in

Oxford New York

Athens Auckland Bangkok Bogotá Buenos Aires Calcutta
Cape Town Chennai Dar es Salaam Delhi Florence Hong Kong Istanbul
Karachi Kuala Lumpur Madrid Melbourne Mexico City Mumbai
Nairobi Paris São Paulo Singapore Taipei Tokyo Toronto Warsaw

with associated companies in Berlin Ibadan

Oxford is a registered trade mark of Oxford University Press
in the UK and in certain other countries

ISBN 0 19 577903 7

Third Impression 2001

Printed in Pakistan at
Mas Printers, Karachi.
Published by
Ameena Saiyid, Oxford University Press
5-Bangalore Town, Sharae Faisal
PO Box 13033, Karachi-75350, Pakistan.

To my grandchildren, Hamzah, Mashal, Hassan, Ali, Faraz, Maha, and Zoya, who, I pray, will live and prosper within peaceful borders.

CONTENTS

LIST OF MAPS AND PHOTOGRAPHS

LIST OF TABLES

FOREWORD

The Taliban phenomenon created a new and puzzling reality when it first appeared in 1994, gathered momentum, and grew into a force that dominated the Afghan landscape. War-hardened adversaries either joined the Taliban or fell back in disarray. Some observers saw them as militant reformists with sword in one hand and the Koran in the other. The rapidity with which they brought large tracts of war-ravaged territory under control, putting an end to crime and disorder, attracted attention abroad and even moral support in certain quarters, until their draconian measures and obscurantist religiosity raised alarm and disappointment in the region and in the world at large.

The story of the capture of Kabul and the triumphal northward advance of Taliban, their reverses in Mazar-i-Sharif, and the subsequent ebb and flow of the tide of conflict is graphically related by the author. It is supported by a military assessment of the scale of engagements, the correlation of forces, and the strengths and weaknesses of either side. The author has described these and other operational aspects with a precision and coherence that has been lacking in the reports so far available to the public. The political and diplomatic consequences of the Taliban phenomenon have been delineated with rare insight and objectivity. Specially praiseworthy is the clear-sighted appraisal of its impact on the foreign policy and the immediate and long-term security concerns of Pakistan. As the country most directly affected by the continuing convulsion and civil strife in Afghanistan, Pakistan's vital interests are engaged in its outcome. The possibility of the over-flow of the civil war into our territory, the continuing presence of more than one and a half million refugees in

the border areas, the eventuality of the dismemberment or
disintegration of Afghanistan, and the perilous ramifications
of such a development, are among the most valuable parts
of the book. Equally weighty is the author's conclusion
that Pakistan as well as other neighbours must resist the
temptation to intervene in the civil war in the hope of
swinging the outcome of the war in their favour. Experience
shows that in the Afghan setting such efforts are likely to
reap a bitter harvest.

This long awaited, meticulously documented work not
only fills a void in the kaleidoscopic picture that
Afghanistan presents, but also brings out the political,
strategic, and economic significance of peace-making efforts
for the Central Asian Republics and the region as a whole.
The convergent interests of the great powers in this area
and linkages with neighbouring states heighten the
importance of the conclusions in the last part of the book.
Faced with a two-front strategic situation, which has
historically been the nightmare of all continental states,
Pakistan has a high stake in an early and lasting peaceful
settlement on the western front. The hypotheses formulated
in the concluding chapter have a special interest for us.
The author is right in highlighting the most unfavourable
setting. It is the one scenario that all concerned must do
their absolute best to avert.

Lieutenant-General Sahibzada Yaqub Khan

PREFACE

During the course of my appointment as the Director General of the Institute of Strategic Studies, Islamabad, besides being the editor of the monthly publication entitled *The Afghanistan Report*, I came into contact with a number of Afghan leaders who were then actively engaged in the Afghan jihad against the Soviet occupation of their country.

Later, I delved into the Afghan problem much more deeply when carrying out research for my book on Afghanistan called *Power Struggle in the Hindu Kush*. I interviewed all the important Afghan leaders and went to Moscow and to Tehran to ascertain their long-term interests in Afghanistan. As a student of international affairs I have kept myself abreast of the developments across our western border since completing my book.

My own views about peace returning to Afghanistan after the withdrawal of the Soviet troops from that country were at odds with many of those optimists who sincerely believed that the Afghans would soon establish an Islamic government in Afghanistan which would be friendly to Pakistan. I had studied the Afghan situation long enough to come to the conclusion that there were major differences between the rival militia and, since all of them were armed and supported by outside powers, the struggle for ascendancy would continue in Afghanistan.

The emergence of the Taliban on the Afghan stage gave further proof of the divisions amongst the Afghans on the question of the future of their country. Ever since the Taliban gained international attention, numerous articles have appeared on their origin, intentions, and capabilities. Many Afghan watchers have expressed their opinions on the strengths and weaknesses of the Taliban, but no comprehensive study has yet been carried out on this new phenomenon which suddenly appeared on the Afghanistan horizon.

A need arose, therefore, to produce a book on the Taliban which could be useful to the casual reader as well as for those carrying out research on Afghanistan at any later date. It is with this end in view that I undertook the task of writing a book on the rise, successes, and failures of the Taliban.

The present book intends to fill the gaps that today exist in presenting the whole picture of the Taliban. It is an attempt to find the source of the Taliban movement and the reasons for their sudden rise. It also highlights the role of the United Nations in trying to bring about a *rapprochement* between the Rabbani regime and the Taliban. The interests of the outside powers and their alleged interference has also been fully covered *vis-à-vis* the Taliban.

Pakistan's Afghan policy in respect of the Taliban movement has been critically analysed. An attempt has been made to look into the future of the Taliban regime by assessing its strength and weaknesses. The impact of an ultra-conservative government in Afghanistan on peace and security in the region has been examined.

ACKNOWLEDGEMENTS

My grateful thanks are due to former Foreign Minister, Lieutenant-General Sahibzada Yaqub Khan, who spared his valuable time to give me his assessment of the Taliban phenomenon and its impact on the geo-strategic environment in the region.

Major-General (retd.) Naseerullah Khan Babar, Interior Minister in the second Bhutto government and an interlocutor between the Taliban and their opponents, gave me his opinion on the Taliban movement in Afghanistan. Ijlal Haider Zaidi, advisor to the second Benazir government on Afghanistan, shared with me his views on the Taliban leadership with whom he had personally negotiated. The former Director-General of the Inter Services Intelligence Directorate, Lieutenant-General (retd.) Hamid Gul, and Qazi Hussain Ahmed, chief of the Jamaat-e-Islami, both of whom have a deep knowledge of Afghan affairs, were very accommodating in granting me interviews.

I am deeply indebted to Dr Azmat Hayat Khan, Director of the Area Study Centre, Central Asia, University of Peshawar, who arranged some very important meetings with both the Taliban and anti-Taliban factions residing in Pakistan. Rahimullah Yusafzai, the well-known journalist, who has several times been inside Afghanistan, was kind enough to give some of the facts concerning the students' militia. Mufti Mohammad Masoom Afghani, the Ambassador-Designate of the Taliban regime in Islamabad, agreed to meet me several times and gave me a detailed account of the origins of the Taliban movement and its future prospects, for which I am deeply indebted.

The United Nations Information Service in Islamabad provided me with relevant material dealing with the United Nations' role in Afghanistan, for which they deserve my special thanks. Mr Percy Abole of the Canadian Foreign Service, who was attached to Ambassador Mahmoud Mestiri during his meetings with the Taliban, related some interesting stories about the situation in and around Kandahar.

Dr Ijaz Shafi Gilani, who has a profound knowledge of Afghan affairs, shared his views on the Afghan phenomenon with me, for which I am grateful. Additional Secretary, Ministry of Foreign Affairs, Iftikhar Murshid and his Director, Mohammad Naeem, were kind enough to provide me with the bio-data of some of the Taliban personalities whom they had met during their meetings in Afghanistan.

My thanks are also due to Lieutenant-General Naseem Rana of the Inter Services Intelligence Directorate for arranging a briefing for me on the current situation in Afghanistan with special reference to the Taliban movement. I am greatly obliged to Professor Ahmed Hasan Dani, the internationally acclaimed archaeologist and historian of the Central Asian region, for going through my initial draft and giving me some valuable suggestions. Faisal Mustafa Siddiqui was kind enough to provide me computer assistance.

Needless to say, the views expressed in this book are entirely mine.

Thank you, Suraiya, for the patience you showed when you found me engrossed in front of the computer for hours on end, unmindful of the assistance needed to do the household chores.

Rawalpindi
14 October 1997

CHAPTER 1

BACKGROUND

Geo-strategic Environment

External Factors

The Afghan state came about as a result of the invasion of
India by Nadir Shah of Persia, after which the Mughals
lost control of all the territories west of the River Indus.
When Nadir Shah was assassinated in AD 1747, Ahmed
Shah Abdali, a twenty-three-year old Durrani Pushtun,[1]
was serving under him as the head of a 4,000-strong Afghan
contingent in Meshad (Persia). On hearing of Nadir's
death, Ahmed Shah fought his way back from Meshad to
Kandahar, where he was proclaimed Shah. It was he who
in AD 1747, founded the kingdom of Afghanistan, with its
capital at Kandahar. Afghanistan then was merely a
confederation of tribes and khanates, with the central
authority confined to the cities only.

The territory north of the Hindu Kush was still a part of
the Bokhara emirate. Later, Ahmed Shah wrested
Badakhshan from the Amir of Bokhara, with the two of
them agreeing to the Amu Darya as the border between
the domains of the Amir and the newly-established
Kingdom of Afghanistan.

Afghanistan is a landlocked country which has stood at
the crossroads of history ever since it was founded. In
present times its location at the junction of three major
powers, Iran, Pakistan, and China, with two other major
powers, Russia and India, only a stone's throw away, makes

it vulnerable to outside interference whenever there is instability within.

Its linkage with Iran goes back to the sixth century BC, when Kabul was included in the Archaemenian empire. Ghazni was part of the Persian kingdom in the tenth century AD. For hundreds of years that followed, present-day Afghanistan was divided between the Mughal and Persian domains, with the cities often changing hands.² Kandahar (the initial seat of the Taliban) and Herat remained Persian towns for centuries, which has given them a distinct Iranian flavour. The Abdalis are half Persian and half Pushtun, and have adopted much of Persian manners and dress, observed Olaf Caroe, who spent a lifetime amongst the Pathans.³ A threat from across the Iran-Afghanistan border is something, therefore, which the Taliban cannot ignore.

The Tsars of Russia had made no secret of their desire to expand their empire southwards towards the warm waters of the Indian Ocean. They were prevented from doing so by Great Britain, which kept them at a safe distance from India. After the defeat of the British at the hands of the Afghans, the new rulers of Russia revived their interest in Afghanistan. In 1921 King Amanullah signed a Treaty of Friendship with Moscow which helped the Soviets to establish a foothold in Afghanistan⁴, leading many decades later, to the actual occupation of that country by Soviet forces. Even after the break-up of the Soviet Union, Russia continues to work towards having a friendly regime below its soft underbelly, which puts it in conflict with the ultra-conservative Taliban of today.

When Sir Mortimer Durand, Foreign Secretary of Great Britain, drew the boundary between Afghanistan and British India in 1893, he bifurcated the Afghan tribes that lived in that region. The Achakzais of Quetta, the Waziris of Waziristan, the Toris and Mengals of Parachinar, the Shinwaris of Khyber, and the Mohmands of the Mohmand Agency have cousins still living in Afghanistan. Except for the Afridis and the Mahsuds, almost all the Afghan tribes have affiliations with their kith and kin in Pakistan. Consequently, they come to each other's help when the need arises, regardless of the international boundary which nominally divides the two Muslim neighbours.

Uninterrupted movement across the Durand Line in both directions has been the norm for centuries. Afghans crossed into Pakistan in large numbers to come to the assistance of the Kashmiris who had revolted against the Hindu maharajah in 1947. Afghan *pawandas* (nomads), known as Kotchis, moved freely between Pakistan and Afghanistan for decades. Millions of Afghan refugees sought shelter in Pakistan. Mujahideen commanders found plenty of brethren in the NWFP and in Balochistan willing to fight along with them for a common cause during the Soviet occupation of their country. It was not uncommon to find Pakistanis being trained in camps in Afghanistan and the Afghans in very large numbers being educated in Pakistani *madaris*.

In spite of the fact that the Afghan rulers, at the behest of the Soviets and the Indians, tried to harm Pakistan, they could not eliminate the strong ties of religious, linguistic, and ethnic affinity that existed between the people of Afghanistan and those living in Balochistan and in the Frontier Province of Pakistan.

Afghanistan needs Pakistan's friendship as it is it's only outlet to the sea. Pakistan requires a stable and friendly Afghanistan for security reasons and commercial benefits. A warm and friendly relationship between them would, therefore, be beneficial for both the countries but is looked upon with suspicion by their neighbours.

India, though a country away, did not put Afghanistan on its political back burner. With quite a few Afghans of Indian origin gainfully employed in Kabul and some other cities, New Delhi continued to take an interest in Afghan affairs, if only to put pressure on Pakistan's western frontier. The bogy of Pukhtunistan was kindled by the Indians and kept alive while the pro-India regime lasted in Afghanistan. The rift between the Rabbani regime and the authorities in Islamabad gave India an opportunity, though shortlived, to get a toe-hold in Afghanistan again.

The Central Asian States, three of which lie just across the northern border of Afghanistan, cannot ignore the developments that are taking place in that country. Turkmen, Uzbeks, and Tajiks are to be found in Afghanistan as well. A natural desire to come to their assistance, therefore, exists amongst the newly independent Muslim republics. Having been under Soviet occupation for nearly seventy years, they are more liberal in their religious attitudes, and are concerned about the possible spillover of the Taliban's rigid interpretation of Islam into their countries.

The Wakhan corridor juts into the Peoples' Republic of China, providing a land link between the two countries. Though passing through very remote areas, it nevertheless allows traffic to go through. China, therefore, does keep a watchful eye on the happenings in Afghanistan, especially with regard to the ideological nature of the conflict in that country. Afghanistan's nearness to the Muslim areas of Sinkiang makes it necessary for the communist leaders of China to see that extremist religious views do not infiltrate into the region from that direction.

Internal Situation

The struggle for power in Afghanistan is not a new phenomenon. It began with the overthrow of King Zahir Shah by his cousin and brother-in-law, Sardar Mohammad Daud, in a bloodless *coup* in 1973. Five years later another struggle took place, and this time plenty of blood was spilled in the presidential palace. Daud and his family were brutally murdered by the pro-Soviet elements in Afghanistan, who were under the false notion that communism was the answer to Afghanistan's backwardness. After Daud, the common enemy, had been eliminated the

Khalq and Parcham, the two communist parties of Afghanistan who had jointly carried out the April *coup*, split up. Now it was a struggle for power between the communists themselves.

Differences between Noor Mohammad Taraki (Khalq) and Hafizullah Amin (Parcham) assumed even greater proportions after Taraki took over the reigns of government in Kabul. Hafizullah Amin, who had helped Taraki to stage the revolution, was waiting in the wings to seize power. Since he had played a significant role in the planning and execution of the *coup* against Daud, he also coveted the topmost position in Afghanistan. Taraki was killed in mysterious circumstances and Amin began his one-man rule over the country. But it did not last long, as only three months later the Soviet-supported Babrak Karmal entered the scene.

The ten long years of struggle against the Soviet occupation of their country did not bring the nation onto a single platform. Although all of the *Islam-pasand* parties fought for the common purpose of evicting the Soviet troops from their land and replacing the communist Afghan government with an Islamic one, they did so separately. Due to the tribal nature of Afghan society, the country could not throw up a charismatic leader who, as an accepted political figure and as the head of a national army, would command the respect of all the anti-communist elements in Afghanistan. The result was that when the common objective was achieved, they began fighting among themselves.

The struggle for power in Afghanistan has, therefore, gone through different phases since 1963. These could be divided as follows:

Phase 1 (1963–73)   Family feuds and Republicans versus Royalists.
Phase 2 (1973–8)   Communists against Republicans.
Phase 3 (1978–9)   Khalq and Parcham fight it out.
Phase 4 (1979–89)   Mujahideen versus the Soviet-backed communists.

Map 1

Afghanistan—Provincial Boundaries

Phase 5 (1989–92) Mujahideen struggle to get rid of Dr Najibullah's communist regime.

Phase 6 (1992–4) Mujahideen jostle for power. The ethnic factor becomes visible.

Phase 7 (1994–) Taliban enter the scene.

As far as the Afghan Mujahideen are concerned, their fratricidal war began on 18 April 1992—the day Dr Syed Mohammad Najibullah was forced to quit the presidency in Kabul. The internecine fighting was expected, as those knocking at the gates of the capital belonged to different tribal groups of the religiously-oriented political parties—each distrustful of the other. Former allies had become competitors for the grand prize. Commander Ahmed Shah Masood (Jamiat-e-Islami) was moving towards Kabul from the north. Engineer Gulbadin Hikmetyar (Hizb-e-Islami) was advancing towards the same objective from the south. General Abdul Rashid Dostum (Jumbish-e-Milli) flew 2,000 of his well trained Uzbeks into Kabul. A head-on clash between all of them was inevitable.[5] There has been no let-up in the fighting since then; in fact, new factors in the power equation have been introduced.

The Afghan jihad was instrumental in the arming of all the ethnic groups. The Tajiks and the Uzbeks, who so far had not had enough clout to demand a share in the running of the affairs of the state, could now do so. With the departure of Najibullah and the arrival of Masood and Dostum's forces in Kabul, the balance of power had visibly shifted in favour of the non-Pushtuns. Kabul, which had always been a Tajik city, despite the fact that the rulers were Pushtuns, was now firmly under their control.

Immediately after the fall of Najibullah, Pakistan's Prime Minister, Mian Mohammad Nawaz Sharif, managed to assemble most of the Afghan leaders and persuade them to sign, on 24 April 1992, an agreement which became known as the Peshawar Accord (Appendix ii). Although Hikmetyar, who at that time was a major player on the Afghanistan scene, did not attend the Peshawar meeting, the government of Pakistan made an announcement that the agreement would ensure a glorious future for Afghanistan. Subsequent events proved how wrong predictions can be, specially when a consensus among factions has not been obtained.

Neither the Pakistan-brokered Peshawar Accord nor the Islamabad Declaration, (Appendix iii) proved effective. The Nangarhar Peace Committee also failed to achieve peace between the rival factions, nor could the OIC or the UN help in settling the issues to the satisfaction of the numerous Afghan blocs. Old enmities came to the surface when the common enemy had been evicted from power: weapons were freely used between the Mujahideen themselves to settle old scores. The members of the former Afghan Interim Government (AIG) fought with each other and quarrelled on the allocation of ministries; there were serious differences also amongst the *ad hoc* cabinet ministers of the provisional administration over the power each would wield. Even the procedure to be adopted for the formation of an Islamic government in Afghanistan became a controversial matter.

The future rulers disagreed on whether elections should be held or not, as some considered elections to be un-Islamic. There was no agreement on whether only elected representatives or a combination of elected and nominated persons should be included in the government-to-be. The composition of the electorate was also a bone of contention, as the definition of a good Muslim was interpreted differently by different militia. Whether the Afghan communists should be included or left out in the cold was another question on which there was no unanimity of thought.[6]

It was most unfortunate that the people of a proud and fiercely independent nation did not have the wisdom to sink their personal animosities when it came to ruling their country along the lines they had been advocating during their combined struggle to get rid of the 'occupation' forces. The result—the jihad against the pro-Soviet components turned into a civil war, with Muslims killing Muslims, contrary to the injunctions of the religion they were determined to protect. Unfortunately, the negative side of the Afghan character comes to the fore when an injury or an insult has to be avenged, even if it be the proverbial cutting off of the nose to spite the face.

Having achieved the impossible by throwing out a superpower from their country—initially almost bare-handed the Afghan Mujahideen, to the dismay of their well wishers, began fighting for the crown. The tasks before the new leaders after the communists had been evicted from their country were: (1) to disarm the militia; (2) to form a single army under the control of the central government; (3) to remove all erstwhile communists from official positions; (4) to obtain the co-operation of all the major members of the *Tanzeemat*; (5) to arrange for a broad-based *shoora* which would elect the new head of state and establish a stable government in their country.

None of these national aims could be achieved. Professor Sibghatullah Mojeddedi, chief of the Jabha-e-Nijat-e-Milli and the first acting President of Afghanistan after the fall of Dr Najibullah, failed to disarm the militia roaming around Kabul. He was in no position to form a national government as he was at daggers drawn with Hikmetyar, whom he had accused of firing at his aircraft when it was coming in to land at Bagram airport. He was also blamed for nepotism as he had inducted two of his sons into the cabinet. Because of his weakness in command he could not achieve any positive results during his short tenure as head of state. 'If we leave, the Hizb-e-Islami would send Mojeddedi packing back to Peshawar,'[7] is how a spokesman of the Dostum militia put it. In spite of his inability to achieve the goals that had been set, he was very reluctant to hand over power to Professor Burhanuddin Rabbani as envisaged in the Islamabad Declaration.

Burhanuddin Rabbani, head of the Jamiat-e-Islami, Afghanistan, who followed him, got involved in a bitter fight against Hikmetyar in which many were killed. Peace under his regime remained elusive. He could not obtain the willing co-operation of other members of the AIG. His *Shoora Hal-o-Aqd*, which had elected him as the President of Afghanistan, was not accepted by the political parties as it consisted of his supporters only. Maulvi Yunus Khalis, head of his own faction of the Hizb-e-Islami, withdrew from the *Qayadi Shoora* (Leadership Council) saying that 'whatever was happening in Kabul was against Islam as all key posts were held by communists'.[8]

The split between Rabbani and Abdul Rashid Dostum, the Uzbek general who controlled the northern provinces of Afghanistan, further reduced the extent of his authority.[9] The head of state and its chief executive had become a lame-duck president.

Rabbani was to hand over power to another transitional government on 28 October 1992. According to the Hizb-e-Islami (H), Rabbani's government had ceased to exist as a legal entity after that date. His term was, however, extended by two years[10] and then by another two months by a hand-picked *Qayadi Shoora*. Rabbani's extended term as President of the transitional government of Afghanistan and as head of the *Shoora* expired on 15 December 1994.

The two and a half years of in-fighting between the old guard brought about the loss of thousands of lives and the destruction of billions of dollars worth of property. Around 45,000 Afghans were killed in the fratricidal conflict between 1992 and 1994. (In the first six months of 1994[11] alone, 2,500 Afghans were killed by their own citizens, another 17,000 were maimed.[12])

Suddenly a completely new element came on the scene. Was it a fresh breeze, a *bad-e-naseem*, that was to blow over the ashes left behind by the warlords? Or was it a hot desert wind, a *bad-e-simoom*, which was to sweep away whatever was left of their ill-fated country? Only time will tell.

Who are these so-called Taliban? Where did they come from? What was their origin? Who organized them into a movement? How did they acquire so much military hardware and where did they learn how to use such sophisticated equipment? What tactics did they apply initially to achieve unprecedented gains on the battlefield? How effective have they been? What is the socio-political philosophy which they would put into effect? What are the fears and reactions of outside powers *vis-à-vis* the Taliban? And finally, was Pakistan's policy of being the first country to recognize the Taliban government in its national interest? These are some of the questions which I have attempted to answer.

The contents of this book are based on published material and interviews with prominent Pakistani and Afghan personalities. Members of the United Nations team which tried to bring about a cease-fire in Afghanistan have also given their views, and so have the ambassadors of the countries concerned.

CHAPTER 2

GENESIS OF THE TALIBAN PHENOMENON

Definition

Talib is an Arabic word, the literal meaning of which is one who is seeking something for himself. It is derived from the word *talab*, meaning desire. In Urdu it is generally affixed with another word to clarify what is being sought, for example, *Talib-e-didar* (one who is seeking the sight of his beloved), *Talib-e-duniya* (one who seeks the pleasures of this world). Hence the Urdu word *Talib-e-ilm* is a person in search of knowledge i.e., a student. *Taliban* is the plural of *talib*. In Pushto the word *taliban* generally denotes students studying in *deeni madaris* (religious institutions).

Deeni Madaris

Religious seminaries in Central Asia, Afghanistan, and in undivided India have played a significant role in the spiritual uplift of the Muslims in the South Asian region for centuries. Well-known institutions like the Firangi Mahal in Lucknow and the *madaris* at Nadwa, Deoband, Bareilly, and Azamgarh (all in UP, India) have produced luminaries who have served the interests of Muslims the world over. They were also, however, instrumental in dividing the *Ummah* into different schools of thought and in narrowing the vision of those who passed through their portals.

Deeni madaris are an offshoot of the old *madrassa* educational system. Some of these led to the formation of religious groups which adopted a very rigid attitude towards the implementation of what they believed to be true Islamic values. Quite a few young minds were brainwashed, by these religious groups into carrying forward the messianic spirit of Islam to other parts of the world. Their dogmatic approach and intolerance of others' points of view often produced fanatics who were recruited for trans-territorial missions.

A BBC documentary screened in 1997 showed some students in chains in one of the *deeni madaris* being taught to memorize the verses of the Holy Koran. What was even more appalling was that the head of that particular institution defended this practice by saying that the chained *talibs* would otherwise run away to their homes.

Though the Taliban phenomenon is of recent origin, *talibs* appeared on the scene several decades ago. They used to go to different *aalims* (religious scholars) to acquire religious knowledge. But that did not prevent them from participating in tribal dances, for which they were well known. Dressed in colourful clothes, with their well-kept hair flowing below their ears, they became part of Afghan folklore.

Many of them rose to become religious teachers and political activists. Fazal Omar Mojeddedi and Sher Agha Naguib were both *talibs*. They were among the religious leaders who had become the foundations of power in Afghanistan between 1929 and 1953.[13] Mullah Shor Bazar, an Afghan fighter famous for having kept the British at bay during the Third Anglo-Afghan war of 1919, was also a *talib*, as was Mir Waiz of Kandahar, who also fought against the foreign occupation of his country.

There were around 2,500 spiritual teachers and leaders enjoying a vital leadership role in the village and tribal society of Afghanistan before the failed attempt to introduce communist ideology in Afghanistan.[14]

Soon after the Soviets sent their troops into Afghanistan in support of the communist regime in Kabul, General Mohammad Ziaul Haq, the then President and Chief Martial Law Administrator of Pakistan, established a chain of *deeni madaris* along the Afghan-Pakistan border. He did so in order to create a belt of religiously-oriented students who would assist the Afghan mujahideen to evict the Soviet forces from Afghanistan.[15] Of course, it was also to satisfy the mullahs who he was building up as his own constituency for political ends.

Soon *deeni madaris* began to sprout in almost all the major cities of the NWFP and Balochistan. Later they spread to Punjab and Sindh as well. They were to be found in as far away places as Gilgit in the north and Karachi in the south. 'I have studied at a *madrassa* in Gujranwala,' said a Persian-speaking *talib*.[16] A survey carried out by the Home Department of the government of Punjab in May 1997 revealed that in Rawalpindi division alone there were a total of 169 *deeni madaris*, and that 17,533 *talibs* were on their rolls. Most of these schools were being used as hide-outs for terrorists attached to foreign mentors, says the report. (For details, *see*, Table 1).

Statistics compiled by Dr Syed Sher Ali Shah of the *Khadim al Hadith al Nabvi*, Miran Shah, gave a figure of 30,000 students from various *madaris* who joined the Taliban movement.

In addition to receiving donations from local philanthropists, the *madaris* were reportedly given grants from Saudi Arabia, Kuwait, and some other friendly conservative Muslim countries. General Ziaul Haq had also authorized the district *zakat* committees to give them money regularly from their *zakat* funds.[17] The report of the Special Branch of the Punjab police indicated that 37.87 per cent of the 169 *madaris* received government aid.

After the fall of Dr Najibullah, religious schools began refunctioning in Afghanistan as well, specially in the eastern provinces and in Herat.[18]

Haji Abdul Qadeer, former governor of Nangarhar, gave a figure of about 2,000 students (*talibs*) in the *madaris* established in the four provinces bordering Pakistan. The students in these *deeni madaris* were a mixture of Afghans and Pakistanis, with the majority being Afghan nationals. According to Mullah Shahabuddin, the Consul General-Designate in Peshawar of the Taliban regime, around 80 per cent of the students were Afghans. The teaching staff were both Pakistanis and Afghans.[19]

The *deeni madaris* which were functioning in Afghanistan before the Soviets entered the country were running classes from Class 1 to Class 12 and were attended by students of all ages. After the Soviet occupation, these seminaries moved to Pakistan and established themselves in all parts of the country.

The syllabi of these schools included the learning of the Holy Koran by heart; *tajweed* (correct pronunciation of the Koranic verses); *tafseer* (interpretation of the Holy scriptures); *fiqah* (Islamic jurisprudence); *shariah* (Islamic Laws); *ahadis* (life and decisions of the Holy Prophet [Peace Be Upon Him]) on various issues brought before him by the faithful); *mantiq* (philosophy); *riazi* (mathematics) and *falakiat* (astronomy); *tabligh* (spreading the word of God) and a smattering of modern subjects. Shahabuddin claims that the subjects ranged from the *Baghdadi Quaida* to *Bokhari Sharif*.

Unlike the well-known religious schools of pre-partition India, which awarded proper degrees to their students, many of these seminaries only gave a nameless certificate at the end of their studies which was not recognized by any other institution or government department, neither in Pakistan nor elsewhere. Mufti Mohammad Masoom Afghani, Ambassador-Designate of the Taliban regime to Pakistan was a product of one such *madrassa* in Gulshan-e-Iqbal, Karachi.[20]

A distinction must be made between a *talib* and a mullah. A *talib* is one who has not completed his studies at the seminaries and has yet to be given the honorific title of mullah. A mullah, on the other hand, has gone through the designated number of years in the *madaris* under different religious scholars. Only then is a proper *dastar bandi* carried out and the recipient entitled to carry the title of a mullah. This allows him to become an *imam, qari,* or *khatib* of a mosque. Many are absorbed as teachers at religious schools, while others become *qazis* and *muftis,* which qualifies them to conduct religious rituals and act as local judges in villages and towns. If this distinction were to be strictly applied, many of those who call themselves mullah amongst the Taliban do not really qualify for this title as they are only half educated and are not fully conversant with the injunctions of Islam and the correct interpretations of the Holy Koran and the Sunna.

The *madaris* not only imparted religious education of sorts, but more than that, they organized the students into militant groups who would be prepared to use force to subdue their rivals. The Taliban were divided into two categories. The first category was prepared and organized to take part in the jihad; the second confined themselves to their studies only.[21]

The size of the schools varied from fifteen students studying in mosques to around 2,000 in proper boarding and lodging institutions. It is the larger of the two types that produced fighters who went into Afghanistan to evict the communists and later fought against those who they believed were not introducing an Islamic regime in their country.

Those selected to fight were associated with various Afghan factions in order to obtain arms. Initially trained in how to fire a rifle, they soon moved on to use machine guns and rockets. During the three months of holidays (*Ramzan, Shawal,* and *Zi Quad*), those above eighteen years of age took part in the jihad against the Soviets and returned to their studies thereafter although many of them were martyred, maimed, or injured. (Shahabuddin denied that military training was being imparted to the students in the *deeni madaris*.) 'After the fall of Najibullah the Taliban came back to the *madaris* and laid down their arms,' said the Consul-General.[22]

The Pakistani Linkage

Some political analysts believe that the institutions where these radical students were being trained to participate in the Afghan jihad were under the control of the Jamiat-i-Ulema-e-Islam (JUI) of Maulana Fazalur Rahman.[23] While this may possibly be true, the Maulana reportedly had personally never met the Taliban leaders. His political party was, however, involved in influencing the minds of these young students, many of whom were remnants of those recruited by the Frontier Corps during the days of the proxy war in Afghanistan.[24] (There was a well-known *deeni madrassa* in Dera Ismail Khan, the home town of Maulana Fazalur Rahman.)

The famous *deeni madrassa* at Akora Khattak (NWFP) known as Jaamiah Darul Uloom Haqqania was founded by *Shiekhul Hadis* Maulana Abdul Haq in 1947. Currently the *madrassa* is headed by his son, Senator Samiul Haq, assisted by his brother Anwarul Haq. Its origins go back to 1937, when a religious school was opened at Akora Khattak by *Sheikul Islam* Maulana Syed Hussain Ahmed Madani. Presently this *darul uloom* alone is imparting religious education, and providing boarding and lodging free of cost, to around 2,000 *talibs* from Pakistan, Afghanistan, and the Central Asian States, with Afghans numbering 700 or so.[25]

The yearly expenditure of the *madrassa* comes to over Rs 60 lakhs, which the organizers say is provided for by donations from Pakistani philanthropists both at home and abroad. Intelligence agencies are, however, aware of the fact that many *madaris* are provided funds from Iraq, Libya, Iran, and Saudi Arabia, each doing so in the hope of retaining their influence in this region and keeping their rivals out.

Table 1
A Sect and District-wise Survey of the Various Deeni Madaris of Punjab

District	Deobandi	Barelvi	Ahle Hadith	Ahle Tashi	Total
Lahore	143	136	41	3	323
Gujranwala	36	87	36	13	140
Rawalpindi	83	64	6	16	169
Faisalabad	47	39	18	8	112
Sargodha	68	64	9	8	149
Multan	127	159	27	12	325
D. G. Khan	133	174	24	30	411
Bahawalpur	335	493	36	19	883
Total	972	1216	174	100	2512

Source: *The News*, 26 May 1997

A Sect and District-wise Survey of Students Enrolled in the Deeni Madaris of the Punjab

District	Deobandi	Barelvi	Ahle Hadith	Ahle Tashi	Total
Lahore	1792	18336	5524	350	42102
Gujranwala	3632	7400	1712	373	13117
Rawalpindi	8367	8307	417	442	17533
Faisalabad	11631	5027	3141	700	20499
Sargodha	6158	6427	1318	341	14244
Multan	11888	10798	2620	138	25966
D. G. Khan	8816	9593	1829	669	20907
Bahawalpur	3220	29302	2319	746	64571
Total	100588	95190	18880	4281	218939

The owners of Darul Uloom Haqqania claim that they have established around 1,000 such *madaris* of different sizes both in Pakistan and in some foreign countries. Thousands of

Afghan *talibs* who passed through the portals of this religious seminary took part in the Afghan jihad. Quite a few of those *talibs* who were in the central *shoora* at Kabul, or who were appointed as governors and deputy governors of the provinces under Taliban control, had passed out from this very institution.

It is here that they were imbued with the spirit of imposing the Islamic *shariah* which, according to Anwarul Haq, is not just derived from the Holy Koran and Sunna, but also includes the *fatwas* (religious edicts) which have been given off and on by religious scholars.[26] It is these religious injunctions which have introduced extremism into the thought process of those Afghans who joined the Taliban movement.

Anwarul Haq supported the directives of the Taliban which made it compulsory for Afghan women to cover themselves from head to foot when they ventured outside their homes. During an interview when I reminded him of the Koranic verse: 'and tell the believing men to lower their gaze and be modest and tell the believing women to lower their gaze and be modest,' verses 24:30 and 24:31. How is that possible if the eyes of the women are not exposed, I enquired from him. His reply was, 'Women's eyes and hands can be the cause of immoral deeds. Many *ulema* have, therefore, given *fatwas* that women must cover all parts of their bodies including the eyes and hands.'[27] It is such *fatwas* given by obscurantist mullahs which portray a wrong image of Islam.

Asma bint Abu Bakar, sister of the Holy Prophet's wife Aisha (RU), one day came to the Prophet's house wearing thin clothes. The Holy Prophet (Peace Be Upon Him) turned his head away and said, 'It is not proper that you should reveal anything except this and this,' pointing towards her face and hands.[28]

Furthermore, Islam not only allows women to be earning members of the family but warns men not to covet the earnings of the women: 'envy not one another but ask Allah for his bounty' (4:32). Religious extremism seeps into one's life when one starts following edicts issued by various mullahs of different schools of thought, in addition to and sometimes contrary to the verses of the Holy Koran and the sayings of the Holy Prophet (Peace Be Upon Him).

Tahara and *Tazeer*, purity and punishment, were emphasized by the teachers in the religious seminaries,[29] but were given an interpretation which binds the student to ritual rather than to the spirit of Islam.

While I did not see any signs of military training being imparted at Darul Uloom Haqqania, a report presented to Prime Minister Nawaz Sharif at a cabinet meeting stated that there were about one hundred *deeni madaris* in Pakistan which were imparting combat and semi-military skills to their pupils, and that in different parts of the country there were about 10,000 foreign nationals studying in these so-called places of religious education.[30]

Another famous *deeni madrassa*, where a large number of foreign students are being imparted religious education, is known as Jamiatul Uloomil Islamiyyah. It was founded by Maulvi Mohammad Yusaf Binnori and is located in Binnori Town in the suburbs of Karachi. The bulk of the Taliban leadership comes from these two institutions.

Madaris where Afghan students were studying were located in large numbers in the surrounding areas of Quetta. The more important ones were in Chaman, Pishin, and Qila Abdullah. Several Afghans who were studying there went back to Afghanistan to participate in the on-going struggle between the various factions in that war ravaged country. They were often joined by Pakistani students who believed that they would achieve martyrdom if they fell while fighting against the anti-Taliban forces. Many of them became prisoners of the anti-Taliban alliance. Those kept captive by Ahmed Shah Masood in the Panjsher valley were released only when their parents personally went to him and asked for their return. He released them on condition that they would not come back to Afghanistan again to fight alongside the Taliban.

When the Taliban were compelled to withdraw from Mazar-e-Sharif and fighting again erupted around the Salang Tunnel, Mullah Omar gave a call to the *talibs* studying in the *deeni madaris* to move to the front lines. Thousands of Afghan students responded immediately.

Origins of the Taliban

The mullahs in Afghanistan came into the limelight when Hazrat Ziaul Mashaiq and, Maulana Mohammad Ibrahim Mojeddedi, were caught by the communist regime of Noor Mohammad Taraki and Hafizullah Amin and imprisoned along with 150 other religious leaders. After their arrest, the mullahs called for a jihad against the pro-communists leaders of their country. Since they feared persecution at the hands of Taraki and Amin they fled to Pakistan. (Masoom Afghani gave this forced migration a religious connotation by calling it a *hijrat*.)[31]

'Initially only one organization existed,' said Afghani. Later, according to him, Professor Burhanuddin Rabbani and Engineer Gulbadin Hikmetyar made their own *tanzeems*, which gave rise to the seven Afghan factions in Pakistan at the time of the Soviet occupation of Afghanistan. The religious students joined six of the seven *tanzeems* as it was through them that they could obtain the arms which they needed to fight for their cause. The majority of them had become part of Nabi Mohammedi's Harakat-e-Inqilab-e-Islami and Yunus Khalis' Hizb-e-Islami. They were even then known as *talibs*.

The exact origin of the Taliban movement is, however, still shrouded in mystery. Although several articles have been written on this so-called 'mysterious army', no researched or authentic material has so far been published on the historical perspective of the Taliban movement. The most widely circulated theory is that the leadership of the Taliban emerged from amongst the disgruntled young Afghan refugees studying in the *deeni madaris* around Quetta and Peshawar (even

Lahore and Gujranwala have been mentioned in this context by some journalists). Senior officials of the Government of Pakistan claimed ignorance about the presence in Pakistan of any *deeni madaris* where the Taliban might have received their early education,[32] though there is ample proof that this was so.

Professor Ahmed Hasan Dani believes that the Taliban received their education at *deeni madaris* in Pakistan and were also being supported by elements in Pakistan. Dani claims that the young students were being prepared for jihad against those who it was felt, were not adhering to the moral code of Islam.[33] That is why they reportedly developed a dislike for the existing Afghan groupings, which they blamed for bringing about much of the death and destruction in their homeland. They realized that the people were suffering because of the power struggle that was going on between their elders.

Immediate Causes of the Rise of the Taliban Movement

By the year 1992, the average citizen of Afghanistan was sick and tired of the civil war that had been raging for three years. Masoom Afghani said that around 50,000 Afghans were killed in the struggle for power between Hikmetyar and Rabbani. The people had lost faith in their leaders, who were making and breaking alliances overnight. They found none of them trustworthy as they were not fulfilling their promises, some of which had been made in the precincts of the Holy Kaaba, the co-sponsors of which were Pakistan and Saudi Arabia.[34] Their bitterness towards the leadership was increasing as they saw no end to the wanton killings which were being perpetrated in their country. Near famine conditions were adding to the anger which was building up against the once 'revered' Afghan leadership.

The popularity of the Afghan mujahideen, therefore, was decreasing with the passage of time. Not only had they been unable to bring about peace in their war-ravaged country, but what was worse was that many of them had begun to engage in unsocial activities. All of them were armed. Quite a few had turned into gangsters and were extracting money from shopkeepers and levying taxes on passenger vehicles passing through areas under their control. According to the BBC, as much as $400 was being taken from every truck driver carrying goods bound for the interior. Passengers were made to pay 100,000 Afghanis ($2 approximately). Even those carrying goods on bicycles were deprived of some of their precious earnings before being allowed to proceed further. There were seventy-one such check points between Chaman and Herat alone.[35] One of the reasons for demanding money, in addition to personal greed, was that the fighters were no longer receiving regular pay from the leaders who had earlier recruited them. Many were even indulging in corruption, looting, drug trafficking, and rape.

The worst-affected area was around Kandahar, where lawlessness had spread to such an extent that shopkeepers could not keep their goods in their shops during the hours of darkness. They used to bring goods to sell by day and take them back to their houses at night as they feared that the would be looted by bandits if they were left unattended after sundown.

Commanders Nadir Jan, Saleh Mohammad, and Doro Khan had bases on the Kandahar-Herat road near Mullah Omar's village. They were known to be abducting and raping women. In July 1994 Commander Mansoor, one of the fighters in the Ismatullah militia, kidnapped three women who were gang-raped and killed. This sent a wave of indignation through the locals in Kandahar. Stories were afloat of tank battles between commanders over the possession of handsome young boys.[36] A marriage between two boys, celebrated with a great deal of jubilation in Kandahar, aroused bitter feelings among the students and teachers of the *deeni madaris.*[37]

There was mismanagement everywhere and the existing mujahideeen leadership was either unwilling or unable to curb the rising trend of anarchy in Afghanistan. Chaotic conditions prevailed throughout the country at that time, with the sole exception of the six northern provinces 'governed' by the Uzbek General, Abdul Rashid Dostum.

Afghanistan had become a failed state, like Somalia, Rwanda, and Burundi. Although physical boundaries still existed and the country did indeed still have a flag, a national anthem, a government of sorts, membership of the United Nations, and embassies abroad, the writ of the government-in-being was not running even inside the capital. Warlords and petty chieftains had taken over the country. There was an economic collapse. Rabbani had no money to pay his 'army'. Food convoys were being looted. Virtually no outside government was willing to do serious business with the regime, with the exception of a few. In the words of a very respectable senior citizen, there was *tawaiful muluki* or a kind of a free-for-all attitude prevailing throughout the country.

Disenchantment, to put it very mildly, with the rotten leadership of the Afghan mujahideen was gradually building up. The harmony that had existed between them during the Afghan jihad had gone to pieces. The ordinary Afghan was looking for a 'messiah'. It did not require much effort therefore, by the Taliban to garner support for ending the fratricidal war and the anarchy which was prevailing in their land.

The education which the Taliban were receiving in the *madaris* from semi-educated *maulvis*, however, converted them into religious fanatics. They were made to believe that none of the then Afghan leaders were sincere about the establishment of what they perceived to be a truly Islamic state in Afghanistan. They were told that the struggle between Rabbani and Hikmetyar and the others was more about grabbing power than an effort to introduce Islamic practices in accordance with their own interpretations of Islam. The blame for the pitiable condition in which the Afghans found themselves was placed at the doorsteps of the existing mujahideen factions.

The Taliban came to the conclusion that neither Dostum nor Ahmed Shah Masood, who was in control of Kabul, had shown any evidence of changing the social set-up to bring it in conformity with Koranic injunctions. Nor, for that matter, had the Hizb-e-Islami chief, who was in the forefront during the Afghan jihad, anything to show in this regard. His sole aim remained the ouster of his political rival and the holding of general elections, which was not enough to pacify the rising religious emotions of the Taliban.

Afghans have traditionally looked up to a tribal elder or a religious figure to solve their problems and so, when one such person came forward to lead them out of the morass, they followed him without any hesitation.

Mullah Mohammad Omar, a jihad veteran from the district of Maiwand just west of the city of Kandahar, who had fought against the Soviets in order to see a truly Islamic government in his country, was most disappointed with the events that followed the ouster of Dr Najibullah. He had come back to resume his studies at the Sang-i-Hisar Madrassa in Maiwand after handing over all the weapons and ammunition he possessed to Abdul Rasul Sayyaf. In late September 1994, however, he decided to give up his studies and work towards achieving the objective of bringing about peace by evicting the pro-communists in his country and introducing Islamic values in Afghanistan.

On 20 September 1994, a Herati family, while on its way to Kandahar from Herat, was stopped at a check point ninety kilometres short of Kandahar by local mujahideen bandits. The men and women were separated. The boys were taken away and molested. The girls were repeatedly raped until they became unconscious. Later all of them were killed and their bodies partially burnt. It was Mullah Omar (sometimes referred to as

Mullah Mujahid) who was the first to arrive on the scene.
He is reported to have gathered some *talibs* who helped
him in collecting the bodies. These were washed and given
a decent burial. He then gathered the students and pledged
to start a campaign to get rid of such criminals.[38]

Some days later, Omar went to a mosque in his village to
gather support for his mission. The seven students who were
studying there did not accept his invitation as they thought the
task was too big for them. But he did not lose hope; he went to
another mosque and this time he was joined by about fifteen
talibs, but they said that they would work for him only on
Fridays as they were not prepared to leave their studies. By
nightfall, however, around fifty students had joined him. The
story goes that one of them had had a dream in which he claimed
that he had seen angels descending from heaven, which to him
was an indication that by following Mullah Omar they were
on the right path.[39]

Omar apprised them of his objectives, but he also told
them that he had neither money nor weapons to offer them.
The next morning one Haji Bashar, son of Haji Isa Khan,
a mujahid commander of Hizb-e-Islami (Yunus Khalis)
opened up his armoury and gave Omar both weapons and
vehicles. The Taliban movement had begun. The formal
name given to the newly-created political faction was
Tehreek-i-Islami-i-Taliban Afghanistan.

The immediate goals of the newly-formed organization
were to: (1) disarm all rival militia, (2) fight against those
who did not accept their request to give up weapons,
(3) enforce Islamic laws in the areas they 'liberated', and
(4) retain all areas the Taliban captured.[40]

Prominent leaders who joined Omar were: *Shaikh Haji
Moawin* Mullah Mohammad Rabbani, Shaikh Haji Mullah
Mohammad Shahid, Shaikh Mullah Mohammad Hassan,
Mullah Borjan, and Haji Amir Mohammad Agha. All of the
above personalities were formerly members of the Yunus Khalis
faction of the Hizb-e-Islami. Others who joined the Taliban
movement were: Shaikh Nuruddin Turabi, Ustad Sayaf, Mullah

Abbas, Shaikh Mullah Mohammad Sadiq, Shaikh Abdus Salam Rocketi (all from Abdul Rasul Sayyaf's Ittehad-e-Islami).[41]

Syed Hamid Gailani, the son of Pir Syed Ahmad Gailani, chief of the National Islamic Front of Afghanistan (NIFA), who is greatly revered and respected by all Kandaharis including the Taliban, stated that NIFA commanders in Kandahar sought permission from their leader to join this new band of black-turbaned Islamic warriors. Permission was given in the hope that the Taliban would bring about peace in Afghanistan,[42] and the strength of the Taliban soon swelled.

The *deeni madaris* in Chaman contributed to the Taliban movement, but it was also in Chaman that some fifty to a hundred like-minded students were organized into a separate group by agencies interested in breaking the deadlock in Afghanistan. They were joined by members of the former Afghan armed forces in Kandahar who had now apparently become devout Muslims.[43] The name of General Shanawaz Tanai, a communist general in the days of the Najibullah regime who had defected some years back and was welcomed by Hikmetyar into his fold, has also been mentioned in some circles as a person who helped in creating this force. He is believed to have grown a beard and claimed to have become a true Muslim.

Demographic Character

The Taliban are mostly Pushtuns and are therefore part of those elements in Afghanistan who have lorded it over this country since the days of its founder, the famous Ahmed Shah Abdali. The robust Pushtuns form 43 per cent of the population (the Taliban claim that the Pushtuns are over 50 per cent, the *Asia Year Book*, 1995 mentions a figure of 38 per cent), with the light-skinned Tajiks only half their number and the rest of the dozen or so ethnic groups comprise 5 per cent or less.[44]

Out of a total population of 18,293,800 (1973 census) the Pushtuns number around 7.5 million. They have traditionally

provided the politico-military elite of the country, and they
have always been keen to strengthen their power and their
sense of identity. The leadership of the Taliban comes
mainly from sub-tribes of the Pushtuns such as the
Noorzais, Barakzais, Mohammadzais, Popalzais, Alizais,
and Hotaks.

The Pushtuns are generally thought of as the real Afghans.[45]
They consider the non-Pushtuns less fortunate than they in the
matter of birth. The Taliban, therefore, could expect support from
a major section of their people based on ethnic and linguistic
affiliations, particularly from the Pushtun-dominated southern and
eastern provinces of Afghanistan.[46] Large pockets of Pushtuns are
also found in the northern provinces where the Uzbeks, Tajiks,
and the Turkomen are the predominant race (*see*, Map 2).

Kabul is a multi-ethnic city which, though located in the
heartland of the Pushtun areas, has a large Tajik and Hazara
Shi'ite population. Persian and Dari along with Pushtu are
the languages, one hears on the streets of the capital.

The Tajiks, who are concentrated in the north-eastern
provinces of Afghanistan, have always complained that they
have been deprived of their share in the affairs of the state
by the Pushtuns, hence they are determined to maintain
their individual identity and fight for their political rights.

The vast majority of the Taliban are Sunnis who follow
the Hanafi *fiqah* and mostly belong to the Qadriya *silsila* of
the famous sufi saint Abdul Qadir Al-Gilani of Baghdad.
They insist that they are neither Deobandis nor Barelvis,
but their pristine methods put them closer to the former.
The Deoband school of thought does not allow any
deviation from the practices followed by the first four
Caliphs and insists on a very strict religious code which
does not permit any accommodation with those who have
even slightly different views on an Islamic way of life. 'It is
this refusal to make any compromises that is evident in the
behaviour of the Taliban,' said a student of Binnori Town
madrassa at Karachi with great pride.[47]

About 14 per cent of the Afghans are Shias; they are concentrated mainly in the central region of Hazarajat and in the province of Bamian. Although Maulvi Khairullah, a Taliban leader, maintained that they had cordial relations with their Shia brethren in the past as well, the fact of the matter is that the Taliban have been perceived as anti-Shia by those who support the latter. This may not be entirely true, but since Saudi Arabia provided funds to many of the religious seminaries where these *talibs* were studying, the young students are likely to have been influenced by the Saudis' negative attitudes towards the Shias.

The agreement which was concluded between the Taliban and Dr Mohammad Sadiq Modabbir, who was a renegade from the main Shia group led by Sheikh Asef Mohseni of the Shi'ite Harakat-e-Inqilab-e-Islami, gave the Taliban, a more representative character. That, however, did not remove the fears of the Iranian leadership, who still considered this student militia to be working against their interests. The four-point agreement justified their contention as it called for a joint political and military struggle to oust the illegal Rabbani regime which Iran was supporting. It also gave freedom of movement to the Taliban in parts of the Shia-dominated Hazarajat region.[48]

The ages of the members of the Taliban movement vary from 15 to 50. It would, therefore, not be wholly correct to refer to them as young students, for they were joined by many war veterans who either were from the disintegrated Afghan armed forces or had taken part in the Afghan jihad against the Soviet troops.[49] Many had defected from the existing mujahideen parties, especially from Nabi Mohammedi's Harakat-e-Inqilab-e-Islami. Haji Abdul Qadeer claimed that the Taliban were joined by erstwhile communists including members of the infamous Afghan secret service Khad, which, according to him, had infiltrated the organization and provided the military faction of the movement.[50] Mullah Shahabuddin, however, stated categorically that no communists had joined the Taliban until the

Table 2
A Population-wise Break-up of Ethnic Tribes in Afghanistan (1973)

Tribe	Sect	Population	%	General Location	General Characteristics
Pushtun	Hanafi Sunni except Turi (Shia)	6.5 million	43%*	Southern and eastern Afghanistan with large pockets in northern Afghanistan	
Tajik	Mainly Hanafi Sunnis; some Ismaili Shias	3.5 million	24%	Scattered through-out but mostly in northern Afghanistan	Sedentary agriculturists
Uzbek	Hanafi Sunni	1.0 million	6%	Northern Afghanistan	
Hazara	Imami Shia; Ismaili Shia; some Sunnis	870,000	5%	Central Afghanistan, (probably arrived in Afghanistan AD 1329-1447)	
Chahar	Aimaqs Sunnis	800,000	5%	Western Afghanistan	
Farsiwan	Imami Shia	600,000	4%	Western Afghanistan	Agriculturists
Brahui	Hanafi Sunni	200,000	1.3%	South-western Afghanistan	Tenant farmers or hired herders for Baloch and Pushtun Khans
Turkomen	Hanafi Sunni	125,000	.7%	North-western Afghanistan	Semi-sedentary and semi-nomadic

Tribe	Sect	Population	%	General Location	General Characteristics
Nuristani	Hanafi Sunni	100,000	.6%	Eastern Afghanistan (Nuristan)	
Baloch	Hanafi Sunni	100,000	.6%	South-western Afghanistan	Caravanners, nomads
Mughals		Several thousands		Central and northern Afghanistan	
Kirghiz		Several thousands		North-eastern Afghanistan (Badakhshan)	

A Population-wise Break-up of Religious Minorities and Other Nationals

Tribe	Sect	Population	%	General Location	General Characteristics
Hindus		20,000	.1%	Kabul, Jalalabad, Ghazni and Kandahar	
Sikhs		10,000	.05%	Kabul, Jalalabad, Ghazni and Kandahar	
Jews		Several thousands			
Arabs		Several thousands		North-western Afghanistan	

Total estimated population 16.5 million

Sources: L. Dupree, *Afghanistan*, Princeton University Press, Princeton, New Jersey, 1973, pp. 59-64; ISI; *Frontier Post*, 17 February 1992.

* Some sources mention a higher percentage, with the Taliban claiming that the Pushtun population is over 50 per cent.

Map 2
Afghanistan—Ethnic Divisions

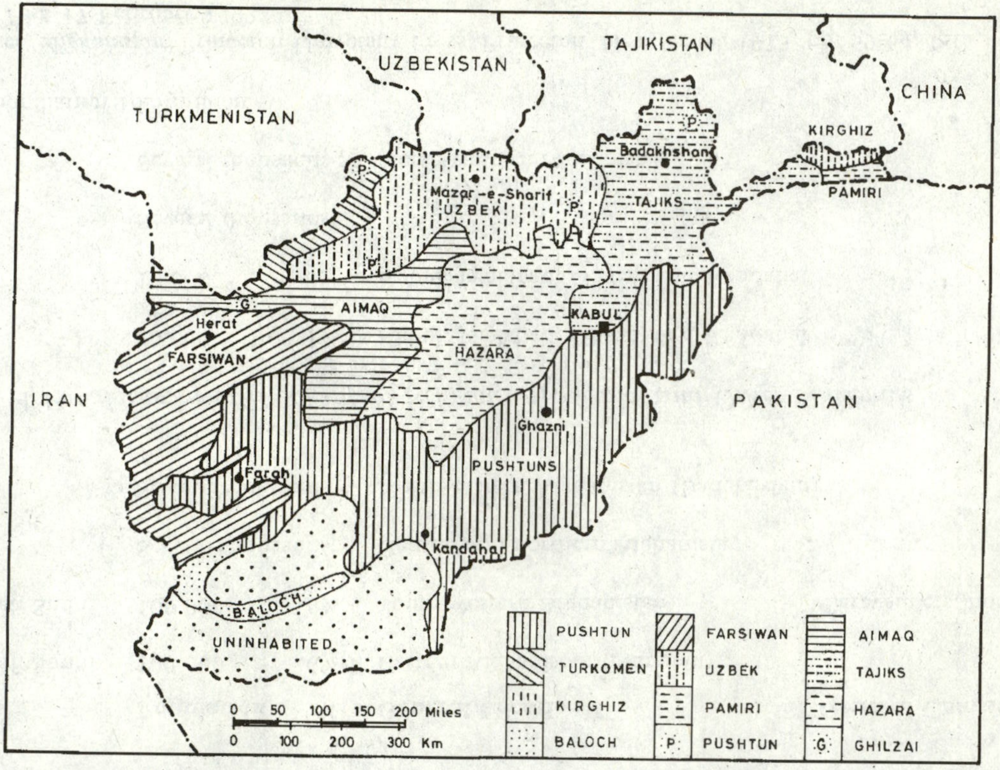

PUSHTUN	FARSIWAN	AIMAQ
TURKOMEN	UZBEK	TAJIKS
KIRGHIZ	PAMIRI	HAZARA
BALOCH	PUSHTUN	GHILZAI

P. = PUSHTUN
G. = GHILZAI

0 50 100 150 200 Miles
0 100 200 300 Km

fall of Kabul. 'Only then were they accepted into our fold,' said the representative of the Taliban regime in Peshawar.[51]

The Taliban are not completely ethnically homogeneous. Mullah Omar is a Gilzai Pushtun and his so-called second-in-command, Mullah Mohammad Durrani, as the name indicates, is a Durrani Pushtun. These two strands of Pushtuns have a history of squabbles amongst themselves which has lingered on in spite of centuries having rolled by. However, this ethnic divide has not caused any rupture in their relationship. It is not likely to do so unless differences arise on a power-sharing formula when and if the Taliban are able to achieve their objective of forming a government of their choice in the whole of Afghanistan.

During their negotiations with representatives of Ahmed Shah Masood and Abdul Rashid Dostum, the Taliban were represented by Uzbeks and Tajiks—just to prove the point that the Taliban did not comprise Pushtuns alone.[52] But despite the efforts to prove their diverse composition, the vast majority of the Taliban are in fact Pushtuns.

Sir Nicholas Barrington, former United Kingdom High Commissioner to Pakistan, was fluent in Persian, Pushto, and Urdu and spent a total of nine years in Islamabad. He is believed in some quarters to have been quite involved in developments in Afghanistan. According to Lieutenant-General Hamid Gul, the former Director-General of the Inter Services Intelligence Directorate (ISI), Barrington inducted both former royalists and erstwhile communists into the Taliban movement.[53] Though this has not been substantiated, it is true that commanders of various Afghan factions, including supporters of the return of King Zahir Shah and former communists did join the Taliban.

The Taliban, like all other Afghans, possess not only physical courage and a capacity to withstand extreme hardship, they also have a strong belief in the verses of the Holy Koran which say that a man killed in a jihad becomes a *shaheed* whose spirit immediately goes to heaven.

The Taliban can be divided into three categories: those who concentrate on religious studies alone and after taking their degrees in theology become *aalims* (religious teachers); the militants, who may or may not have completed their studies but are willing to take up arms against the anti-Taliban forces; and the followers of the various other political factions, ex-communists, and former members of the Afghan armed forces who changed their loyalties out of fear or conviction, or for monetary gains.

The Taliban's Religious Attitude

While the vast majority of Afghans are devout Muslims and to a large extent live their life in accordance with Islamic principles diluted with their code of Pushtunwali and their local culture, their views on the implementation of the shariah differ. They too have liberal, conservative and orthodox elements within themselves. Although some Afghan rulers did try to introduce radical reforms, including the abolition of the veil and the introduction of western dress for women, the deeply-rooted Islamic values and tribal traditions did not permit these changes. Nevertheless, many of the educated elite of Afghanistan would still like to have leaders with a modern and liberal outlook.

The statements of the Taliban leaders and the actions they have taken in the areas they control put them in the category of extremists. Girls are being denied education; women have been prevented from working; if they leave their houses they have to be covered from head to foot with a veil (*burqa*); besides being veiled, women have to be accompanied by a male relative when they venture out on the streets. Shopkeepers have been directed not to sell goods to unveiled women. Rickshaw drivers are not to pick up women passengers unless they are fully covered.[54] Women caught violating these rules are imprisoned, as are the shopkeeper and the rickshaw driver.

Doctors have been compelled to cut off the hands and feet of thieves in accordance with the *shariah*; killers have been tried by the local *qazis* and the punishment has been handed down in a matter of hours. The place of the crime is immaterial— Saifullah, a Pakistani, had killed two persons in Pishin, a district in Pakistan, some two years earlier. When he crossed into Afghanistan, the Taliban arrested him and promptly hanged him in Spin Boldak on the Afghan-Pakistan border.

Cinemas have been closed and their buildings turned into mosques. Taking photographs and displaying portraits, posters, and pictures is banned to prevent idolatry. The Taliban even vowed to destroy the world-famous, sixty metre high statue of the Buddha, carved out of rock on the side of a hill in Bamian province in the fifth century BC, once that province came under their control. (This intention was later denied by the Taliban leadership.)

A Taliban delegation allegedly refused to sit in a room in Chitral (Pakistan) on the occasion of the signing of a transit agreement just because a photograph of the Quaid-i- Azam was hanging there.[55] Taliban leaders attending the Pakistan Day parade in Islamabad remained seated when the national anthem of Pakistan was being played. This unprecedented action was not because they wanted to be discourteous to their hosts, but because it was in keeping with their religious dogma.

Video shops were destroyed not only in Taliban- controlled areas but also in Zhob (Pakistan), where they were raided by the Taliban and forced to shut down. No cassette was to find its way into shops, hotels, vehicles, or anywhere else. Violaters would have their businesses closed.

Television sets have been used for firing practice. The Taliban are reported to have marched a boy with a rope around his neck for playing football, which they considered an un-Islamic practice.[56] Similarly chess, is frowned upon as an idle occupation. Kite flying and keeping of pigeons and other pets is forbidden and the birds have been killed.

Those found engaging in such pursuits are jailed. Gambling has been banned. Celebration of the Western new year and the Iranian Nauroz is not allowed. Radio Kabul changed its name to Voice of Radio Shariat. No music and songs are broadcast from the new radio station. This, according to the Taliban elders, is in keeping with the Koranic verse *Amr Bil Maruf Wa Nahi anl Munkir* (invite people to benevolence and goodness and stop them from bad and evil deeds). The sixteen-point set of rules, incorporating most of the points mentioned above, was handed over to the UN agencies, foreign funded NGOs, and all the concerned government departments.

Frederick Michael and Jose Daniel Llorento, two French aid workers with the French NGO Contre La Faim (Action Against Hunger) were arrested for violating the law against attending mixed parties. They were found in the company of women workers who had given a farewell lunch to a woman aid worker in Kabul.[57] What the press did not reveal was that these Frenchmen had with them TV cameras and were allegedly wanting to shoot a few scenes, which was against the injunctions issued by the Taliban. (Nancy Dewolf Smith, writing in the *Asian Wall Street Journal* of 25 March 1997, mentions that the foreigner grapevine has it that the raid on the French agency turned up a soft porn video cassette).

The European Commissioner for Humanitarian Aid, Emma Bonino, who had gone to Afghanistan to assess the requirements for aid, was detained by the Taliban authorities for over three hours for taking photographs of Afghan women while on a guided tour of a women's hospital in Kabul. Bonino should have known that respecting local customs is necessary for foreigners if they want to avoid getting into trouble.

Twelve murderers were hanged in public between November 1994 and April 1997; relatives of victims have been asked to personally shoot the killers. A woman was given the freedom to slay the murderer of her husband in the presence of onlookers. Dur Mohammad, condemned by a makeshift Islamic court, was shot by the father of the deceased on the lawns of Ali Sher

Hotel. Subedar (retired) Faizullah Khattak of Mianwali, Pakistan, was asked to come to the Afghan border town of Khost in order to personally take revenge from those Afghans who had earlier looted and killed his son, a taxi driver.

Four Afghans were killed and their tortured bodies were hung in the streets of Kabul in October 1997—they had allegedly committed the sin of selling out frontline positions to Ahmed Shah Masood. This kind of interpretation of Islam may not be acceptable to many in Afghanistan.

Maulvi Yar Mohammad, the Taliban Governor of Herat, ordered all men to sport a beard and to cover their heads with a turban when outside their homes. Mullah Nuruddin Turabi, the Minister of Justice, saw to it that men with trimmed beards were beaten with rubber hoses and even jailed till they grew a beard long enough for the Taliban's liking. The 400 or so religious police, headed by Mullah Qalamuddin, patrolled the city and established check posts to ensure compliance of religious edicts issued by Mullah Omar. Over a thousand citizens were thrown out of jobs, beaten, and jailed in 1997 alone for being seen without a full-grown beard. (Sporting a beard and wearing a turban was part of Kandahari culture even before the Taliban appeared on the scene, but it was not binding.)

Praying was made compulsory. Roads adjacent to mosques were closed to traffic at prayer time. Young people seen in their shops after the *Azaan* were to be arrested. Maulvi Wakil Ahmed, Secretary to the Taliban movement, emphasized the fact that when they came to power all the provisions of the Koran and Sunna would be strictly enforced, including an interest-free banking system.

John F. Burns of the *New York Times* aptly described the areas under Taliban control as a 'terrifying picture of puritanism at a brutalizing extreme. A place governed by illiterate teenage boys. They have never been to school (non-religious) but they believe they know the absolute truth—and enforce it with kalashnikov rifles'.[58] This western view of the Taliban smacks of prejudice as those at the helm of affairs are not illiterate teenage boys but middle-aged students of religious seminaries. They are all ultra-strict puritans, no doubt, but with good intentions.

Since the new rulers were fully occupied with bringing about peace within the areas they occupied, no attention was paid towards revitalizing economic activity. An elderly Islamic scholar in Herat, whom Burns had met while he was there after the Taliban had captured it, said, 'We are ruled by men who offer us nothing but the Koran, even though many of them cannot read....we are in despair'.

This view was confirmed by those Afghan refugees who left their country three months after the Taliban had overrun Kabul. When questioned as to why they decided to leave their country although peace had returned to those areas under the control of the Taliban, they were unanimous in saying that they did so because they had been jobless since the Taliban entered the capital.[59] Mohammad Yunus, Director of Afghan Refugees at Peshawar, rightfully described the new refugees as 'economic migrants'.

Anthony Lewis, a columnist of the *International Herald Tribune*, writes that in Afghanistan every modern institution has been destroyed except that people with little or no education have the most technically sophisticated weapons in their hands.[60] This tallies with the unverified impression of Qazi Hussain Ahmed about the Taliban.

The Taliban are, however, strong willed and very dedicated to the cause they have set out to accomplish. They lead a very simple and austere life and practice what they preach. Most of the ministers and government servants draw no salary and continue to live in their modest dwellings. 'A guest is not entertained by slaughtering the fatted sheep but by a loaf of dried bread and curry diluted with water,' said Anwarul Haq, Deputy Administrator of Darul Uloom Haqqania, who was the guest of Mullah Hassan, a member of the Central *Shoora* in Kabul.[61] Mullah Omar received visitors sitting on the ground in a small house in Kandahar.

No distinction was noticed between the ruler and the ruled. All were equal in the eyes of the Taliban.

One positive action by the Taliban in the areas they occupied was the banning of drug trafficking. Drug addicts were to be arrested and a proper investigation made to reach the supplier, who was to be severely punished.[62] This fact was reiterated by Mullah Mohammad Rabbani, Chairman of the Caretaker Council of Afghanistan, while giving his government's policy at the Extraordinary Session of the OIC held at Islamabad on 23 March 1997. However, directives on banning poppy cultivation were not implemented as that was the only source of revenue for many in Afghanistan. Mullah Rabbani also informed the members of the OIC that his government was giving due consideration to the need to revive the educational institutions. He is reported to have said, 'Despite having certain financial constraints we have re-established the Kabul university'. As far as the question of female education was concerned, Rabbani said that the Taliban leadership believed in compulsory education for all male and female Muslims, and that the state was determined to start special schools for women subject to the availability of finances and suitable conditions.[63]

Qazi Hussain Ahmed, Chief of the Jamaat-i-Islami, Pakistan, does not accept the credentials of the religious teachers in the *deeni madaris* where most of the Taliban have received their early education. On being told that these schools were not imparting modern education (*jadeedi talim*) and the Taliban, therefore, would find it difficult to run the affairs of the state if and when they came to power, he remarked that even the traditional education (*qadeemi talim*) was not being properly taught as the teachers were uneducated *maulvis*. (This is not entirely true as the syllabi of these schools include a profound study of Islam. The library at Darul Uloom Haqqania at Akora Khattak, where hundreds of Afghan *talibs* were found studying, has about 3,000 books on various aspects of Islam in Arabic, Persian, and Urdu). Qazi Hussain Ahmed cited the example of

all girls' schools being closed and watching of television
having been banned in areas under Taliban control, which
even he thought to be an incorrect interpretation of the
Holy Koran and Sunna. He therefore doubted their ability
to interpret the *shariah* in keeping with the objectives of
progress and prosperity in a Muslim country.[64]

Organization

Many amongst us were not prepared to believe that a group
of young Afghan students living in Quetta would be able to
organize a movement on such a large scale by themselves.
After all, it was not an easy task for raw hands to implement
the stupendous task of overthrowing an established regime,
however motivated they might be and however weak the
de facto government in Kabul appeared to be. They surely
must have received the tacit approval of, and financial support
and training from, some other agency.

The ISI, the Ministry of Interior, Saudi Arabia, and the United
States have all been mentioned off and on, but with no
credible evidence to prove that any of them was actually
involved. Pakistan has denied having organized the Taliban,
and its reasons for allegedly supporting them will be
discussed later; the other two countries would not be major
beneficiaries if the Taliban came into power, particularly
as it has generally been seen that the recipients of aid do
not necessarily remain 'loyal' to their benefactors—in fact
they have been known to turn against them when realpolitik
so demands.

One thing is certain: that without an outside agency the
Taliban by themselves did not have the ability to organize
a full-fledged fighting force. The training needed to operate
sophisticated military hardware and the logistics required
to sustain a conflict for so long were surely beyond the
capability of these new entrants to the battlefield. Supply
of ammunition, provision of fuel and rations at far-off

places, maintenance of aircraft and modern weaponry, all these need money, organizing ability, and an expertise which these raw hands did not possess. Granted, they were not fighting a regular war on the pattern of modern conflicts, but even guerrilla warfare requires logistical support and outside assistance for it to succeed.

What observers failed to realize initially was that the young students were soon joined by experienced hands who had been fighting against the Soviets during the Afghan jihad. It is they who were helping in organizing the 'war effort'.

A central *shoora* had been established in Kandahar, with Mullah Omar designated as the *Amirul Momineen*. The 'war effort' and all policies were being directed from his headquarters in Kandahar, which virtually became the capital of the Taliban-controlled areas of Afghanistan. According to a UN official, Mullah Omar remained in the background, and most of the time mediators in the conflict had to content themselves with meeting second stringers. Representatives of the Taliban frequently met UNHCR officials in Islamabad and negotiated on behalf of their *shoora* as far as the administration of the twenty-two provinces under their control was concerned.

The ten Taliban who initially formed the *Shoora* were:

1. Mullah Mohammad Omar Akhund, (Gilzai Pushtun) *Amirul Momineen*
2. Mullah Mohammad Rabbani (Pushtun), Chairman of the Caretaker Council and Deputy Commander of the Taliban movement
3. Mullah Mohammad Fadel, (Pushtun), Minister of Defence
4. Mullah Mohammad Ghaus, (Pushtun), Minister of Foreign Affairs
5. Mullah Mohammad Hassan, (Pushtun), Minister of Security

6. Maulvi Ghayasuddin Agha, (Uzbek), Minister of Education
7. Maulvi A. Raqeeb, (Uzbek) Minister for Refugees
8. Qari Deen Mohammad, (Tajik) Minister for Planning
9. Mullah Abdul Razzaq, (Tajik) Member Supervisory Council
10. Maulvi Abdul Salam, (Uzbek) Deputy Minister of Education

The Taliban, however, lacked a state structure. Ministries, departments, bureaucratic machinery, and an organized army or police force, which are symbols of modern governments, were not initially functioning in Taliban-controlled areas. The educated officials needed to run ministries had mostly fled the country, and filling their vacancies was not a priority. The first task was to establish law and order and to ward off threats from anti-Taliban forces. The trappings of government were to come later.

In May 1997 the Taliban claimed that twenty ministries had begun to function and that they were engaged in long- and short-term development programmes. However, almost all of them existed on paper only, as the trained manpower needed to run the affairs of state along modern lines was absent.

Aims and Objectives

The aim of the Taliban is to establish an Islamic government in Afghanistan where the *shariah* law, as interpreted by them, will be the law of the land. The country is to be called the Islamic State of Afghanistan and will be governed in accordance with the Sunni Hanafi *fiqah*. A nominated *shoora* is to run the affairs of the state in keeping with the edicts of the *Amirul Momineen*.

The Taliban believe in non-interference in the affairs of other countries and similarly desire no outside interference in their country's internal affairs. No body or organization, whatever its identity or goals may be, will be allowed to carry out any terrorist or criminal activities in other Islamic countries, says their unwritten 'constitution'.

The official handout circulated by the Taliban regime in May 1997 lists the objectives of the Taliban as follows:

- Restoration of peace
- Collection of weapons
- Implementation of the *shariah*

The Taliban leaders also call their movement a jihad. According to Mullah Syed Abdullah, the Taliban Governor of Khost, 'the jihad is against sins, corruption, and cruelties'. Omar wishes to re-create the times of the *Khulafa-e-Rashideen* by emphasizing equality amongst all citizens and simplicity in leading one's life.

Their fury, however, was mainly directed against Rabbani, as he was holding on to power in spite of his term of office having expired in October 1994. They felt that he was responsible for the fighting in Afghanistan since he was not prepared to step down despite the fact that that was the demand of the majority of the Afghan factions. His use of force to stay on as the head of the country was causing considerable suffering, not only to the Kabulis, but also to those living in other parts of Afghanistan. The Taliban considered him to be the main stumbling block in the way of peace returning to their country. However, even after Rabbani was compelled to flee from Kabul the warring factions continued to fight against each other.

Another reason for their determination to oust Rabbani was political in nature as their aim appeared to be to oust a non-Pushtun government in Kabul. (The only non-Pushtun ruler in Afghanistan's history was the Tajik upstart Bacha Saqao, who could sit on the throne for only ten months. He was ousted by General Mohammad Nadir Khan on 17 October 1929 and later executed.)

Ahmed Shah Masood, Rabbani's right-hand man, his Defence Minister and Commander-in-Chief of his forces, was also disliked by the Taliban—they blamed him for all the killings and destruction in Afghanistan. In this they were not too far wrong; Masood did believe in solving issues by coercion. His general attitude towards others is known to be harsh and blunt—having fought against the Soviets without the support of the United States or that of Pakistan, he developed a superiority complex.

Masood, however, did not have the strength to nip the new arrivals on the Afghan scene in the bud so far away from his stronghold. His *Shoora-e-Nazar* was the only faction available to him to stem the Taliban tide as no other force was supporting him. There was nothing much he could do, therefore, except to watch with dismay their further gains and await their arrival on his doorstep. Thus a new factor of great significance was introduced into the already complicated situation in Afghanistan.

Table 3

The Taliban Cabinet (1 May 1997)

Cabinet Member	Designation
Mullah Mohammad Omar Akhund	*Amirul Momineen*
Mullah Mohammad Rabbani	*Naib Amir*
Haji Mohammad Ghaus	Foreign Minister
Commander Abdullah Akhund	Defence Minister
Mullah Khairullah Khairkhwa	Interior Minister
Mullah Amir Khan Muttaqi	Information Minister
Mullah Nuruddin Turabi	Justice Minister
Maulvi Syed Inayatuddin Agha.	Education Minister
Haji Mullah Mohammad Abbas Akhund	Health Minister
Mullah Allah Dad	Communications Minister
Qari Deen Mohammad	Minister of Planning
Maulvi Abdur Raqeeb	Muhajireen Affairs
Maulvi Abdul Shakoor Rehmani	*Haj* and *Auqaf*
Mullah Qalamuddin	Head of the Anti-vice Department
Maulvi Wakil Ahmed	Secretary to *Amirul Momineen*

Kabul's Six-man Supervisory Council

Mullah Mohammad Hassan Akhund
                    (Vice Chairman)
Mullah Mohammad Rabbani
Mullah Mohammad Ghaus
Mullah Syed Ghayasuddin Agha
Mullah Ghazi Mohammad
Mullah Abdul Razzaq

Source: Afghanistan Forum;
                  Frontier Post, 24 February 1995

CHAPTER 3

THE MILITARY DIMENSION

Military victories on the battlefield have generally been the result of superiority in numbers or firepower at the point of engagement of the forces concerned. But numerous cases can be cited where a smaller number of ill-equipped fighters have managed to throw back an aggressor or have been able to overrun positions occupied by a larger body of men.

The Afghans in particular have demonstrated this ability several times. The Anglo-Afghan wars of the late nineteenth century resulted in the defeat of the British Indian army at the hands of Afghans armed with relatively lighter weapons. The Afghan mujahideen succeeded in evicting the Soviet troops even though they were pitched against the might of a superpower.

The military situation in Afghanistan was not quite the same when the Taliban came on the scene as there were no foreign troops occupying their country. However, the ruling clique had more or less lost the support of the majority of the people of Afghanistan, and the mujahideen, who had for long struggled to evict Soviet soldiers from their land, had begun to behave like occupation forces themselves. It was, therefore, not very surprising that the war weary people joined a movement which promised them security from the self-appointed warlords.

Military Strength

The order of battle of the Afghan armed forces during the days of the Soviet occupation of their country was as follows:

1	Corps Headquarters	Kabul
8	Infantry Division	Kabul
9	Infantry Division	Kunarh
11	Infantry Division	Jalalabad
4	Armoured Brigade	Kabul
46	Artillery Regiment	Kunarh
2	Corps Headquarters	Kandahar
15	Infantry Division	Kandahar
17	Infantry Division	Herat
18	Infantry Division	Mazar-e-Sharif
20	Infantry Division	Baghlan
7	Armoured Brigade	Kandahar
43	Mountain Regiment	Zabul
3	Corps Headquarters	Gardez
12	Infantry Division	Gardez
14	Infantry Division	Ghazni
25	Infantry Division	Khost
91	Artillery Regiment	Jalalabad
6	Artillery Regiment	Khost

The Afghan air force consisted of around 140 aircraft and about 73 helicopters on 1 January 1985. These were stationed as under:

Airbase	Aircraft
Bagram (Kabul)	3 Fighter Aircraft Squadrons (40 MiG 21s)
	3 Fighter-Bomber Squadrons (Su-7/22)
Shindand (Farah)	3 Bomber Squadrons (ILL 28)
	1 Fighter-Bomber Squadron (MiG 17s)
	1 Helicopter Squadron (Mi 8)

Dehdadi (Balkh)	3 Fighter-Bomber Squadrons (MiG 17s)
Kabul airport	3 Helicopter Squadrons (12 Mi 4/6/8)
	4 Helicopter Squadrons (6 Mi 25, 25 Mi 17)
	2 Transport Squadrons (1 ILL 18, 12 An 14)
	Attack Helicopter Squadron (c. 15 Mi 24)
Jalalabad	Attack Helicopter Squadron (c. 15 Mi 24)

Source: Mark L. Urban, *War in Afghanistan*, St Martin's Press, New York, 1988, pp. 223–5

Afghan infantry divisions were equivalent to a standard infantry brigade. The strength of the infantry divisions in 1985 varied between 1,500 and 4,500[65] i.e., less than one-third that of a similar formation in any modern army. Many were without their normal complement of supporting arms and services.

The strength of the Afghan armed forces on 1 April 1992, the day the Afghan mujahideen entered Kabul, comprised:

Army

Main battle tanks	700 (T54–55), 170 (T62)
Towed artillery	1,000 (85mm, 100mm, 122mm, 130mm, 152mm)
Multi-barrel rocket-launchers	185 (122mm, 140mm, 220mm)
Mortars	1,000 ((82mm, 107mm, 120mm)
SSM (Scuds)	30
Air defence guns	600

Air Force

Ground attack fighter	30 MiG 23, 80 Su 7/17/22
Fighters	80 MiG 21 F

| Armed helicopters | 25 Mi 8, 35 Mi 17, 20 Mi 25 |
| Transport aircraft | 2 ILL 18 D, 50 (An 2, 12, 26, 32) |

(An unknown number of these aircraft were shot down or destroyed on the ground during the civil war of 1994-7.)

Source: *Military Balance*, Institute of International Strategic Studies, London, 1996/97, p. 157

The mujahideen factions inherited these formations and kept the same designations but turned them into *lashkars* (irregular forces) of varying sizes. While the amount of military hardware that came into the hands of the rival militia depended on the territories they controlled, their operational effectiveness was determined, to a great extent, by the supporting arms, logistic elements, and maintenance facilities each could manage to obtain.

Their morale and the support each of them received from the local population also played a significant role in their fighting capabilities. Battle fatigue and the inability of the leaders to meet the expenses of maintaining their militia, both had an adverse impact on their followers.

The loyalty of the mujahideen to their respective factions was, therefore, not very strong. They could be purchased or persuaded to switch sides whenever they found it in their interest to do so.

Sources of Weapon Supplies

The Taliban obtained their first military hardware from a well-wisher who opened his armoury for Mullah Omar. This was soon augmented by raiding an arms and ammunition dump belonging to Hikmetyar at Spin Boldak. As they succeeded in overrunning province after province, more and more weapons fell into their hands. According to one source, the Taliban possessed around 200 tanks, 12 MiG 23s, and over a dozen helicopters by April 1995.[66] Twelve aircraft were seen at Kandahar airport by a member of the UN team when he visited Kandahar in June 1995.

According to reliable sources, the military hardware left behind by the Russians amounted to billions of US dollars. At the height of the Afghan jihad the Soviets had 257 aircraft and 335 helicopters of all types stationed at different airfields in Afghanistan.[67] Many of these were left behind by the Soviets as they wanted to strengthen the hand of Dr Najibullah so that he could remain in power after they withdrew their troops from Afghanistan.

In addition to the weapons of Soviet origin lying around in different places, US-supplied military hardware was also held by the various mujahideen factions. The arms and ammunition pipeline which had been established by the ISI during the Afghan jihad had not totally dried up. In spite of the fact that the United States had discontinued its military aid to the mujahideen, there were plenty of American weapons in the hands of the various factions— the Ojhri camp disaster notwithstanding.

Since disarming the militia was a priority task of the Taliban, their stockpile of weapons kept increasing every time they overran a province. These were handed over to the Taliban at their request by the rival militia to avoid further bloodshed. The largest source of military hardware came into their hands when they captured Hikmetyar's stronghold of Charasyab.

Replacement of weapons and ammunition expended was also not much of a problem. Merchants of death in western nations have no hesitation in selling these wares if they get the price they ask for. Chartered aircraft from East European countries bringing in arms for the Kabul regime had been intercepted by the Taliban. It is quite possible that they too were obtaining their weapons from outside sources. Smugglers and the drug mafia operating from outside Afghanistan were also a source of arms supply to the Taliban.

Weapons of Russian Origin Held by the Various Afghan Militia (1994)

Infantry

9 mm pistol (Markov)
7.62 pistol
7.62 mm sub-machine gun (Sudayev)
7.62 mm light machine gun (Deztyarer)
7.62 mm general purpose machine gun (Kalashnikov)
7.62 mm modernized (Goryunor)
12.7 mm heavy machine gun (Dehska)
AGS 17 grenade launcher
Smoke hand grenade RDG 1 and RDG 2
RG-42 anti-personnel hand grenade
FI anti-personnel hand grenade
Rocket-propelled anti-tank hand grenade RPG 6
Anti-tank (A/Tk) recoilless launcher (RL)
RPG 2
RPG 7
82 mm A/Tk RL
82 mm recoilless rifle (RR)
107 mm RR
RPG 16,18, and 22 (Shamy)
SPG 9

Mortars

81 mm, 82 mm, 107 mm, 120 mm, 160 mm

Heavy Weapons

57 mm A/Tk , 76 mm self-propelled (SP) gun,
100 mm gun MI 944 (towed)
122 mm howitzer M 30 (towed)
122 mm gun D 30
130 mm gun, M46 (towed)
152 mm gun, D-1 (towed)
BM 21, 13, 16, 27
Single-barrel rocket-launcher 122 mm
Multi-barrel rocket-launcher (MBRL)

Tanks
   T-34, T-54, T-55, T-62

Armoured Personnel Carriers (APC)
   BTR-40, BTR-50 (tracked), BTR-60 (wheeled)
   BRDM-2 (command vehicle), BMP-1

Anti-Tank Guided Missiles
   AT-1 (Snapper), AT-3 (Sagger), AT-4 (Spandrel)
   Milan

Air Defence Weapons
   Deshika AA MG 12.7, 1
   4.5 AA Hy MG
   23 mm ZSU-24 (Shalka)
   37 mm gun AA, Hydra 2.5, 57 mm, 85 mm, 100mm
   Surface to air missile (SAM)
   SA-2, SA-3, SA-7, SA-9
   Surface to surface missile (SSM)
   SCUD-A, SCUD-B, FROG-7 (LUNA)

Source reliable, name withheld

Weapons of Other Origins Held by Various Afghan Militia (1994)

US Origin

Infantry
60,000 rifles from Turkey
100,000 .303 rifles from India
8,000 light machine guns from Turkey
10,000 pistols from Turkey
122 mm rocket-launchers from Egypt

Air Defence
Stinger shoulder-fired anti-aircraft missiles
20mm Orlikon anti-aircraft guns

Chinese Weapons

Artillery
Multi-barrel rocket launchers (MBRL)
Single-barrel rocket launchers (SBRL)
82 mm mortars

British Origin
Anti-aircraft hand-held Missile (Blowpipe)

Source: M. Yusuf, (Brigadier) and Adkin, M., *The Bear Trap,* Jang Publishers, Lahore, 1992, pp. 84–7

Table 4
Strength of Various Factions in Afghanistan During the Afghan Jihad

Faction	Strength
Jumbish-e-Milli (Abdul Rashid Dostum)* Mainly Uzbeks. Area of operation: Northern provinces	50,000
Jamiat-e-Islami (Ahmed Shah Masood) Mainly Tajiks. Area of operation: Panjsher, Herat	30,000
Hizb-e-Islami (Gulbadin Hikmetyar) ** Mainly Pushtuns. Area of operation: Nangarhar	20,000
Harakat-e-Inqilab-e-Islami (Nabi Mohammedi) Mainly Ahmedzai. Pushtuns. Area of operation: Logar	20,000
Mahaz-e-Milli-Islami (Syed Ahmed Gailani) Mainly Pushtuns. Area of operation: Wardak, Kandahar	15,000
Hizb-e-Islami (Yunus Khalis) Mainly Pushtuns. Area of operation: Paktia, Kabul	10,000
Ittehad-e-Islami (Abdul Rab Rasul Sayyaf) Mainly Pushtuns. Area of operation: Paktia	4,000
Jabha-e-Nijat-e-Milli (Sibghatullah Mojeddedi) Mainly Pushtuns. Area of operation: Kunarh, Kandahar	3,500
Hizb-e-Wahdat (Abdul Karim Khalili) Mainly Shia. Area of operation: Bamian	Not available
Taliban, estimated (1997)	50,000

* Estimated strength in 1997. Well equipped, well trained, well organized.
** Strength considerably reduced due to defections after being defeated at the hands of
the Taliban. Almost a non-entity in 1997.

Sources: Institute of Strategic Studies, Islamabad.
Urban, Mark, *War in Afghanistan*, St Martin's Press, New York, 1988, pp. 241–3.

Defections have taken place in all other parties. Except for
Jamiat-e-Islami (Masood) the strength of all other factions
in 1997 was far below what it was during the Afghan jihad.

Table 5.1
Strength of Personnel Belonging to Various Factions

	Faction	Strength
1.	Taliban	50,000
2.	Jumbish-e-Milli	35,000
3.	Hizb-e-Islami (H)	10,000
4.	Hizb-e-Wahdat (Khalili)	5,000
5.	Jamiat-e-Islami	35,000
6.	Ittehad-e-Islami	8,000
7.	Mohsini	4,000
8.	Hizb-e-Wahdat (Akbari)	3,000

Recent information - source reliable

Table 5.2
Air Power Capabilities of the Various Factions

Faction	Fighters	Helicopters	Transporters
Taliban	23	32	2
Jumbish	11	9	3
Jamiat-e-Islami (Ahmed Shah Masood)	10	12	10

Recent information - source reliable

Availability of Money

Where did they get the money to maintain the fighters that came under their fold as they advanced further into Afghanistan? 'In one word it is smuggling,'[68] said Ijlal Haider Zaidi, former adviser to the second Benazir government on Afghanistan. Eyewitnesses claim that they have personally seen Kandahar airport full of consumer items coming in from Dubai. Stacks of foreign cigarettes, Sony televisions, frigidaires, washing machines lay one above the other in the hangers. In a country where electricity connections were then non-existent, why were these goods being imported? According to a reliable source, these items were checked and payment was taken for allowing the vehicles with their cargo to proceed onwards to Pakistan through Chaman and Jalalabad.[69] The profit so made was allegedly used for the purchase of weapons from outside sources.

Rahimullah Yusufzai, a well-known columnist and one who has been going into Afghanistan every now and then, claims that, 'the Afghan car economy is booming'. He mentions a figure of 200 to 300 vehicles of every description being smuggled into Pakistan every month. He says that they were brought from the United Arab Emirates via Iran. While talking to a businessman in Taliban-controlled Herat he was told, 'business has never been so good, the demand in Pakistan for our cars is growing'. Rahimullah says that, 'Vehicle smuggling has received a boost since the emergence of the Taliban Islamic movement as it has restored peace which in turn has re-invigorated the informal Afghan economy.'

The profit made in these shady car deals is enormous. According to a car dealer in Kandahar, a car that he purchases in Dubai for Rs 22,000 sells for 600,000 in Pakistan. 'The Taliban charge Rs 18,000 customs duty for a 1986 model Toyota Corolla car in Herat and a little more on mini-buses, Pajeros, and Land Cruisers of 1990 origin', writes Yusufzai.[70] The Taliban perhaps do not believe that they are doing anything wrong as, according to them, Islam encourages trading with no regard to international borders between Muslim countries, and that is what they are doing. There was, therefore, enough money available to the Taliban to buy their weapons from those willing to sell them.

The Gulf states are believed to have been funding the Taliban and, according to one source, the UAE Sheikhs on one occasion left behind 100 Mitsubishi Pajeros after their annual hunting trips to Pakistan.[71] Petro-dollars, or to be more precise, Saudi money, is said to be the life-blood of this new outfit, claims Afrasiab Khattak.[72] His pro-Najibullah feelings and his disagreement with Pakistan's Afghan policy notwithstanding, there may well be some truth in his assertions as the Saudis have been funding the *deeni madaris*.

Khattak goes on to blame Pakistan for organizing, training, and arming the Taliban and for continuing the policy of the Silent Soldier (a reference to the covert operations of the ISI during the Soviet occupation of Afghanistan) though he does not produce any concrete evidence to prove his assertion.

Training

How is it that these Taliban, who until yesterday were mere students in religiously-oriented schools in another country, learnt to use weapons effectively on a battlefield? It takes a long time to teach a recruit to drive a tank or to fire an artillery piece accurately—leave alone fly a bomber or a fighter aircraft, which needs hundreds of hours of flying experience and practice firing.

Training camps had been established inside Afghanistan by different factions during the jihad. They continued to function even during the civil war which engulfed the country after the fall of Dr Najibullah. Those in operation in Taliban-controlled areas were at Kandahar, Khost, Logar, and Herat.

One such training camp was fully operational in the south-eastern province of Khost on the border of Pakistan. The camps known as Al Badar I and Al Badar II are reported to have been started by Gulbadin Hikmetyar and his ally, the Jamaat-i-Islami of Pakistan. Yusafzai, who visited the camp, writes that hundreds of Afghans, Pakistanis, and Muslim militants from other Muslim countries were receiving training there.

Both of these camps were closed by the Taliban on 17 September 1996 as they believed that those receiving training there were to be used against them. Later they were handed over to Harkatul Ansar, a militant Islamist group.[73] Jalaluddin Haqqani, a famous military commander in Khost from the days of the Afghan jihad against the Soviets, has been running a training camp in Khost as well.

Modern arms and weapon systems however, need considerable training. How is it that the Taliban have become so efficient in their use so quickly? I put this question to a member of the UN Secretary General's special mission for Afghanistan and Pakistan who had been talking to them during frequent visits to Afghanistan. According to him, former communists who were in the Afghan armed forces during the days of Dr Najibullah joined the Taliban movement, including pilots, trained artillerymen, and tank crews.

Haji Abdul Qadeer, Governor of Nangarhar, who was forced to flee to Pakistan when the Taliban attacked Jalalabad, claims that several erstwhile communists joined the Taliban movement and that it is they who were operating the sophisticated weapon systems.[74] He was not far wrong, as many old communists had indeed defected and joined the Taliban, whether through fear or a genuine change of heart is not known.

During one of his visits to Afghanistan Major-General (Retired) Naseerullah Khan Babar, former Interior Minister in the second Benazir Government, was flown by a Taliban-owned aircraft to Mazar-e-Sharif. The black-turbaned pilot was a *talib* dressed in the usual *shalwar qameez*. Babar was surprised to find that the so-called *talib* had logged 1,500 hours of flying.[75] He seemed to have exaggerated his flying hours, nevertheless, he was obviously one of those who was part of the Afghan air force and had now defected. It is these elements who are training the Taliban. Many of the Taliban took part in the Afghan *jihad*, where they would have been operating some of these weapon systems.

In any case, the Afghans are known for their fondness for weapons, which they learn to handle as soon as they can stand on their own feet. It was, therefore, not difficult for them to operate the newly found military hardware.

Tactics Used

The Taliban are not to be compared to an organized army. Their commanders do not carry out a military appreciation. There are no assembly areas, forming-up places, or start lines before an attack is launched. No fire plans are made. A large number of rockets are fired in the general direction of the objective, accompanied by a hail of bullets from automatic weapons, and hopefully the rival militia surrenders. The war booty so obtained helps them to fight another day.

If the 'enemy' does not melt away, an attack of sorts is put in. Initially, nowhere was a force of more than 500 fighters used.[76] It was only when they met very stiff resistance, or were faced with the well-trained and well-disciplined militia of Abdul Rashid Dostum, that they felt the need to assemble thousands of their Talibs. That was also the case with the opposing militia.

More often than not, guerrilla tactics have been resorted to for instance, a surprise attack from the flanks, a short sharp engagement, and then a rapid retreat. Generally there would be an exchange of artillery and rocket fire without any forward movement. Aerial bombardment has been sparingly carried out and is confined to a single, or at the most two, sorties at a time. Since the pilots generally remain out of range of anti-aircraft fire they have not been very accurate in their bombing.

Poor maintenance facilities, lack of spare parts, fuel shortages, and hardly any regular training are some of the reasons for the limited aerial attacks on both sides of the shifting front lines.

The Taliban tried to avoid fighting as much as possible in the days before they reached Kabul. Their usual tactic when closing on the opposition was to send their trusted Mullahs, carrying the Taliban flag (pure white, with the *kalima* written in green) and the Holy Koran, to the opposing militia fighters and ask them to lay down their arms as the Taliban had come to restore peace and end all fighting in that area. In most cases the opposition did so, as the Taliban seemed to be a neutral force with no axe to grind, and power would be transferred peacefully. More often than not, they took control of the cities without a shot being fired. In these early days of their forward movement, they were by and large following the traditional Afghan method of solving disputes, namely agreement by consensus.

The fighting in Afghanistan between the Taliban and their opponents has been correctly described as small, low-risk engagements.

Major Military Engagements:

Capture of Spin Boldak Arms Depot

The first military skirmish that they undertook was to capture an arms and ammunition dump in a remote area that was only lightly held by one of the Afghan factions. The newly-formed body did not have enough arms and ammunition to achieve their objectives. When they found out that a huge arms depot belonging to the Hizb-e-Islami (Hikmetyar) was located at Toba Achakzai, fifteen kilometres north of Spin Boldak, close to the Pakistan border town of Chaman, they decided to raid it to obtain the necessary military hardware.

In May 1994 about forty or fifty *talibs* mounted on two trucks moved out from Maiwand towards Spin Boldak. To avoid being detected, they covered the trucks with tarpaulins and bypassed the town of Kandahar. When stopped by local commanders manning the various check-points on the way to their objective they told them that the trucks were loaded with cattle. A small bribe at each barricade ensured that their secret plan was not leaked out. On reaching the arms depot they suddenly dismounted and raided the ammunition dump. A brief scuffle took place, after which Commander Sarkatib of Hizb-e-Islami, whose men were guarding the depot, surrendered. Four or five *talibs* were killed in the raid.

Incidently, on that very day the UNS-G's Special Representative for Afghanistan was holding a meeting of some Afghan factions and Afghan expatriates in Quetta in an attempt to make the various groups agree to a broadbased government in Afghanistan. After the successful raid of the Taliban on the Spin Boldak arms depot, the military situation on the ground had changed, and the meeting broke up without any progress on the formation of the interim government which was being planned to replace the Rabbani regime.

The depot contained around 3,000 metric tonnes of arms and ammunition. A very large amount of weapons, including 80,000 Kalashnikovs, and hundreds of thousands of rounds of ammunition, belonging to Hikmetyar's Hizb-e-Islami, fell into the hands of the Taliban without much fighting.[77] Having captured the depot, they sent word to the Afghan students studying in the *madaris* around Quetta, who willingly joined them.

The successful raid on the arms depot at Spin Boldak was due to deception and surprise. The Taliban first deceived those manning the check-points by posing as traders and hence went on towards their objective unnoticed. The guards at the depot were totally surprised when the Taliban suddenly swooped upon them from nowhere. With reinforcements arriving in time, the task was accomplished with very little loss of life.

Taliban Come to the Rescue

Mullah Salam Rocketi, a local warlord, operated along the road leading to Kandahar from Chaman. He and the Government of Pakistan fell out when some of his supporters, including his brother, were arrested by the Pakistani security agencies in Quetta. He took his revenge by kidnapping two Chinese and eight Pakistanis working on a project in Balochistan. It was only after the Saudi Ambassador in Islamabad went to Kabul that Mullah Rocketi agreed to release the hostages.[78] Many of Rocketi's followers, however, continued to bear a grudge against Pakistan.

Ever since the civil war around Kabul had intensified, Pakistan had been keen to establish contacts with the newly-independent Muslim republics of Central Asia, using the western route which appeared not to have been affected by the internecine conflict to a great extent.

Herat is an important communication centre on the highway leading to Turkmenistan, lying as it does on the main trade route to Central Asia and Iran. Herat has a rich Islamic culture, and Pakistan was keen to establish its presence in western Afghanistan. The Government of Pakistan therefore sought and received permission from President Rabbani to open a mission in Herat. Sultan Amir (generally known as Colonel Imam by the mujahideen and the Taliban), formerly of the Inter Services Intelligence Directorate (ISI), was posted as the first head of the Pakistani mission in Herat on 1 August 1994. The formal opening ceremony of the mission was performed by General Mohammad Ismail, Rabbani's divisional commander in Herat, in mid-September 1994. General Babar also attended the function.[79] At that time the Rabbani regime in Kabul was friendly towards Pakistan.

In the last week of September Babar decided to visit the Central Asian States by land, along with Major-General Hidayatullah Khan Niazi, Director-General of Pakistan's National Highway Authority. They took the western route. The fifteen-day trip through Afghanistan, the Central Asian Republics, and China was meant to assess the possibility of opening up trade with the newly-independent Muslim republics via Kandahar and Herat.

On his return via the Karakoram Highway (KKH), Babar announced that Afghanistan was returning to normalcy and it was time to help the Afghans meet their socio-economic needs. (Infact the assessment applied only to south-western Afghanistan, as Hikmetyar and Rabbani were locked in a life-and-death struggle in Kabul, with casualties rising with each passing day.)

Babar and Imam apparently discussed the chances of rehabilitating the western route to the trans-Oxus region. Imam also suggested to Babar that Pakistan should give some humanitarian assistance to the Afghans. 'They deserve our help,' said Imam. Babar asked for a consolidated report on the type of assistance which Pakistan could provide to alleviate the sufferings of the Afghans living around Kandahar and Herat. An aid package for the two cities was eventually worked out, and it was agreed that a convoy of vehicles could be taken through, and then proceed to the Central Asian Republics.

While arrangements for the convoy were being finalized, Babar took a number of ambassadors to Herat with the intention of encouraging some of them to invest in the improvement of the western highway. Seven ambassadors— those from the USA, China, Japan, Spain, France, Germany, and Rabbani's ambassador to Islamabad—flew to Herat on 20 October and found the conditions there relatively peaceful. The possibility of winning contracts for the construction of an oil and gas pipeline from

Turkmenistan to Pakistan through Afghanistan attracted some multi-national firms. Babar's hopes did not materialize, however, as no company was prepared to invest till durable peace returned to Afghanistan.

Ten days later a convoy of thirty National Logistics Cell (NLC) vehicles laden with flour, rice, sugar, X-ray machines, surgical instruments, and medicines, under the command of Major Jehangir of the NLC, crossed the Pakistan-Afghanistan border at Chaman on its way to Central Asia. Two vehicle-loads each were meant for Lashkargarh (capital of Helmand), Kandahar, and Herat, and the rest for Turkmenistan and Uzbekistan. Some ISI personnel accompanied the convoy.

To give wider publicity to the newly-established contacts between Pakistan and the Muslim republics north of the Oxus (Amu Darya), the convoy was timed to reach Ashkabad, capital of Turkmenistan, during the Prime Minister's visit to that country, which was scheduled for 22–6 October 1994. However, all did not go well and the convoy was not only delayed; it also created a diplomatic row between Islamabad and Kabul.

Rabbani's regime in Kabul, which considered itself to be the *de jure* and *de facto* government of Afghanistan, objected to the plan as permission to transit through the country had not been obtained from them. Pakistan, however, was relying on a Trade and Transit Agreement signed between the two countries in 1965 which allowed the movement of goods through their respective countries without any special permission. This did not satisfy the authorities in Kabul and they, presumably, decided to have the convoy disrupted.

Colonel Imam, who joined the convoy at Spin Boldak, maintained that he had obtained written permission from all the senior commanders in Kandahar, which was still under the nominal control of the regime at Kabul, allowing the convoy to pass through all the check-posts on the way. Neither he nor the Ministry of Foreign Affairs informed Amir Usman, the then Ambassador and Plenipotentiary of Pakistan in Kabul, about the planned operation. According to Usman, he had no knowledge of a convoy of Pakistani vehicles passing through Taliban-controlled areas.[80]

On 2 November 1994 the convoy was detained and looted by local warlords allegedly belonging to the Achakzai militia. When the convoy crossed Takhta Pul, twenty-five kilometres short of Kandahar,[81] and was between the airport and the city, the leading vehicle was stopped. The driver was told to get off the road and the convoy was forced to move towards a deserted place a few kilometres away from the main highway. This was reportedly done at the instigation of commanders Mansoor, Aamir Lale, Ustad Alim, and Hikmetyar's local commander, Sarkatib. A militia belonging to Ismatullah Muslim, an independent warlord who had loose affiliations with Pir Syed Ahmed Gailani's National Islamic Front of Afghanistan (NIFA), was also involved in the highjacking of the convoy.

Colonel Imam, who was travelling in the centre of the convoy, told the drivers not to resist and do as the captors directed. He himself left the convoy and went on to Kandahar to negotiate the release of the hijacked vehicles. He received a message from the hijackers that the militia in that area had jointly decided to stop the convoy and would not allow it to proceed until the Government of Pakistan assured them that the Taliban studying in Quetta would not be permitted to join their colleagues in Kandahar. The commanders also asked to be given a huge sum of money as ransom.

Akhunzada Abdul Ghafoor, the powerful commander of Helmand province, tried to negotiate with Mansoor because some of the items being carried in the vehicles were to be delivered at Lashkargarh, the capital of Helmand. However, he was told to obtain a guarantee from Pakistan that it would not support some religious students in Kandahar against Rabbani's administration in that city.[82]

General Babar blames the Indians and the Iranians for disrupting the movement of the convoy as, according to him, it would have affected their plans to deny this route to Pakistan.[83] His views were not, however, confirmed by any other source.

While Akhunzada was talking to the hijackers, Mullah Borjan, a Taliban leader, approached Imam at his consulate in Kandahar and promised to have the convoy freed. Around 200 students, who had been studying in the *deeni madaris* in Balochistan, suddenly swooped down from nowhere. The fighting between the Taliban and the local commanders commenced on 2 November and continued uptil the forenoon of 4 November while negotiations in Kandahar continued. The hijackers surrendered after one of their commanders was killed in the ensuing 'battle'. The convoy was freed on 4 November and allowed to proceed on its northward journey, but not before fifty per cent of the goods it was carrying were looted. According to Imam, the Taliban saw to it that most of the looted items were located and returned to the convoy.

Eight students were killed in the encounter while twelve others lost their lives.[84] A spokesman for the Taliban in Chaman claimed that forty persons from the other side were killed.[85] The ISI personnel and the PTV team were also rescued.

This act of theirs brought the Taliban into the limelight. It also endeared them to General Babar, who was trying to prove that he had succeeded in opening the western route to the newly-independent countries north of Afghanistan. It is because of this that the Taliban were referred to by some journalists as 'Babar's private army'.

Check-Posts Removed

Another successful Taliban operation was the removal of the numerous check-posts between Chaman and Kandahar which had been established by the local Afghans. The main purpose of these check-posts was to extract money from the drivers of vehicles plying between the two cities. A dozen or so students armed with light weapons went to each barrier and demanded that it be dismantled. In most cases, those manning them did so without offering any resistance. Wherever there was some hesitation, a few shots fired in the air were enough to make them comply.

By eliminating these hurdles and allowing free movement of goods along the Chaman-Kandahar highway, the Taliban gained considerable popularity amongst the people of Kandahar, as they could now carry out trade freely without having to pay heavily for taking their goods across every checkpost.

Kandahar 'Liberated'

The Taliban then sent word of their success to their colleagues in Quetta. Soon they were joined by about 2,000 Taliban from various *madaris* in and around the city. Thus reinforced, they drove back towards Kandahar. Having brushed aside all resistance between Chaman and Kandahar, the Taliban decided to overrun Kandahar itself. Their first action inside the city was to capture two barricades which had been set up by the Governor, Gul Agha. Clashes between government forces and the Taliban took place inside Kandahar city, with both sides using rockets and other heavy weapons freely.

Dagar-General (Lieutenant-General) Naqib Akhunzada, was commanding 2 Corps at Kandahar. The Corps consisted of 7 Armoured Division, 15 Infantry Division, and 7 Mechanized Division. Its firepower comprised 120 tanks, 80 to 90 artillery pieces, and 6 MiG 21s, four of which were serviceable. Six Mi8 helicopters gave the Corps added mobility.

With such a strong force available to him, Rabbani could not only have defended Kandahar against an assault by a group of untrained, ill-equipped young students but could also have sent them packing back to their *madaris*. But he had not catered for the possibility of loyalties changing in the midst of a battle: Naqib, Rabbani's military commander in Kandahar, defected and joined the Taliban along with his 20,000 troops. Commander Mansoor and his supporters put up a fight near

Kandahar but they were soon over-powered. After three days of fighting and the loss of around fifty lives, Kandahar fell to the Taliban on 5 November 1994. Mansoor was caught and killed. His body was hung from the barrel of a tank and paraded along the streets of Kandahar.[86] This was meant to teach others a lesson.

These half-educated students found fertile ground in Kandahar, the second largest city of Afghanistan (population 300,000) and its former capital. From then on the royal city became their headquarters.

Mullah Mohammad Omar Akhund, a thirty-three-year old veteran of the Afghan jihad, who had lost his left eye while fighting against the Soviets, formally assumed the leadership of the 'young bloods'. He formed them into a regular militia with the specific object of bringing about peace in Afghanistan and enforcing the Islamic *shariah*.

The fall of Kandahar shocked Rabbani. Instead of accepting the fact that he was becoming unpopular amongst his own people, he blamed the ISI for the defeat he had suffered at the hands of the Taliban. He alleged that Pakistan was encouraging the student militia to fight against him and was supplying them with weapons. The Taliban refuted the allegation. Although no evidence existed of Pakistan's involvement in the struggle for power between the Taliban militia and the Kabul regime, the fact that they were being given prominence by Islamabad gave rise to the general impression that the Taliban were Pakistan's baby.

Causes of the Fall of Kandahar

Kandahar was host to various mujahideen factions. Sarkatib and Wali Shah were members of Hikmetyar's Hizb-e-Islami. General Naqib owed allegiance to Burhanuddin's Jamiat-e-Islami. Ustad Abdul Halim was loyal to Sayyaf's Ittehad-e-Islami. Gul Agha and Amir Lale were disciples of Pir Syed Ahmed Gailani, and Commander Mansoor belonged to the infamous Ismat militia. But none of these well-known Afghan political parties had complete control over Kandahar. Disunity amongst the old guard was one of the causes of the fall of Kandahar.

The locals were tired of the in-fighting and the corrupt mujahideen commanders. It was not difficult, therefore, for Mullah Omar, who had emerged as the self-appointed leader of the Taliban movement, to convince the Kandaharis to lay down their arms and live peacefully amongst themselves.

The game was up when General Naqib defected along with his entire Corps. Many of the commanders of the older militia also changed sides and joined the Taliban, either through fear of reprisals or because they had been yearning for the peace in their city which the Taliban were able to achieve.

Being far away from Kabul and tucked away to one side of Afghanistan, with easy access to safe havens inside Pakistan, Rabbani and Masood could not play an effective role in suppressing the Taliban movement in Kandahar, so it did not take long for Omar and his band of religious students to consolidate their position in and around the city.

The fact that Kandahar was close to the Pakistani border, and had a reasonably good motorable road from Quetta, helped in getting reinforcements from among the Afghan students studying in the religious schools in Balochistan.

The Taliban Spread Their Wings

After enforcing their authority in Kandahar, and having found that the people welcomed the change, the Taliban moved out of the city towards their next objective. Lashkargarh, on the Kandahar-Herat road, and the neighbouring provinces of Zabul and Uruzgan were taken without any fighting. According to one source, the governors of neighbouring provinces sent delegations to Mullah Omar accepting his leadership.

As more and more volunteers joined the newly-formed force, Mullah Omar organized training centres for the young recruits. The older mujahids, and even some trusted ex-communists who had served in the Afghan army of yore, were brought in as instructors. Many of them had already won their spurs in the crucible of the eleven-year-old war against the Soviets. Soon the ranks of the 'people's army' began to be filled with properly trained and thoroughly motivated *talibs*.

Advance Towards Kabul

The Taliban movement picked up considerable momentum within a very short period. After consolidating their hold over Kandahar in November 1994 in just four weeks they 'overran' four provinces. In the next three months they were in control of another five. By January 1995 their strength had grown to around 4,000 and they were in occupation of seven Afghan provinces: Kandahar, Helmand, Uruzgan, Zabul, Ghazni, Wardak, and Logar. On their way to Kabul, city after city was 'captured' without a fight. As the advance continued, they gained more and more adherents to their cause. By the time they reached Maidan Sheher, close to Kabul, they could count on around 25,000 supporters. A fair amount of military hardware also fell to their lot as most of the rival militia gave up their weapons.

Not surprisingly, they were joined in this new jihad by their brethren living in the tribal areas of Pakistan, to whom the Durand Line had no significance whatsoever. Moving across it to fight a common enemy presented no problem. Many Pushtuns living on either side of an invisible international border consider themselves to be part and parcel of one 'nation'.

Counter-attack on Ghazni

Hikmetyar, once the strong-man of Afghanistan, whose faction had received the maximum military assistance from the ISI during the Afghan jihad, and who brooked no rival during his heyday, was now on the receiving end. A group of young militants had picked up enough strength to challenge his overlordship. Hikmetyar had by now begun to accept that the student militia was a force to reckon

1. A Talib on duty at Kandahar's money exchange market.
Rahimullah Yusufzai. Courtesy *The News*

2. The Taliban targetting forces loyal to the former defence minister, Ahmed Shah Masood in Jabal-us-Siraj, north of Kabul.
Syed Haider Shah. Courtesy *The News*

3. Mullah Stanakzai, Deputy Foreign Minister, March 1997.

4. The Taliban in Kabul. Courtesy *The News*

5. Hizb-e-Wahdat soldiers at a march to commemorate Mazari's death anniversary, 12 March 1997. Chris Weiss.

6. The destruction of Kabul. A view of the Karte Seh Area, Kabul, March 1997. Megan Reif.

7. A BM-12 multi-barrel battery patrolling the frontline in Rishkhor, 3 kilometres away from Kabul city. Syed Haider Shah. Courtesy *The News*

8. The author with Professor Burhanuddin Rabbani, 1991.

with, but thought that they were no match for him. He promised to teach them a lesson if they dared to attack Ghazni.

The Taliban initially bypassed Ghazni and swept through the territories beyond it. A few weeks later they turned back to overrun Ghazni itself.

When Ghazni, the third largest city of Afghanistan, came under the threat of the advancing Taliban, Hikmetyar decided to pre-empt the attack on the city by launching an offensive against them. A fierce fight ensued between the two forces on 19 January 1995. Qari Baba, who had been nominated by the Rabbani regime as the Governor of Ghazni, defected to the Taliban because Rabbani and Hikmetyar were bitter rivals by that time. Consequently Ghazni fell to the Taliban without much fighting.

Hikmetyar realized that if Ghazni was not retaken, the students from the *deeni madaris* would soon be knocking n the doors of his stronghold in Charasyab. He decided, therefore, to put in a counter-attack in a bid to reverse the flow of the Taliban tide. He did manage to recapture some parts of Ghazni, but his followers were soon repulsed. In keeping with the Afghan tradition of siding even with a potential adversary in order to deal with the immediate enemy, Rabbani's forces and those of Nabi Mohammedi (Harakat-e-Inqilab-e-Islami) came to the support of the Taliban. Rabbani's air force bombed Hikmetyar's forces around Ghazni. The two militia together crushed Hikmetyar's counter-attack. Hikmetyar is reported to have lost hundreds of his fighters outside the city.

The Taliban had no love for Rabbani and Masood, but they were clever enough to accept assistance from wherever it came. Having removed one thorn from their side, they had no qualms about demanding the overthrow of their supporter in the encounter at Ghazni.[87]

'Battle' for Maidan Sheher

The town of Maidan Sheher lies about forty-five kilometres south of Kabul. It was being held by the Hizb-e-Islami militia and served as an outpost to Hikmetyar's main base at Charasyab. On their way to Kabul the Taliban had to deal with Hikmetyar's men as they were entrenched south of the capital. When the previous tactic of demanding a peaceful surrender of weapons in lieu of 'general amnesty' was not successful, the Taliban made a full-fledged attack on Maidan Sheher in February 1995.[88]

The pressure on Hikmetyar's forces was severe, because the Taliban had succeeded in cutting off Hikmetyar's main supply-line from Jalalabad. The fighting lasted several days and around 200 people were reported killed before Maidan Sheher came into the hands of the Taliban.

Charasyab Falls

The Taliban's major victory was the storming of Charasyab, twenty-five kilometres south of Kabul and the stronghold of Hikmetyar's Hizb-e-Islami, in February 1995.[89] The one-time favourite of the ISI, who was known to be a fighter *par excellence*, had to flee to Sarobi, further north, to avoid capture. Many of his supporters defected, others melted away. Whether it was a tactical withdrawal to put added pressure on his main rival in Kabul, or fear of losing his military clout, that compelled Hikmetyar to give in without putting up any resistance is open to question.

Whatever the reason, Hikmetyar's defeat at the hands of the Taliban pleased his arch-rival Rabbani. 'His men could not contain their glee when the Taliban evicted Hikmetyar from Charasyab,' reported a correspondent in Kabul.[90]

In spite of having suffered a humiliating defeat, Hikmetyar put up a brave front. When asked whether he was concerned about the rapid advances of the Taliban, he is reported to have said, 'I have had my whole family from babies to grandparents jailed and my father and two brothers murdered. I have had the death sentence proclaimed against me. I have never worried about any of these things. I am not worried about the Taliban now.'[91]

The ease with which the newly created force was able to drive out even strong men like Hikmetyar from his stronghold in Charasyab sent shivers down the spine of some weak-kneed mujahideen leaders. The stories of their successes, and the harsh punishments they meted out to offenders and anti-social elements, spread far and wide. Children in Jalalabad frightened each other by saying, 'The Taliban are coming, better mend your ways.'

Those government forces which had tried to infiltrate into the area vacated by Hikmetyar's men were surrounded by the Taliban. As a measure of goodwill they were allowed to return to their previous positions after being disarmed. By August 1995 the Taliban had occupied the hills overlooking Kabul. They were at the gates of the capital.

Capture of Herat

The province of Herat lies on the north-western border of Afghanistan close to the Iranian border. It straddles the main highway to Turkmenistan from Kandahar and contains the important airbase of Shindand. Unlike other areas of Afghanistan, the terrain around Herat consists of lowlands. The majority of people in the Herat province are Farsiwans and Taimuri Aimaqs. A small stretch in the north is inhabited by Turkomens. The few pockets of Pushtuns (Alizais and Popalzais) that are found there are also Dari-speaking.[92]

The local mujahideen commander was Lieutenant-General Mohammad Ismail Khan, who was a member of the Jamiat-e-Islami and allied to Rabbani. During the Afghan jihad he claimed to have built up a force of 12,000 fighters. The troops under his command were as follows:

Headquarters 4 Corps, Lieutenant-General Mohammad Ismail, at Herat.

17 Infantry Division, Major-General Alauddin Khan, at Herat.

21 Mechanized Division, Major-General Shah Ghazi, at Shindand.

4 Armoured Brigade, Commander Nasir

Some elements of Hikmetyar's Hizb-e-Islami and Nabi Mohammedi's Harakat-e-Inqilab-e-Islami were also present in Herat.

The sizes of the Afghan formations and units, even before the fall of President Najibullah, were around one-third of those in modern armies; in other words, the strength of an Afghan infantry division was no more than the strength of a normal infantry brigade, and the same applied to all other formations and units.

The organization and composition of the Afghan armed forces after the Mujahideen had taken over the country underwent a radical change. While the designation of the formations and units remained the same during the civil war that followed, they were converted into *lashkars* of varying sizes. So one came across an Afghan general or a black-turbaned mullah sitting in the office of an erstwhile regular Afghan army formation calling himself Commandant, *firqa-e-chahar zar-e-dar* (Corps Commander 4 Armoured Division), or Commandant *qila-e-urdu* number 4 (4 Infantry Division), with an undetermined number of ill-clothed, ill-trained, ill-equipped, but thoroughly motivated fighters under his command.

General Ismail's military strength and his capabilities were, therefore, very much less than would seem to be indicated by the formations he commanded in Herat.

The Taliban initially had no intention of attacking Herat, but when Ismail gave protection to elements who had fled from areas occupied by the Taliban, they sent a message to Ismail asking him not to give them shelter. When Ismail did not pay any heed to their request they decided to march on his stronghold as well.

In March 1995 the Taliban pushed northwards towards the strategic town of Herat, 500 kilometres from Kandahar, on the Afghan-Iran border. On the way they captured Dilaram, some 200 miles south of Herat, and continued their advance towards that strategic city. While they were on the move they were bombed and rocketed by Ismail's 'air force'. Ismail asked Masood for help, and he airlifted 1,000 of his crack *lashkars* from Bagram airbase to Herat. With fresh reinforcements having arrived, Ismail was able to push the Taliban back to Dilaram. The student militia managed to withstand all subsequent attacks against them and maintained their presence on the Dilaram line for a number of months. However the pressure continued to increase and when Mullah Mohammad, who had taken over as the corps commander of the Kandahar corps, was killed, panic spread in the Taliban camp. In late August they were uprooted from Dilaram and were pushed south to the banks of the Helmand river not far from Kandahar. A frantic message was then sent to Kandahar asking for immediate reinforcements. The citizens of Kandahar were told that the Panjsheris and the Tajiks were moving towards their city and the danger of its falling to their 'foes' was increasing. Thousands of Kandaharis rushed forward to stem the tide. Weapons were collected, vehicles were offered, money was distributed, and soon the Taliban were on the march again.

Mullah Omar had been able to augment his force by the addition of 500 volunteers from each district of Kandahar This had increased his strength to around 10,000. A hand to hand fight took place at Grisk, a small town on the banks of the unfordable Helmand river, which went in favour of the Taliban. Having overcome the resistance at Grisk, they reached Dilaram again.

General Mohammad Ismail had by now consolidated his forward defensive line at Dilaram. He had also established road-blocks every 50 or 60 kilometres by placing tanks on the road. Since the area on either side was not tankable, the

Taliban had to force their way through the obstacles, which they succeeded in doing by sheer determination. A bold and courageous attack on Ismail's positions saw the Panjsheris running for their lives. They left the road to avoid being captured by the Taliban but perished in the waterless desert of Helmand and Farah. According to a well-informed source, around 2,000 of Ismail's supporters were killed in the many encounters with the Taliban. The casualties on the Taliban side were also heavy.

While the Taliban were chasing the Panjsheris, President Rabbani removed Ismail from his command and replaced him with Said Nurullah Hammad. The new commander, however, was not able to bring normalcy back to the confusion that was prevailing in the ranks of 4 Corps.

The Taliban reached Shindand airbase, 130 kilometres south of Herat, on 3 September 1995 and met no resistance as the troops guarding it had become demoralized and gave up the base without any resistance. Only four aircraft managed to fly away. The remaining fifty-two MiG 21s, some helicopters, and around sixty pieces of artillery were part of the *maal-e-ghaneemat* (war booty) which fell into the hands of the Taliban.

Surprisingly, General Mohammad Ismail, who had withstood the combined attacks of the Soviet and Afghan armies in 1984-5, just melted away against the oncoming tide of the Taliban. He, along with his men, had to take shelter in Iran. Herat was in Taliban hands on 5 September 1995.

Flushed with success, the Taliban moved on towards the Iranian border and established their presence right up to Islam Qila on the Afghan-Iran border. They could not stay there long, however, as the Heratis loyal to Ismail made a comeback with Iranian assistance. The see-saw battle continued for some time until the Taliban finally and firmly occupied the entire area between Herat and Islam Qila with the support of the locals.

Causes of the Fall of Herat

General Ismail stretched his forces along the road to Kandahar, thus weakening his defences and exposing his troops to a defeat.

Differences arose between his commanders on the plan for the defence of Herat.

The rise of the Taliban and their success in bringing about peace in Kandahar had diluted the resolve of the Heratis to put up a strong resistance against them.

Commanders Azmi and Alauddin had developed differences with Ismail and did not give him their wholehearted support.

Some of the local people in Herat were dissatisfied with the manner in which Ismail was running the affairs of his domain and defected to the Taliban. They had been blaming him for corruption, nepotism, and for living lavishly.

The morale of the Taliban was much higher than that of their opponents as they sincerely believed that they were engaged in a jihad against their corrupt leaders.

Impact of the Fall of Herat

By capturing Herat and its surrounding areas, the Taliban increased their source of income as they could now levy duties on all goods passing through Torghundi on the border of Turkmenistan and Afghanistan. In addition a great deal of arms and ammunition, including aircraft, fell into the hands of the Taliban.

However, this move of theirs brought the Taliban into direct conflict with the Iranians. Not only had they been instrumental in pushing yet more Afghan refugees into Iran, but their sectarian and ethnic hues were unpalatable to the Ayatollahs in Tehran. This only strengthened the resolve of the Iranians to back the Rabbani-Masood duo in Kabul, which went against the Afghan policy of Pakistan at that time.

The Taliban had now reached the outskirts of the area controlled by the Uzbek commander General Abdul Rashid

Dostum, who would not brook any intrusion into his domain.

The capture of Herat by the Taliban sent shock waves as far as Moscow; Russia was now concerned about the possibility of the Taliban exporting their ideology into the Central Asian Muslim republics, which it still considered its preserve.

The sacking of the Pakistan Embassy in Kabul in September 1995, at the instigation of Ahmed Shah Masood, was the direct result of the fall of Herat to the Taliban. Rabbani and Masood were convinced that Pakistan had not only encouraged the Taliban in this venture but had also given them military support. It was to vent their anger that they decided to pull down the Pakistan Embassy in Kabul and manhandle Ambassador Humayun Khan. It is an irony of fate that such an unfriendly act should be carried out against a country which had given shelter to over three million Afghans for ten long years and was continuing to do so when this dastardly act was carried out on a wrong premise.

It pushed Rabbani into the hands of India. He needed political and military assistance, and New Delhi was looking for an opportunity to get back into Afghanistan. The capture of Herat by the Taliban provided that opening.

Soon after the fall of Herat, parleys between Iran, Russia, and India began to take place as they now found a common objective, that of keeping the Taliban in check.

Since the western route to Central Asia was now in friendly hands some multi-nationals based in Islamabad revived their interest in constructing an oil and gas pipeline from Turkmenistan to Pakistan through Afghanistan.

Ghor

The province of Ghor is a desolate mountainous area of north-western Afghanistan which has little strategic importance except that, like Herat, it prevented a linkage between Rabbani's forces and Iran. Faryab, which was Dostum's domain lay on its north. Since Dostum and

Rabbani were still not reconciled, the Taliban could expect direct military assistance from Dostum if needed.

As events turned out, that help was not needed since the militia in Ghor surrendered without putting up any resistance.

Khost Falls to the Taliban

The Afghan province of Khost lies on the borders of Pakistan's North Waziristan Agency, to which it is linked by two jeepable roads. Before the province fell to the Taliban it was the headquarters of Hizb-e-Islami(H). Along with Pakistan's Jamaat-i-Islami, Hikmetyar had established two camps in Khost. The camps were called Al-Badar I and Al Badar II. According to an eyewitness, hundreds of Afghans, Pakistanis, and other Muslim militants were receiving military training in these camps. They came from various towns in Sindh, Azad Kashmir, Punjab, and NWFP (Swat). Most of them were volunteers who had run away from their homes in Pakistan to take up the cause of Islam. One hundred and seven Pakistanis were among those who were receiving military training at these camps. These misguided youths had fallen prey to over-zealous mullahs who had promised them a place in heaven if they picked up a gun to fight for the establishment of what they considered to be the one and only true path.

Despite the presence of hundreds of fighters in these camps who were loyal to Hikmetyar, they did not resist the arrival of the Taliban, who took over the control of the city without any fighting whatsoever.

For quite some time after the capture of Khost the Taliban allowed the camps to remain open because they believed that they were imparting religious education. It was much later that they began to suspect that those trained at these camps were being used against them. Mullah Syed Abdullah, the Taliban Governor of Khost, is reported to have said that the camps had become centres of anti-Taliban planning and activities. He further stated that Hikmetyar and Qazi

Hussain Ahmed were jointly running these camps. The Taliban, therefore, closed these camps on 17 September 1996 and handed them over to the Harakatul Ansar, a militant Islamic group acceptable to the Taliban.[93]

The Siege of Kabul

After overrunning Charasyab the Taliban succeeded in besieging Kabul from three sides. They brought in heavy weapons, including large calibre guns, heavy mortars, and rockets-launchers, and deployed them on the hills surrounding Kabul. From these well-entrenched positions in the mountains they could shell the city and be safe from a counter-attack.

The rapid advances of the Taliban came to a grinding halt, however, in front of Kabul. Their luck had run out. So far they had met little or no opposition, but now they were face to face with Ahmed Shah Masood and his Panjsheris, who had given a very good account of themselves during their struggle against the Soviets. Notwithstanding the sincerity, dedication, strength, and popularity which the Taliban initially enjoyed, they could not prove their mettle when it came to facing a battle-hardened and well organized force. It was only when they reached the outskirts of their main objective that they found the nut too hard to crack.

Commander Ahmed Shah Masood with his 20,000 well trained and fully-motivated troops proved more than a match, at that point of time, for the Taliban. Rabbani's strong-man was equipped with plenty of arms and ammunition, and more kept coming from outside sources. The Taliban realized that they might have to fight pitched battles in built-up areas, something of which they had had no experience so far. It appeared to be a no-win situation for the Taliban. If they engaged in a long drawn-out battle with Ahmed Shah Masood there would be much bloodshed and destruction, which would place them on a par with the rest of the mujahideen leaders. They would thus lose the sympathy of the populace.

After five months of besieging Kabul, the Taliban found themselves unable to launch a final assault on the capital

In fact, they were quite vulnerable in the open ground around Charasyab where they were being shelled and rocketed by Rabbani's forces. They, therefore, decided that prudence was the better part of valour and withdrew their heavy weapons from Charasyab, redeploying them on higher ground.

The Taliban regularly bombed, strafed, and rocketed Kabul and other government positions in the vicinity of the capital as part of a process of softening up the target before the final assault. Unfortunately they were not able to avoid civilian casualties, which, as they had feared, placed them in the same category as the other Afghan militia. Merely causing death and destruction, without the ability to deliver the final blow, was beginning to have an adverse impact on their credibility among their supporters and their popularity amongst the average Afghans.

Even when Kabul fell there was no guarantee that they would reach the end of the line. General Abdul Rashid Dostum, whose Jumbish-e-Milli was the strongest force in northern Afghanistan, would not be an easy person to deal with. Being an erstwhile communist, he would not be very happy with the religious zeal of the Taliban, and it was doubtful if he would give up without putting up a strong fight. An open war between the Pushtun-dominated religious extremists and the Uzbek liberals could draw in the neighbouring Central Asian Republic of Uzbekistan and possibly the Russians as well. The Taliban were conscious of the fact that it would not be easy to overrun northern Afghanistan even after Kabul came under their sway.

Counter-attacks by Rabbani's Forces

Kabul

Afghan government forces stationed in Kabul used their long-range artillery and aircraft to keep the Taliban out of gun range from their positions around the capital. Three

Russian-made SU-22 jets bombed a Taliban camp south of Kabul on 26 March 1996, destroying several buildings and killing at least thirty people. An ammunition dump about thirty kilometres south of Kabul was also hit. A Defence Ministry spokesman called it a defensive measure because, according to him, the Taliban were preparing an assault on the capital.

Ghor

General Ismail, who had been evicted from Herat and had taken shelter in Iran, was making plans to retake his lost territory with Iranian assistance. Instead of attacking Herat from across the Iranian border, he decided to do so from the neighbouring province of Ghor, one district of which was still not in Taliban hands. This was done to make the operation look indigenous in character. A *lashkar* of around 1,500 Heratis were gathered and flown to Bagram airbase, from where they were taken to the front line in July 1996. The force was led by Alauddin Khan, and Ghulam Yahya, the ousted Mayor of Herat and the ousted Governor of Ghor.

When Omar came to know of Ismail's intentions, he despatched Mullah Brader to Ghor from Kandahar. Brader decided against putting in a spoiling attack and chose to fight a defensive battle instead. He even lured the attackers into the mountainous terrain where he succeeded in breaking up wave after wave of the oncoming rival militia until the opponents, after suffering heavy casualties, were forced to disperse without having been able to evict the Taliban from Ghor.

Ismail lost Alauddin and the former Governor of Ghor, who were both killed in the counter-attack against the Taliban in Ghor.

Herat

After a gap of several months, during which the intermittent fighting was confined to around Kabul, government forces launched an offensive towards the strategic town of Herat. They claimed to have entered Herat province after pushing the Taliban back from their mountain strongholds in the adjacent province of Ghor. Their aim was to evict the student militia entirely from Herat, and initially they boasted that their troops were making steady progress towards their final objective. 'Our men have moved several kilometres into Herat in the general direction of Herat city,' stated a government official.

However, the Taliban Governor of Herat, Maulvi Yar Mohammad, said that the Taliban immediately put in a counter-offensive and not only pushed Rabbani's forces back from the entire province of Herat but also recaptured the capital of the adjacent province of Ghor. The Taliban were assisted by the forces of Abdul Rashid Dostum. General Rasul Pehalwan, who is believed to be the right-hand man of Dostum, sent his troops to help the Taliban in retaking Chaghcharan and driving the government forces further eastward. Karim Khalili, chief of his faction of the Hizb-e-Wahdat (a Shia-dominated militia) also supported the Taliban from the areas controlled by him in central Afghanistan as he too had not yet mended his fences with Rabbani and Masood. Khalili, installed as Governor of Ghor by the Kabul regime, was killed in the encounter. Some districts of Ghor however remained out of reach of the Taliban.

Wardak

The province of Wardak lies immediately to the west of Kabul. It was overrun by the Taliban during their advance to the capital, and it was from here that the Taliban continued to harass the forces of Ahmed Shah Masood. Facing the threat of a final assault by the Taliban militia, Masood continued to push them as far back as possible from Kabul. In the middle of May he succeeded in retaking two districts deep inside Wardak province. General Muslim, a senior military commander of the forces under the control of the government, claimed that the air, artillery, and rocket attacks on Taliban positions in the districts of Chak and Daimirdad had caused severe damage to their defensive installations. According to the General, government forces captured a great deal of weapons, ammunition, and vehicles, besides killing around a dozen Taliban.

On the March Again

After a lull of almost twelve months the Taliban were on the move again. Having surreptitiously sent his men into the neighbouring provinces and finding the situation in favour of the Taliban, Mullah Borjan gathered a group of around 700 fighters and moved forward to try and gain control of a few more provinces. One by one the strongholds of Hikmetyar fell by the wayside. Jaji Maidan, in the province of Paktia, which was the scene of intense fighting between the mujahideen and the Soviet forces in 1986, was taken over by the Taliban without any opposition from the Hizb-e-Islami. The remaining strong-points in the neighbouring province of Logar also melted away.

The Jalalabad Offensive

The Taliban now turned their attention further eastward and headed towards the strategic city of Jalalabad, capital of Nangarhar province, which borders Pakistan. Nangarhar had so far remained peaceful as Governor Haji Abdul Qadeer had managed to create amity between the various Afghan factions represented in his area. Hizb-e-Islami (Khalis), a faction supporting the Kabul regime, was in control of the Jalalabad airport; Pir Syed Ahmed Gailani's NIFA was controlling another portion of Nangarhar. Qadeer was following a neutral policy and not supporting any one particular Afghan group.

The movement of goods and personnel between the Afghans living on both sides of the Durand Line was, therefore, reasonably satisfactory. All material assistance to the beleaguered city of Kabul passed through Jalalabad. The Pakistan Embassy, which had been forced out of Kabul because of an attack against it, had been functioning from Jalalabad. This too had to be closed when the Taliban moved in.

On 11 September 1996 the Taliban, under Mullah Borjan, entered Jalalabad and occupied the city without much resistance by forces loyal to the Governor. Qadeer did not put up any struggle and avoided becoming a prisoner by moving to Pakistan before the city surrendered.

According to Haji Qadeer, he had all the strength and means to fight against the Taliban but when the Taliban placed local people, whom they had forcibly brought from the outlying areas, in front of their fighting elements, the Nangarhar *Shoora*, of which he was the head, decided not to resist. 'If we had decided to fight back we would have been shedding the blood of the locals and not the Taliban,' said Qadeer.

The *Shoora*, after coming to the conclusion that they would not put up any resistance, hand over control of Nangarhar to the Taliban peacefully. Since the Taliban already controlled sixteen provinces, the *Shoora* hoped that they would ensure peace in all the other areas of Afghanistan. 'Which is what all Afghans are wanting,' opined Qadeer. The former Governor hinted that suggestions not to resist the Taliban had also come from outside Afghanistan.[94]

The real reason for throwing in the towel seems to have been an unwillingness to fight against an ideologically-motivated group who were willing to sacrifice their lives for a cause they believed to be just. The various Afghan factions were also not very sure of the support they would receive from the locals if they decided to fight against the Taliban, as the latter had earned a good name for themselves in the areas they were controlling. The Nangarhar *Shoora*, therefore, felt that discretion was the better part of valour. Since it was easy for them to cross into Pakistan and still continue to carry out their trade, they decided to enjoy the comfort of living in more peaceful surroundings rather than live a spartan life under the Taliban.

Laghman and Kunarh Fall to the Taliban

The fall of Nangarhar to the Taliban was followed up with amazing speed. The eastern province of Laghman, which was held by Hikmetyar's men, fell on 3 October 1996. By now the people in the adjoining province of Kunarh had heard about the rapid advances of the Taliban and, deciding not to resist, they raised white flags on the approach of the student militia. Another victory was achieved without any fighting.

Sarobi Occupied

Sarobi, which lay half way between Jalalabad and Kabul, was their next objective. It was Hikmetyar's stronghold and was considered a very difficult objective to achieve. Masood's forces had also reinforced the Sarobi garrison. The recent victories, however, had raised the morale of the Taliban, and they did not waste any time in attacking Sarobi from three directions. The determination and courage shown by the attackers was unprecedented. The ferocity with which wave after wave rushed forward regardless of the numbers being martyred broke the back of the defenders.

The battle for Sarobi, unlike all other military engagements, took a heavy toll of life, but the road to Kabul from then on lay open.

Onward to the Capital

The Taliban had by now built up a force of around 30,000. They were so sure of their prowess that they attacked the capital from three different sides simultaneously, which took the defenders completely by surprise. Rabbani and Masood made a half-hearted attempt to keep the Taliban away from Kabul, but the loss of Sarobi had demoralized their troops to such an extent that they decided to abandon the city without a fight. Their excuse was that they did not want the civilians to suffer any casualties.

The tactical move of outflanking Kabul and capturing Bagram airbase, north of the capital, before attacking Kabul itself lowered the morale of Masood's men, who felt that they were being trapped in the city. It was a psychological victory for the Taliban, who reached the outskirts of Kabul on 26 September and triumphantly entered the capital on the morning of the next day. Masood's forces, which had been reduced to around 10,000 by now, retreated in a hurry to their stronghold in Panjsher, leaving behind a lot of arms and ammunition. Foreign correspondents reported seeing a stream of guns, tanks, and rocket-launchers moving towards the Panjsher valley as Masood went to his famous hideout to lick his wounds before coming back to fight another day.

The first step the Taliban took on occupying Kabul was to arrest and assassinate Dr Najibullah and his brother, who had taken shelter in the United Nations' compound after being forced to quit the Presidency in 1992. At about 0130 hours on 27 September a group of the Taliban militia forced their way into the UN compound and at gunpoint compelled Najibullah to get into their vehicle. About two hours later another group of Taliban took Ahmedzai, Najibullah's brother, who had also taken refuge in the UN compound. At about 0600 hours the UN mission was informed that the bodies of Najibullah and his brother were hanging in Ariana Square in the city centre.[95] Passersby were hitting the dead bodies with shoes and spitting on them.

This brutal act drew immediate and severe criticism from many world leaders. The western media and those opposed to the Taliban condemned the wanton killing of the former president with no form of trial whatsoever. It was indeed not in keeping with Islamic injunctions, as Islam forbids the desecration of dead bodies. Mullah Mohammad Rabbani, the head of the Kabul *Shoora*, had apparently ordered the assassination of Dr Najibullah to avenge the killing of his own brother by Najibullah. Mullah Omar is believed not to have appreciated this hasty decision by his nominee and Mullah Rabbani was relieved of his post 'for health reasons' soon thereafter. (He was reinstated after some months.)

Causes of the Fall of Kabul

No one amongst those who had been following the rise of the Taliban could have predicted that Kabul would fall so easily to the student militia. Since the *talibs* had not fought a single pitched battle against the seasoned troops of Ahmed Shah Masood, their ability to capture the capital had been doubted by almost all Afghan watchers.

What, then could, have been the reasons for the most significant and the easiest of all successes?

By now the relative strengths of the Taliban and Masood had swung very much in favour of the former. Masood's *Shoora-e-Nazar* was now only around 10,000 strong, while the Taliban had gone up to about 30,000. The Taliban, therefore, had a numerical superiority of 3:1 by the time they put in their attack on Kabul.

The morale of the Taliban after their success at Sarobi had risen to new heights. The Panjsheris, on the other hand, had begun to feel insecure on seeing the phenomenal rise of the Taliban.

Some of Rabbani's commanders changed sides, thus exposing a flank of the defences of Kabul.[96] (The practice of winning over the loyalties of the Afghans by paying them money has been in vogue for centuries. The Mughals and the British paid regular stipends to Afghan *maliks* to keep them out of harm's way. The Government of Pakistan continues to dole out thousands of rupees annually to local chieftains in order to retain their loyalty. The Taliban have also been known to capitalize on this human weakness.)

The threat to the only route of withdrawal hastened the decision of Rabbani and Masood to pull back from Kabul to avoid losing all their heavy weapons.

Kabul was under the command of several different factions. Uzbeks were holding the Kwaja Rawash airport; Masood's forces were deployed along the road to Khair Khana; Hikmetyar's men were defending the area south of the capital; Sayyaf was positioned in Paghman, north-west of Kabul; a faction of the Shias were stationed on the western outskirts of the city; the southern half was in the hands of Hizb-e-Wahdat; and the surrounding hills had been occupied by the Taliban. Even when moving around inside Kabul one had to pass through check-points manned by different militias.[97] Kabul was, therefore, a divided city, which made it easier for the Taliban to occupy it without much resistance.

Impact of the Fall of Kabul

The fall of Kabul to the Taliban raised certain hopes or fears in different parts of the world depending, on how people saw their respective national interests being served or denied by this unexpected development in Afghanistan.

With two-thirds of the country and the capital now in the hands of the Taliban, their long-term presence in Afghanistan began to be taken note of by the world community. It was hoped that after their entry into the capital, and having consolidated their hold over most of the country, the Taliban would be recognized as the new rulers in Afghanistan by those nations which had been helping them.

Since the Taliban had demonstrated their ability to evict Masood's forces from the capital, Pakistan hoped that it would not be too long before a friendly regime was able to control the whole of the country. Furthermore, Pakistan could now expect to make further progress towards its

primary objective of establishing commercial contacts with
the Central Asian Muslim republics.

The capture of Kabul had considerably weakened the
claim of Rabbani's government to be the only lawful
authority in the country.

With one political faction having gained ascendancy over
the rival factions, some military analysts felt that the
chances of peace returning to Afghanistan had somewhat
increased.

The Taliban had not shown any indication of being
hostile to the United States and so there was no adverse
reaction in the White House. Indeed, US interests in the
region seemed to be served, because the US believed that
the Taliban would exercise a check on Iran's ambitions of
increasing its presence in Afghanistan.

Unlike Iran, the Taliban did not give the impression of
wanting to export their revolutionary zeal to other
countries. However, the spectre of a Muslim extremist state
emerging on the borders of the Central Asian Republics
became a matter of great concern for Russia.

The fall of Kabul caused the Ayatollahs in Tehran a
great deal of apprehension as they had been opposing the
rise of the Taliban ever since they had come on to the
Afghan scene.

India was dismayed that the government they had been
supporting all along had been pushed out into the cold.
This did, however, bring India closer to Iran and the anti-
Taliban alliance.

It was feared in some Pakistani circles that if the Taliban
were unable to overrun the whole of the country but
managed to retain what they had so far occupied, the ethnic
division of Afghanistan would come closer to becoming a
reality.

With no experience of running a modern state, the
possibility of mismanagement in all government
departments was expected by Afghan watchers in Pakistan.

Exploiting Success

Having gained full control of Kabul, but without waiting to consolidate their victories, the Taliban pushed forward so as not to give any respite to their opponents. Masood's rearguard action at Charikar, forty kilometres north of Kabul, could not stop the Taliban from overrunning it with ease. The next important city to fall was Jabal-us-Siraj at the mouth of the Panjsher valley.

The Taliban had still, however, a long way to go before they could achieve their objective of total victory. Masood had to be evicted from the Panjsher valley and Dostum had to be politically won over, failing which he had to be forcefully evicted from the northern provinces.

The Panjsher Valley

The Panjsher Valley runs along the Panjsher river about 100 kilometres north-east of Kabul and within a day's march of the strategic Salang Pass. It is about seventy kilometres long and some three to five kilometres wide, at a height of 7,000 feet. The hills on either side rise steeply to about 15,000 feet. The entrance to the valley can be blocked to vehicles by dynamiting the only road that goes through it. Numerous places within the valley are also suitable for road-blocks and guerrilla action. In winter most of the valley is snow-bound. The Panjsheris can, therefore, keep the Taliban out of Panjsher if their morale does not totally break down.

The Hardest Nut to Crack

The most difficult issue was dealing with former communist, General Abdul Rashid Dostum, whose troops numbering around 50,000 were well-equipped and well organized into a proper fighting force, having been trained by the Soviets. Russia, sceptical of the Taliban, would not let them reach the borders of their soft underbelly. In fact there was a strong possibility that Moscow would have aided Dostum with the necessary supplies to counter a Taliban offensive. Ethnically too, Dostum was linked with Uzbekistan in the north, whose support they could also expect if the military situation went against them.

Hindu Kush Proves to be a Major Hurdle

The Taliban had by now reached the Hindu Kush, which divides the country into two distinct geographical identities. Only two major passes cross the mountain range. Sibbar Kotal was the gateway to the Shia-dominated province of Bamian. An unmetalled road had been made through it in 1937 with local labour, but it was left unattended. It was the Soviets who linked the north and the south by a modern highway. The Salang Tunnel was begun by them in 1960 and completed in 1964. The three kilometre long Salang Tunnel, at a height of 11,100 feet (3,363 metres), became the world's highest man-made mountain pass. Blizzards and snowstorms close it to all traffic for several days at a time in winter.

Crossing the Salang Tunnel, the northern end of which was controlled by Abdul Rashid Dostum was, therefore, not going to be an easy task. Instead of coming to some kind of understanding with him, the Taliban stuck their necks out by challenging the strongest force in Afghanistan. By creating a threat to the six northern provinces, they pushed Dostum into an alliance with Masood, which tilted the balance of power in Afghanistan much against the Taliban.

The Ignominious Retreat

The unexpected counter-offensive by Masood supported by Dostum's forces found the Taliban overstretched and incapable of holding ground which they had recently seized from the government forces. First Jabal-us-Siraj and then

Charikar were lost as swiftly as they had been taken. Bagram airbase, thirty kilometres north of Kabul, changed hands a number of times. Masood and Dostum drove the Taliban back to the outskirts of Kabul, having reportedly inflicted 500 casualties.[98]

The struggle to gain the heights around Kabul continued, with the opposing militias determined to regain the ascendancy.

The Second Offensive

After the Taliban were driven back to Kabul, it was expected that they would not have the strength to retake what they had lost. With winter setting in and the hills covered with snow, it was generally believed that the Taliban would lie low and consolidate what they actually controlled. But neither snow nor the harsh winter of Afghanistan could stop their determination to force the Panjsheris into their den and to nibble away at Dostum's fiefdom in the north.

In January 1997, at the height of winter, the Taliban not only recaptured the crucial Bagram airbase but also went on to take Charikar and Jabal-us-Siraj, seventy kilometres north of Kabul, at the mouth of the Salang Tunnel and at the head of the Panjsher valley. They also took parts of the Ghorbund valley in the province of Parwan adjacent to Dostum-held areas, which sounded alarm bells in Mazar-e-Sharif.

Despite the severe winter, the Taliban continued on their forward march and were soon 130 kilometres north of Kabul. Bamian, under the control of the Shia leader Karim Khalili, was under threat. Most of the successes were due to the fact that there was very little resistance from the forces loyal to Masood. In fact, many of them deserted and joined the Taliban in their fight against Masood because they believed that 'the Taliban were struggling for the sake of Islam'.[100]

All was not well, however, for the Taliban as they were not so easily acceptable in non-Pushtun areas. The Taliban for the first time forced the local population—in this case

Tajiks—out since they feared a repeat of the October '96 Rebellion. Even in Jalalabad, which the Taliban had 'liberated' many months earlier, there were clashes between them and those opposed to the student militia.

The main issue on which there was resentment was the insistence of the Taliban that all militia lay down their arms.

Reverses in Kunarh

The barren and mountainous terrain of Afghanistan is barely capable of supporting its population. Most of the Afghans, living in the province adjacent to the Pak-Afghan border, earn their living by smuggling goods into Pakistan. Whenever this practice is checked there is trouble on the border. Peace was shattered in the Taliban-controlled province of Kunarh in February 1997 when they tried to prevent the smuggling of timber. Malik Zarin (Sibghatullah's party) and Haji Kashmir Khan (Hikmetyar's faction) were the two timber barons most affected by the banning of the illegal timber trade. Supported by two anti-Taliban groups viz. the Hizb-e-Islami (H) and Jabha-e-Nijat-e-Milli they decided to challenge the new administrators and attacked the student militia. In the fight that ensued the Taliban are reported to have suffered heavy casualties. They also lost four districts to the anti-Taliban forces in Kunarh.

It seems that this rebellion was indirectly also supported by Haji Abdul Qadeer, ousted governor of Nangarhar Province, who tried to reassert his authority in the areas he had once controlled[101] but without success. Although he denied having anything to do with the rebellion in the areas previously under the control of his eastern *Shoora*, the Taliban blamed him for instigating the mini-insurgency in Kunarh. Not being able to lay their hands on him as he was living in Pakistan, they arrested his son for anti-Taliban activities. Pakistan was asked not to harbour anti-Taliban elements, several of whom were located in Peshawar. Islamabad is reported to have warned Qadeer to desist from getting involved again in developments in Afghanistan.

Badghis Front

The northern province of Badghis was overrun by the Taliban in December 1995, but they had not been able to consolidate their position fully in that area. About 2,000 Dostum and Ismaili fighters carried out a major offensive in March 1997 and pushed the Taliban back about twenty kilometres from the Murghab river towards Qila-a-Nau. The Taliban thereafter halted all further movement towards the capital, although their morale was reportedly boosted when they downed one of Dostum's MiG 21s in a dogfight over Qila-a-Nau.

Rebellion in Dostumland

'Soon the forces of the Islamic State of Afghanistan will cross the Hindu Kush ranges to uproot Dostum,' announced Radio Shariat in January 1997. Mullah Omar had appealed to the people of that area to rise against the Uzbek warlord. Five months later they fulfilled their promise.

Diplomats in Islamabad believed the statement, and had been hinting for some time at the possibility of the student militia overrunning the northern provinces as well. Military analysts, however, dismissed their prediction as it was generally accepted that Dostum had the strongest force in Afghanistan—some 50,000 well-equipped, well-trained and battle-hardened soldiers. He had himself commanded an armoured division in the Afghan army and was professionally competent to deal with a newly-cobbled force of students and renegade Afghan soldiers. In addition, he had the support of Russia, Uzbekistan, Iran, and India. Dostum appeared to be certain of being able to defend his territory against the Taliban militia.

But he should have known that the Afghan jihad had not yet run its full course, and that changing loyalties had become the name of the game in Afghanistan. General Shanawaz Tanai, a die-hard communist, had been won over by

Hikmetyar during the Soviet occupation of his country. General Naqib, Rabbani's garrison commander in Kandahar, decided to join the Taliban when they entered the royal city. Dostum himself had changed sides frequently.

Not long ago Dostum had been backing the Taliban against Rabbani. During his visit to Islamabad at the invitation of the Government of Pakistan in February 1996, Dostum is reported to have said, 'An attack on the Taliban would provoke a counter offensive against Rabbani'. He warned Rabbani that he would retaliate if the Taliban were attacked by Masood.

In April 1996 Dostum paid a visit to the United States to gain Washington's support for the ouster of President Rabbani. He was still determined to retain the *Shoora-e-Ham-Ahangi* (Council of Understanding) in spite of Hikmetyar's betrayal. In fact, a new military alliance between him and the Taliban was in the offing after Hikmetyar's Hizb-e-Islami was expelled from SCCIRA.

The possible understanding between Dostum and the Taliban evaporated, however, when Mullah Rabbani assassinated Dr Najibullah and his brother immediately on taking over the control of the capital. Dostum, who was also a communist and had probably been instrumental in the murder of a large number of Afghan mujahideen, had reason to fear for his own life if the Taliban seized the northern areas as well.

Despite that, he did not appear to be keen on joining the anti-Taliban elements as long as the student militia did not try to evict him from the areas he was controlling. When the overtures of the Taliban began to be accompanied by threats, Dostum decided to join Rabbani and Masood. An agreement to this effect was signed at Khinjan in the Hindu Kush mountains in October 1996. He now felt strong enough to withstand any pressure from the Taliban.

Dostum ruled over his six provinces as if he was the head of an autonomous region. He was more than just another warlord. He operated his own airline (Balkh Air), which carried his emblem to the Gulf and to the Central Asian Republics.

He had his own currency, allegedly printed in Russia. He often visited foreign lands and signed agreements with them. He traded freely with his northern neighbours and was able to keep the shops in his fiefdom full of imported goods. He held complete sway over 78,980 square kilometres of territory inhabited by about three million people. His liberal views were appreciated by his allies and by the elite in his domain. Women moved about freely in Mazar-e-Sharif, with or without veils as they pleased. Cinema houses were showing Indian movies of all description. Russian vodka and German beer were openly available. What then was the reason for the rebellion?

His way of governance did not make him as popular as he was made out to be. Although every shop carried his photograph and every official building displayed his portrait, behind the scenes he was being blamed for corruption, nepotism, and maintaining a lifestyle far beyond what even the northern provinces could afford. Prices of essential commodities had begun to rise. The Afghani had depreciated substantially. He did not have enough money to pay his Jozjani militia. His communist past had not been forgotten. Large pockets of Gilzai Pushtuns, the same Afghan tribe to which Mullah Omar belongs, within his Uzbek population were looking over their shoulders towards the Pushtun-dominated Taliban movement. Dissatisfaction and disillusionment had crept into Dostumland.

Shiberghan Occupied

The Taliban were already in control of half of the neighbouring province of Badghis, where the frontline had crystallized. The opportunity of breaking the stalemate came when the Trojan-horse tactics of the Taliban succeeded. Troops loyal to Dostum mutinied and declared their allegiance to General Abdul Jamil Malik.

Malik had been blaming Dostum for the murder of his stepbrother General Rasul Pehalwan, who was killed in

Mazar-e-Sharif in 1996 in mysterious circumstances. *Badal* being a strong trait of the Afghan character, he was waiting to take his revenge. He rebelled against Dostum on 19 May 1997 and in a sudden sweep captured and disarmed 5,000 men of the Jumbish-e-Milli.

General Ismail Khan, the former Governor of Herat, who had taken shelter in Iran after he was ousted by the Taliban, had come back to Faryab and had managed to raise a force of around 2,000. His attempt to retake Herat was foiled, however, when he along with all his supporters were captured by Malik, who later handed 700 Heratis including Ismail to the Taliban in a gesture of goodwill.

In an apparently co-ordinated move the Taliban and General Malik attacked Dostum's forces stationed in the northern province of Jauzjan on 23 May. The attack was led by Mullah Abdul Razzaq and Gul Mohammad Pehalwan (Gulo), brother of General Malik. By around 11 a.m. next day, Dostum's home town of Shiberghan, 140 kilometres to the north, was in the hands of the combined troops of the Taliban and General Malik.

Not much resistance was met during the advance as nearly all of Dostum's commanders had deserted him and joined Malik. Dostum's main strength was his air force, yet throughout the battle for Shiberghan no aerial sorties were flown. In fact one of Dostum's pilot who did take off landed in Mainama, the capital of Faryab, which had already been taken over by Malik's troops. Three other jets which had been ordered to bomb Faryab strafed Shiberghan instead. One of his jet fighters landed in Kabul, sending a clear signal to Dostum that the game was up.[102]

Mullah Amir Khan Muttaqi, the Taliban Information Minister, praised Gul Mohammad for his courage and bravery, and Malik congratulated the student militia for helping in 'achieving such a big victory'.[103] The *bonhomie* displayed by both unlikely allies seemed to promise that peace would returning to Afghanistan.

On to Mazar-e-Sharif

By about 5 p.m. on 5 May troops loyal to Malik, along with Jumma Khan Hamdard, who had been a member of Hikmetyar's Hizb-e-Islami, entered Mazar-e-Sharif, which by then had been vacated by the remnants of Dostum's Gilam Jam militia. Those who managed to escape went across the Oxus into Uzbekistan. Reports of shops being looted and panic on the streets were received by the advancing columns of the Taliban, and Malik's forces. The locals hastened to raise white flags to save themselves from the wrath of the oncoming troops.

Dostum was forced to flee Afghanistan and take refuge in Turkey along with his family. Flushed with a victory which was handed to them on a plate, as there was no resistance in Mazar-e-Sharif itself, the Islamic warriors went on to overrun another three provinces which had been under Dostum's control. They even succeeded in planting their flags in Takhar and Kunduz, on the borders of Tajikistan, compelling Rabbani to flee to Iran, where he joined Hikmetyar in temporary exile.

The Taliban forces which had been held up for months at the mouth of the Salang Tunnel crossed over the Hindu Kush and into Baghlan in large numbers. This was made easy by the surrender of Masood's commander guarding this route into northern Afghanistan.

The Taliban were now in control of twenty-seven out of thirty-two provinces. It was only a matter of days before the Taliban would be able to claim control of the whole of Afghanistan, as the formidable Hindu Kush had been crossed and the supply lines to Masood and Karim Khalili in Bamian, the only two opponents left in the field, had been cut. So it seemed on 24 May 1997

Mullah Abdul Razzaq, the Governor of Herat, was made the political and military head of northern Afghanistan, and General Malik was named as the Deputy Foreign Minister by Mullah Omar.

The Taliban Suffer a Major Setback

Only three days after the famous victory, however, in a dramatic turn of events, allies became enemies overnight. The Taliban were pushed out of all the territories they had occupied north of the mountain range by the very forces which had co-operated with them in the capture of Mazar-e-Sharif. General Abdul Malik, who had mutinied against Dostum a week earlier, turned against the Taliban and captured Mullah Abdul Razzaq. Mullah Mohammad Ghaus, the Taliban Foreign Minister and State Bank Governor; Maulvi Ehsanullah along with hundreds of Taliban fighters were also taken prisoner.

Heavy fighting also broke out between the Taliban and the Shi'ite Hizb-e-Wahdat in which the Taliban were reported to have suffered heavy casualties. While the Taliban leadership conceded having lost twenty of their fighters, their opponents claimed to have killed six hundred Taliban troops.

Causes of the Reversal

A week before the fighting started for the capture of Mazar-e-Sharif by the combined forces of the Taliban and those loyal to General Malik, a three-point proposal, put forward by Malik, had been agreed between them regarding the future status of the northern areas. According to the agreement, the northern parties were to have complete control over northern Afghanistan; the Taliban were to desist from disarming northern troops; and Malik would co-ordinate with the Taliban to bring about an Islamic dispensation.

Because of their determination to control the whole of the country and enforce their interpretation of the *shariah* in totality, the Taliban went back on the agreements they had allegedly made to Malik. These included: (1) no separate understanding with the opposition; (2) establishment of a military council in the north along with the Taliban; (3) Jumbish-e-Milli to remain in control of

the northern areas until a central government was
established through general elections; (4) Jumbish-e-Milli
to abide by the Islamic *shariah*; (5) Jumbish-e-Milli to be
given proportional representation in the cabinet; and all
military actions against the opposition to be co-ordinated
between the Taliban and the Jumbish-e-Milli.[104]

The Taliban, however, offended their allies by nominating
their own man to be the political and military head of
northern Afghanistan and insulted General Malik by offering
him the post of Deputy Foreign Minister.

Taking weapons away from any Afghan even in peace-
time amounts to discrediting him in the eyes of his fellow
beings. The attempt to disarm the fighters who had rebelled
against Dostum was, therefore, the height of folly. By
insisting on disarming Malik's forces they pushed a reliable
friend into the lap of the enemy. While disarming the people
in Pushtun areas created little or no resentment, it was
certainly not acceptable to the Uzbeks.

Closing all schools for girls and enforcing the strict
Islamic code on a liberal section of Afghan society further
alienated them from the rest of the population in their
newly-won provinces.

The firing of weapons over the grave of the revered Shia
leader, Abdul Ali Mazari, by some unknown persons
angered the Hizb-e-Wahdat. Whether it was a deliberate
act by some of Malik's forces, or whether it was indeed done by
the Taliban, is not clear, but it resulted in a major fight
breaking out between the Taliban and the Ismaili Shi'as
headed by Naderi.

Ahmed Shah Masood seized the opportunity of the rift
between Malik and the Taliban to reopen the front at Jabal-
us-Siraj at the mouth of the Salang Tunnel, which put further
pressure on the student militia.

It is for these reasons I do not believe that the Taliban
fell into a trap laid by some foreign power, as is alleged by
some political analysts.

Kunduz

About 2,000 Taliban were trapped in the northern province of Kunduz when those *talibs* who had reached upto Mazar-e-Sharif were forced to give up the territory which they had overrun in May. However, with the support of the local Pushtuns they not only managed to stay on in Kunduz, but remained a thorn in the side of the opposition.

Though surrounded on all sides by Masood's men and those of General Malik, the besieged Taliban continued to launch probing attacks against their foes in and around Kunduz to keep up their morale. They managed to win over a well-known Pushtun commander in Kunduz by the name of Ghulam who had previously been a member of Rasul Sayyaf's militia. This strengthened their position in Kunduz.

Mullah Amir Khan Muttaqi, who was amongst those who had been trapped in Kunduz, led a joint attack on 4 July against Taloqan, the capital of the neighbouring province of Takhar. The attack did not succeed, but it kept the enemy at bay.

Back to Square One

The anti-Taliban forces, emboldened by the breaking up of the newly-formed alliance between the Taliban and General Malik, launched a major offensive across the Salang Tunnel and recaptured Charikar, sixty-four kilometres north of Kabul, on 20 July. Bagram airbase fell to them soon thereafter.

By 25 July Masood forces and those of Hizb-e-Wahdat were once again at the outskirts of Kabul. The front lines now were around Hussain Kot, a small town some fifteen kilometres from the capital. Masood warned the Taliban to quit Kabul within twenty-four hours or face the wrath of his troops. However, he did not have the strength to evict the Taliban from Kabul by force of arms.

After eighteen days of deadlock, fighting again erupted north of Kabul, but the positions on the ground did not change substantially. Casualties continued to mount, and Kabulis fled to safer havens in Pakistan.

In the meantime, Malik's forces and those loyal to Dostum clashed in Mazar-e-Sharif. On 23 August Abdul Rahim Ghafoorzai, the newly-appointed Prime Minister of the northern alliance and formerly Rabbani's eloquent representative at the United Nations, died in a plane crash. These two events considerably weakened the strength and morale of the anti-Taliban militia.

The Third Offensive

Taking advantage of the in-fighting in erstwhile 'Dostumland' between troops loyal to Dostum and those supporting Malik, the Taliban who had been encircled in Kunduz broke out and launched a major offensive against their friend-turned-foe. To make matters more difficult for Malik, simultaneous uprisings took place in the neighbouring provinces of Samangan and Baghlan.

The Taliban succeeded once again in winning over some of the local commanders in Balkh, with whose support they cut off Mazar-e-Sharif from all directions. The main road to Kabul was also cut, thus denying the supply of arms and ammunition to Masood's forces from the north. 'A former mujahideen commander, Majeed Bacha, led the uprising in Tashkurgan and then called in the Taliban,' said Mullah Omar from his headquarters in Kandahar. He claimed that the Taliban had captured 300 of General Malik's fighters and that around 150 of his men had been killed. Casualties suffered by the Taliban were not disclosed.

After capturing the nearby town of Tashkurgan on 9 September they pushed forward and took control of the bypass running towards the river port of Hairatan on the Oxus, thus threatening Mazar-e-Sharif from the rear. Omar had predicted that it would be only a matter of time before the Taliban scored further military victories, and he was not far wrong as, led by Mullah Khairullah Khairkhwa, they entered Mazar-e-Sharif a day later with the support of Majeed Bacha, Bashir Khan, and Jumma Khan Hamdard, all of whom belonged to the Hikmetyar faction of Hizb-e-Islami. Hikmetyar himself had fled Afghanistan and had taken refuge in Tehran. Such was the fluid situation amongst the different rival groups in war-torn Afghanistan.

There was panic in the city and thousands fled to safer places. Malik and Rabbani were amongst those who had to leave Mazar-e-Sharif lest they too fell into the hands of the Taliban. They reportedly took refuge in Shiberghan, capital of Jauzjan. Unscrupulous elements of the Jumbish-e-Milli, taking advantage of the fighting on the streets of Mazar-e-Sharif, looted and ransacked the offices and homes of the international aid-giving agencies. This act of savagery compelled the UN agencies to pull out their workers from Mazar-e-Sharif.

In the confusion that prevailed around Mazar-e-Sharif, six Afghan pilots belonging to the northern alliance defected with three aircraft. Two of them landed in Shindand and the third in Herat. During interrogation they claimed that Malik and Rabbani had flown to Kulyab in Tajikistan to avoid being taken prisoner. This unsubstantiated statement of the pilots led Mullah Omar to warn Tajikistan not to interfere in the internal affairs of Afghanistan.

When Dostum who had fled to Turkey, came to know that General Malik had left the country, he decided to come back to Afghanistan and re-establish his authority over the areas he once controlled in northern Afghanistan. With the unexpected arrival of Abdul Rashid Dostum in Mazar-e-Sharif the Taliban were pushed out of the city and had to fall back to Tashkurgan, but a few days later they were hammering at the gates of Mazar-e-Sharif again.

Hairatan Changes Hands

Despite the presence of Dostum, who not long before had been considered invincible in his own domain, the Taliban managed to occupy the strategic town of Hairatan. The city lies opposite the Uzbek town of Termez and is on the traditional trade route between Central Asia and Afghanistan.

The Soviets had built the Friendship Bridge across the river at this point, and used it for moving their troops into Afghanistan in December 1979. It was also where the Commander-in-Chief of the Soviet forces in Afghanistan, Lieutenant-General Boris Gromov, crossed on 15 February 1989, marking the last phase of the de-induction of the so-called limited military contingent from Afghanistan.

Its capture on 20 September raised the morale of the Taliban sky-high as it enabled them to cut off the main supply route to the opposition from the north. (The other two routes, one from Torghundi in Turkmenistan and the other from Shah Khan Bandar, in Tajikistan were already firmly in their hands.) It could also provide a source of income to the Taliban as they could levy duties on goods passing through this check point. With Hairatan under their control, Mazar-e-Sharif could now be threatened from the rear as well. Assistance from Saudi Arabia would now be more easily available as the chances of their overcoming the anti-Taliban forces appeared to be brighter after the capture of Hairatan.

The Uzbeks, however, were not comfortable with the Taliban right on their doorstep. They must have heaved a sigh of relief when parts of Hairatan passed back into the hands of Dostum and his allies two days after they had lost it.

With Dostum and Malik again reconciled, the pressure on the Taliban began to increase. The anti-Taliban forces not only recaptured Mazar-e-Sharif, but by the middle of October they had pushed the Taliban back into Kunduz, from where they had started the counter-offensive. According to unconfirmed reports, military assistance from Iran helped in turning the tables against the Taliban in the Mazar-e-Sharif sector.

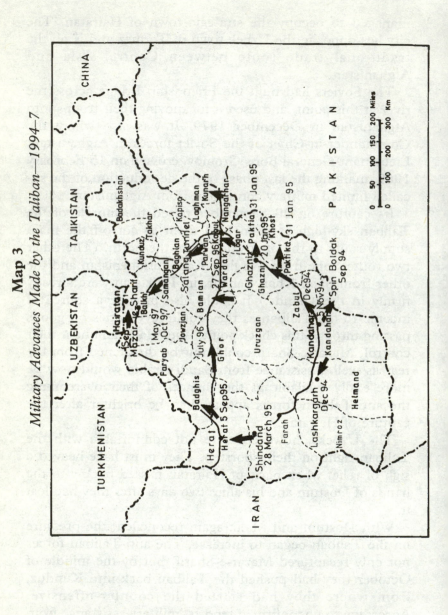

Map 3

Military Advances Made by the Taliban—1994–7

Map 4

Military Situation on 1 May 1997

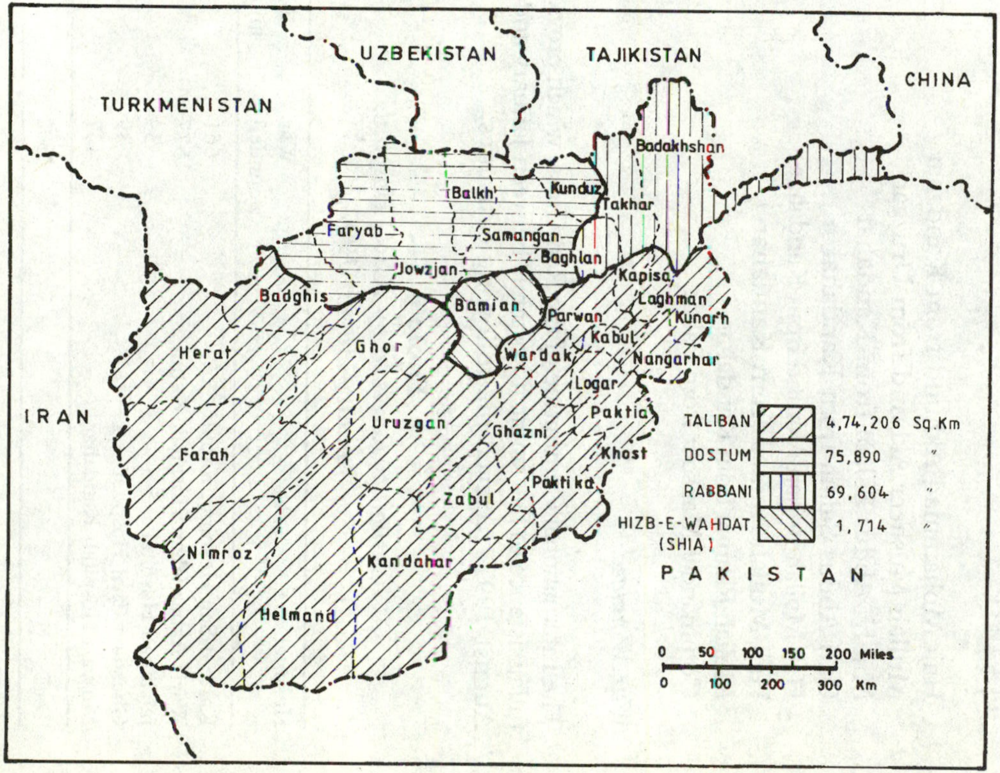

TAJIKISTAN

CHINA

Badakhshan

Takhar

Kunduz

Baghlan

Faryab

Jowzjan

Balkh

Samangan

Bamian

Parwan

Kapisa

Kabul

Laghman

Kunarh

Nangarhar

Logar

Wardak

Paktia

Khost

Ghazni

Pakitka

Zabul

Ghor

Uruzgan

Kandahar

Helmand

Nimroz

Farah

Herat

Badghis

UZBEKISTAN

TURKMENISTAN

IRAN

PAKISTAN

TALIBAN		4,74,206 Sq.Km
DOSTUM		75,890 "
RABBANI		69,604 "
HIZB-E-WAHDAT (SHIA)		1,714 "

0   50   100   150   200 Miles

0   100   200   300 Km

Casualties

The following is a list of prominent Taliban commanders who were killed during the period from November 1994 to April 1997[105]:

Haji Mohammad Akhund from Kandahar
Mullah Musheer Akhund from Uruzgan
Maulvi Abdus Salam from Kandahar
Qari Abdus Salam from Kandahar
Haji Mullah Borjan Akhund from Kandahar
Haji Mullah Ahmed from Kandahar
Mullah Rahmat from Kandahar
Commander Mansoor from Paktia

War Wounded

The International Committee of the Red Cross, which provided full assistance to five surgical hospitals between January and 15 August 1997, recieved the following casualties:

Table 6
Casualties Received by ICRC Hospitals
January-August 1997

Hospital	War wounded	Mine injuries
Karte-e-Seh Hospital, Kabul	661	299
Wazir Akbar Khan Hospital, Kabul	1577	155
Jalalabad Hospital	39	20
Ghaznavi Civil Hospital	39	20
Mirwais Hospital, Kandahar	437	96
Total	3302	727

There were 3,531 newly-registered amputees in the same period.

Prisoners

According to unconfirmed reports, over 1,000 Taliban were taken prisoner by General Malik's forces when the two allies-turned-enemies clashed around Mazar-e-Sharif in the last week of May 1997. Another 3,500 *talibs* found themselves besieged in Phul-e-Khumri by the Hizb-e-Wahdat.[106]

The Taliban claimed to have 750 prisoners in Herat who were handed over to them by General Malik when he overthrew General Dostum.[107]

Massacred

It was alleged that around 3,000 *talibs* were massacred by General Malik's forces and dumped into wells and shallow graves during the Taliban's retreat from Mazar-e-Sharif.

CHAPTER 4

RECONCILIATION EFFORTS BY RABBANI'S GOVERNMENT BEFORE THE FALL OF KABUL

Overtures to the Taliban

President Rabbani was keen to hold peace talks with the Taliban. In fact, to prove his sincerity, he formed a special team in December 1995 to hold the first direct negotiations with his co-citizens who were demanding his ouster. He was responding to the proposal of the United Nations' Special Envoy, who had suggested a meeting between the Taliban and the Kabul regime in the eastern city of Jalalabad, which was generally considered to be neutral ground then. Almost all factions had some presence there, and the Governor, Haji Abdul Qadeer was known not to take sides in the power struggle in post-Najibullah Afghanistan. The peace talks could not be held, however, because the 1,500 Taliban *ulemas* who had gathered in Kandahar declared Rabbani's regime illegal, although a spokesman for the Rabbani regime maintained that indirect talks between the Taliban and Kabul were continuing through the intermediary of a neutral political group whose identity he failed to disclose. The spokesman added that the only way for the Taliban was to carry out peaceful negotiations with the government as 'they would be unable to seize Kabul from us'. The Taliban also kept their options open. Mullah Abdul Jalil, a spokesman of the Taliban, is reported to have said, 'We are ready to work with Rabbani if we are satisfied that he would establish Islamic rule in Afghanistan since we have no quarrel with individuals.'[108]

In the meantime, a four-party anti-Rabbani alliance was formed comprising Sibghatullah Mojeddedi's Jabha-e-Nijat-e-Milli; Hikmetyar's Hizb-e-Islami; Dostum's Jumbish-e-Milli, and Abdul Ali Mazari's Hizb-e-Wahdat. As with numerous other alliances, however, this arrangement also did not last long. Mojeddedi quit, Hikmetyar was expelled, Dostum deserted, and Mazari was killed.

Pakistan Initiates Peace Talks

Ever since the Taliban had set out on their own in an attempt to take over control of the whole of the country they had been on a collision course with the rest of the Afghan groups. However, as their strength grew, overtures were made by different factions who were willing to come to terms with them. The first round of talks was held in Peshawar with the Hizb-e-Islami in January 1996. The common objective was to work out a political arrangement which would be acceptable to the majority of the Afghan factions and ensure a durable and lasting peace in the country. Not much progress was achieved as neither of the two were willing to give up their claim to a bigger slice of the cake. Another round of talks was scheduled for March but it did not take place.

When it became known that Hikmetyar was trying to mend fences with Rabbani and had asked him for billions of Afghanis in compensation for the losses he had suffered at the hands of the Taliban, the latter decided to have nothing to do with Hikmetyar. They then turned to another anti-Rabbani faction, the Jumbish-e-Milli of General Dostum. An alliance with him, they believed, would be much more useful as Dostum had the strongest force in Afghanistan under him whereas Hikmetyar had become almost a non-entity after losing his territory and weapons.

The Supreme Co-ordination Council of the Islamic Revolution of Afghanistan (SCCIRA) held a meeting in February 1996 to work out the modalities of forming a broad-based interim administration to replace the Rabbani regime in Kabul. All the Afghan leaders opposed to Rabbani were to gather in Islamabad to strengthen their own alliance and co-ordinate their efforts to remove Rabbani. Hikmetyar and Dostum were given wide publicity by the national authorities in Pakistan, but the absence of any representative from the Taliban negated the importance of the gathering. Although it was intended to form a grand alliance against the Kabul regime, which was the goal of the Taliban as well, their absence from the meetings highlighted the differences between the Taliban and the anti-Rabbani combine.

The Islamabad conference of Afghan leaders opposed to Rabbani came out with a five-point agenda to resolve the conflict in their country. The five points were: demand for an immediate resignation of the Afghan President; transfer of power to a broad-based government; demilitarization of Kabul; election of a new leadership and formation of a system to solve Afghan problems. The proposals were not new as all of them had been stated many times before, but on each point there was a difference of opinion.

Hikmetyar appeared to be playing a double game. During his meetings with Dostum he proposed joint military action against Rabbani if the latter continued to be stubborn, but when talking to others he was prepared to discuss the transfer of power with Rabbani without him resigning. 'We no longer put that condition,' confided Hikmetyar. The Taliban, on the other hand, continued to insist that Rabbani must quit before they could become a party to the new deal.

The SCCIRA did realize the necessity of including the Taliban in their parleys for, 'without their participation, the objective of removing Rabbani would be delayed or obstructed,' said a member of the anti-Rabbani alliance.

On the other hand, Hikmetyar was willing to sit with Rabbani to solve the Afghan crisis. He asked Pakistan to host another summit meeting and to invite all the Afghan leaders, including Rabbani, to sit together and hold a sincere dialogue for the solution of the Afghan problem. Having done so twice and failed, Pakistan did not accede to Hikmetyar's suggestion.[109]

The reliability of the Afghan leaders can be judged from the fact that, although the decision of the Supreme Co-ordination Council was that in future none of its component parties would talk to the Kabul regime individually, just two months later Hikmetyar, an important member of the Council, did so. He not only talked to the Kabul regime individually, but also accepted Rabbani as President of the future government of Afghanistan with himself as the Prime Minister. The Taliban were left out in the cold by Hikmetyar.

In order to find a political settlement to the Afghan problem, the Taliban invited some three hundred Muslim clergymen from all over Afghanistan, including areas not under Taliban control, to meet in Kandahar. Maulvi Mohammad Muttaqqi, head of the Information and Cultural Department, said that the leaders of the Taliban movement wanted the religious scholars to guide them on how to break the political and military stalemate in the country.[110] A week-long session was held in the Taliban stronghold, beginning on the Afghan New Year's Day (21 March). After a great deal of deliberation, they supported the Taliban stand that the Rabbani regime was illegitimate and must be forced to step down so that a truly Islamic government could be installed in Kabul.

Unfortunately, all rival groups in Afghanistan, whether Rabbani's Jamiat-e-Islami or Hikmetyar's Hizb-e-Islami or Abdul Rasul Sayyaf's Ittehad-e-Islami, are unprincipled and change their stance to achieve temporary gains.

Winning over Hikmetyar

Having failed to win over the Taliban, Rabbani sought to strengthen his position *vis-à-vis* the Taliban by offering money and ministerial positions to Hikmetyar in the future political set-up in Afghanistan. Rabbani is reported to have been willing to pay him 40 billion Afghanis (US $4 million) as compensation for the loss of Charasyab to the Taliban. Hikmetyar's men, however, deny having made any such demand as the price for defecting to Rabbani's regime.

Rabbani invited Qazi Hussain Ahmed, chief of the Jamaat-e-Islami, Pakistan, who is known to be a long-standing friend of Hikmetyar, to mediate between him and Hikmetyar. Hussain Ahmed, along with Lieutenant-General (retd.) Hamid Gul, the former head of the ISI, had a good rapport with both Hikmetyar and Rabbani and even tried several times to bring about a reconciliation between the two. Neither Hussain Ahmed nor Hamid Gul considered the Taliban to be the saviours of Afghanistan; indeed they felt that they had played into the hands of the Americans and had further destabilized the situation in Afghanistan.

Given this background, and the fact that Qazi Hussain Ahmed had been involved in Afghan affairs since the days of General Ziaul Haq and was respected by almost all Afghan leaders, Rabbani sent his special plane to bring him to Kabul from Jalalabad. After several days of shuttling between Jalalabad, Kabul, and Sarobi, the Jamaat-i-Islami chief succeeded in bringing about a reconciliation between the two, much to the annoyance of the Taliban, whose position was weakened somewhat by this new alliance.

An agreement along the lines of a power-sharing formula between Rabbani and Hikmetyar was under discussion. According to the understanding reached between the two rival factions, Rabbani was to retain his position as the President of Afghanistan; Hikmetyar would be reappointed Prime Minister, the important ministries of defence, foreign affairs, and interior would be held by Hikmetyar's Hizb-e-

Islami; and there would be a joint military action against the Taliban. Consequently around 1,200 of Hikmetyar's fighters reportedly reached Kabul to strengthen the hand of Masood. They believed that the two combined forces would not only be able to keep the Taliban away from Kabul, but would also be able to recapture some of the lost territory around the capital.

The newly-forged alliance between Rabbani and Hikmetyar was merely to prevent the Taliban from seizing power. There was no principle involved—only a year earlier Rabbani's forces had joined the Taliban in overrunning Hikmetyar's base at Charasyab. At that time the inexperienced students were naive enough to believe that Rabbani had come to their assistance because he was willing to accept that the Taliban would have a role in the future set-up in Afghanistan. They should have realized then that Rabbani was playing his own game of using one 'enemy' to remove another foe.

Hikmetyar joining Rabbani irked the Taliban greatly— they had earlier accused Hikmetyar of lacking in principles and befriending anyone and everyone in his lust for power.[111] Maulvi Khairullah, a Taliban leader based in Maidan Sheher, accused the Hizb-e-Islami chief of wanting to decide about the future government set-up even before the fall of Kabul. His prediction that Hikmetyar was likely to find new alliances in future in a bid to share power came true when Hikmetyar finally accepted a key post for himself, and some other ministries for his party, when these were offered to him by Rabbani, who he had once vowed to oust.

Professor Sibghatullah Mojeddedi, one-time head of the Afghan Interim Government (AIG) and former President of the interim Afghan regime, did not appreciate Hikmetyar's attempts to join the 'illegal' Rabbani government. He felt that the enmity between Rabbani and Hikmetyar ruled out the possibility of a *rapprochement* between the two for long.

A spokesman of the Pakistan Ministry of Foreign Affairs (MFA) dismissed the news about Hikmetyar joining Rabbani, saying that Rabbani had achieved only a minor gain by bringing Hikmetyar into his fold as the Hizb chief did not have many fighters or weapons with which to boost the strength of Rabbani and Masood, while on the other hand, Hikmetyar's action had led to Dostum signing a military alliance with the Taliban and other small ethnic and sectarian groups opposing Rabbani. What the MFA forgot was that only a month earlier Hikmetyar's visit to Islamabad had been given wide publicity: He was on the front pages of most of the dailies, he was received by the President, and his statements were given a great deal of importance. The public was given to understand that the MFA had isolated Rabbani and Masood altogether, and that Dostum and Hikmetyar would now be able to unseat Rabbani.

With Hikmetyar accepting a ministerial post under Rabbani, the MFA reversed its earlier estimate of Hikmetyar's strength, which amounted to eating humble pie. Rabbani may not have gained a great deal of military strength, as Hikmetyar had lost most of his when ousted from his stronghold at Charasyab, but his joining Rabbani had changed the character of the Rabbani regime. It could no longer be dubbed a purely Tajik outfit now that a faction Pushtun had become a part of it.

Qazi Hussain Ahmed had apparently also been invited by Rabbani to try to bring about a reconciliation between him and Pakistan; he succeeded to the extent that an agreement was reached by both sides to hold direct talks to end the wanton confrontation between them. An Afghan government delegation arrived in Islamabad in May 1996 to discuss the resumption of relations as they had existed before the ransacking of the Pakistan Embassy in Kabul by government agencies.

Dostum Switches Sides

Dostum, who had earlier decided to support the Taliban against Rabbani and Hikmetyar, switched his loyalties.

When the overtures of the Taliban were accompanied by threats he gave up his neutrality and decided to join hands with Rabbani and Masood against them.

It is an irony of fate that in a country with an almost hundred per cent Muslim population, the vast majority of which belongs to one sectarian community, could not accept one another's credentials on the question of establishing an Islamic regime in their own country. With ninety per cent illiteracy, the fiercely independent nature of the Afghans, and the very strong grip of the semi-educated mullahs on them, they fell victim to their own dogmatic religious beliefs. This, coupled with the availability of weapons, made arriving at a consensus on who should be entrusted with the reins of power in Afghanistan very difficult.

CHAPTER 5

THE DRUG PROBLEM IN TALIBAN–CONTROLLED AREAS

Poppy was first introduced into Afghanistan by Alexander the Great as a medicinal plant, and Afghanistan is now reported to be one of the two largest producers of illicit opium in the world.[112] The notable increase in opium production during the years of conflict is largely due to the extra money needed to sustain the war effort against the Soviets in the first instance, and later to maintain rival militia.

Opium is produced in ten out of the thirty-two provinces of Afghanistan. The area under opium poppy cultivation during the 1995–6 season ranged between 55,000 and 58,000 hectares. The yield was between 2,200 and 2,300 metric tonnes of dry opium, which is estimated to be 40 per cent of the global illicit opium production.[113]

The Taliban control eight out of the ten opium-producing provinces in Afghanistan. These are Farah, Nimroz, Helmand, Kandahar, Uruzgan, Zabul, Nangarhar, and Kunarh. The other two provinces where the opium poppy is grown, i.e., Balkh and Badakhshan are ruled by Dostum and Rabbani respectively, these last two provinces produce only 4 per cent of the total.

The opium used to be processed in heroin laboratories in the tribal belt of Pakistan; when these were closed down because of the strict action taken by Pakistan, they were moved into Afghanistan. The International Narcotics Control Board, in its report for the year 1996, noted that heroin manufacturing was taking place in Afghanistan mainly in the areas along its borders with Pakistan.[114] Most of the laboratories were small and could easily be moved about, making detection and elimination quite difficult. UN anti-narcotic teams claim to have seen heroin-producing laboratories in the provinces of Helmand, Nimroz, Kandahar, and Nangarhar.

Abdul Rahim Ghafoorzai, former Deputy Foreign Minister in the Rabbani regime, said in a speech to the UN Security Council that the Taliban faction was producing morphine and heroin in regions under its control to boost its war machine. He also implicated Pakistan in the Taliban drug business by saying that the politico-military mafia of the adjacent country helped the Taliban obtain portable drug processing and refining machinery. He stressed the fact that the Taliban were encouraging the production of drugs, complaining that, 'Accordingly, for the first time in the history of Afghanistan, opium is now being processed into morphine and heroin inside the country in the Taliban-controlled areas of Helmand and Kandahar.' He went on to assert that poppy cultivation in the Taliban-held areas had dramatically increased and that in the five months from December 1995 to April 1996, more than 200 tonnes of the drug had been exported from Taliban-administered regions.

The Taliban denied the charge, saying, 'There is not an iota of truth in the Kabul government's claim and the allegation is part of a propaganda to defame the Islamic government.' According to a high-ranking US official, however, the Taliban are directly involved in drug trafficking. It is alleged that most of the heroin available in the world comes from Afghanistan, and that the Taliban allowed the processing laboratories to be moved from the tribal areas of Pakistan into Afghanistan, when the Pakistani authorities cracked down on the manufacture of narcotics in their country.[115]

The statement of the Taliban regarding opium production in Taliban controlled areas is nearer the truth. An opium poppy survey carried out by the regional office of the United Nations Drug Control Programme (UNDCP) in September 1995 revealed that in Helmand, Uruzgan, and Kandahar the production of opium had decreased. The surveyors attributed the fall to 'higher wheat prices and the fear of reprisals by the Taliban forces'. On the other hand Badakhshan, which was one of the few areas still controlled by Rabbani's regime, was the only province to have sharply increased its opium production.[116]

However, the September 1996 UNDCP report stated that the provinces with the sharpest increase in opium poppy cultivation were Uruzgan and Kandahar,[117] indicating the fact that the Taliban had not been able to implement their objective of banning opium production. A UN survey carried out in September 1997 indicated that the production of opium poppy in Taliban-controlled areas went up by 25 per cent in 1997. According to the report, 96.4 per cent of the total opium production originated in territory under the jurisdiction of the Taliban regime, Mullah Omar's home bases, Helmand and Kandahar, being the provinces which registered substantial increases.

Mullah Omar is reported to have conveyed to the governors of the twenty provinces under the control of the Taliban that poppy cultivation should be banned. 'There is going to be a complete ban and we mean it,' said Abdul Mannan Niazi, head of the security agencies in Nangarhar.[118] General Mohsin Ansari of Iran, however, claimed that the Taliban leaders do not oppose the growing of narcotics in Afghanistan and that it passes through his country on its way to Europe, which has created security problems for Iran on its eastern border.[119]

Ahmed Rashid, a well-known journalist, maintains that, 'all the warring factions depended heavily on the heroin trade to fund and maintain their armies'.[120] The reason why poppy cultivation continues in Afghanistan is that no alternative means of livelihood is provided to the farmers. The Taliban also recognize this difficulty in imposing a ban on poppy cultivation.

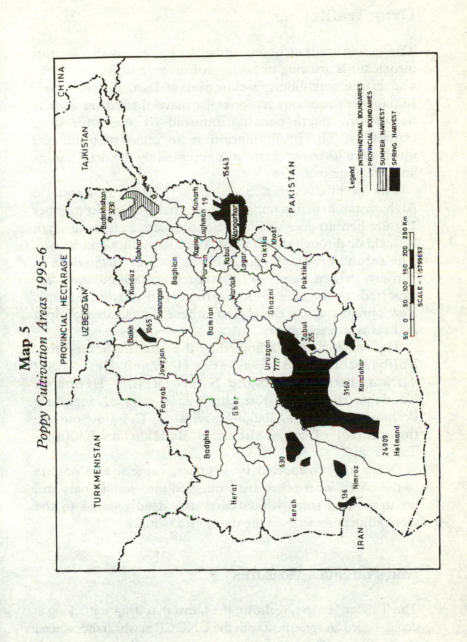

Map 5
Poppy Cultivation Areas 1995-6

Legend
INTERNATIONAL BOUNDARIES
PROVINCIAL BOUNDARIES
SUMMER HARVEST
SPRING HARVEST

PROVINCIAL HECTARAGE

SCALE – 1:5799692

50   0   50 100 150 200 250 Km

CHINA

TAJIKISTAN

UZBEKISTAN

TURKMENISTAN

PAKISTAN

IRAN

Badakhshan 3230
Takhar
Kunduz
Baghlan
Samangan
Balkh 1065
Jowzjan
Faryab
Badghis
Ghor
Bamian
Parwan
Kapisa
Laghman 19
Kunarh
Kabul
Wardak
Logan
Nangarhar 15643
Paktia
Khost
Paktika
Ghazni
Zabul 255
Uruzgan 7777
Kandahar 3160
Helmand 24909
Nimroz 136
Farah 630
Herat

Drug Trafficking

The heroin trade is booming because the demand for this intoxicant is growing not only in Europe and America, but also in the neighbouring countries of Iran, Pakistan, and India. Ultra religious nations also have their drug addicts despite the death penalty imposed by them for drug trafficking. The profit margin is so great that the risk involved in its transportation is accepted by the drug barons and the drug peddlers.

The eventual destination of the heroin produced in Afghanistan depends on its refined quality. Heroin number 1 (pure heroin) goes to Europe and America either through Karachi or through the Central Asian Republics and Russia. The second grade, morphine, finds its way to markets in Turkey, where some of it is further refined and 're-exported' to the well-to-do customers in western Europe. Raw opium stays in the region, where the number of drug addicts is increasing.

The routes usually followed by the drug traffickers from Taliban-controlled areas are: Helmand-Herat-Iran/Turkmenistan; Helmand-Nimroz-Iran; Helmand/Kandahar-Balochistan-Karachi/Makran coast; Nangarhar-Peshawar; Nangarhar-Balkh-Uzbekistan. The route outside the control of the Taliban is Badakhshan-Kunduz-Tajikistan.

Drugs are transported by vehicles, camels, and porters to the coast, where they are smuggled into small boats and on to waiting ships which carry the deadly cargo to the more affluent societies in the developed world.

Anti-Narcotics Measures

The Taliban leaders, realizing the harm that drug trafficking is doing, signed an agreement with the UNDCP in which they agreed to eliminate cultivation of the opium poppy and severely punish drug traffickers (*see*, Appendix iv). However, until such time that money is no longer needed for the continuation of the conflict against their opponents, the Taliban are likely to turn a blind eye to this unIslamic practice—the ten per cent tax collected on opium augments the meagre sources of revenue for the Taliban so they are reluctant to enforce the ban on the cultivation of poppy.

Loss of popular support is another reason why the clerics look the other way when they come across a poppy field right in their midst. 'Everyone is growing poppy. If we try to stop this immediately, the people will be against us,' said Abdul Rashid, Drug Control Director for Kandahar province.[121]

The Taliban regime had been seeking international recognition ever since they settled down in Kabul, but with little success. They seem to have been under the false impression that their willingness to co-operate with the UN Drug Enforcement Agency and to relax the rules banning women from working outside their homes could be used as a bargaining chip towards this objective.

Map 6
Poppy Cultivation and Trafficking Routes

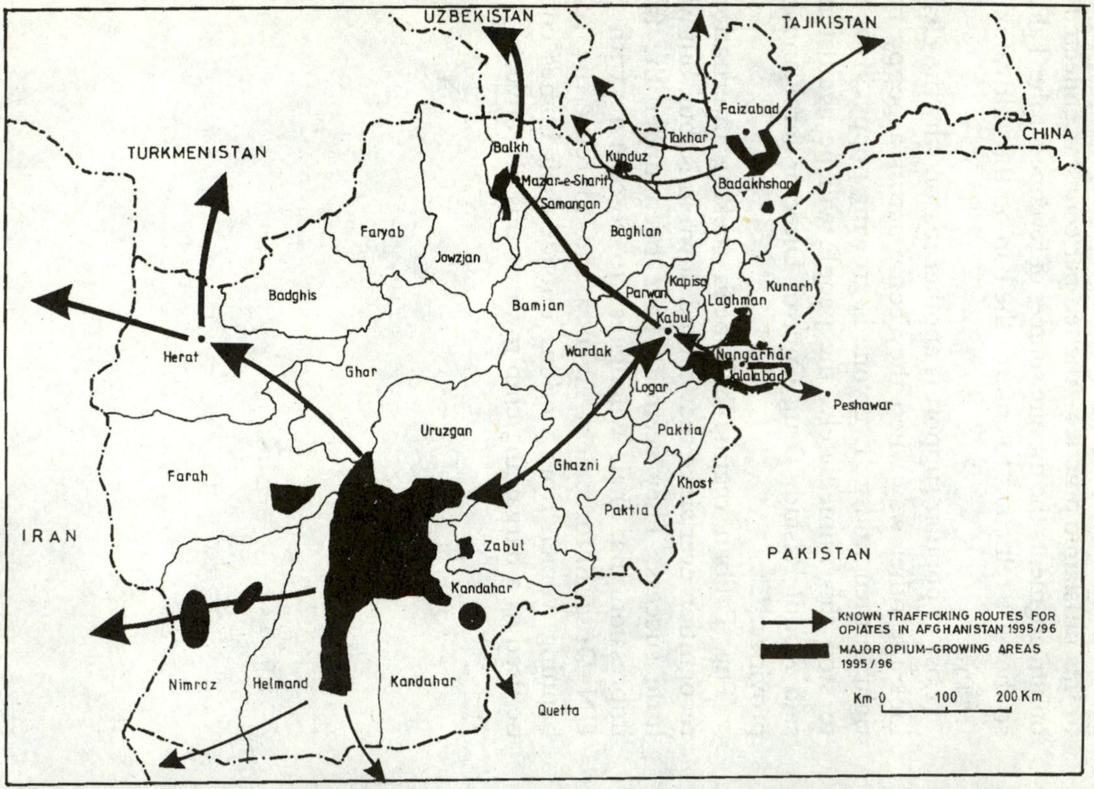

**KNOWN TRAFFICKING ROUTES FOR
OPIATES IN AFGHANISTAN 1995/96**

**MAJOR OPIUM-GROWING AREAS
1995/96**

Km 0   100   200 Km

CHAPTER 6

PAKISTAN'S POLICY TOWARDS THE TALIBAN

Disenchantment with President Rabbani

Burhanuddin Rabbani, like all other members of the Afghan *Tanzeemat*, was indebted to Pakistan for the help and assistance it had given to the Afghan cause during the Soviet occupation of his country. He was also conscious of the fact that Pakistan had been bearing the burden of over three million Afghan refugees since their exodus in 1979.

However, he was, from the very beginning, somewhat unhappy at not being given the same importance as Gulbadin Hikmetyar, who he believed, rightly or wrongly, to be the favourite of the ISI in matters of weapons supply. Rabbani's field commander, Ahmed Shah Masood, who had great influence over him, had always been bitter against Pakistan. The western media had built him up as the lion of Panjsher, but the ISI continued to belittle his contribution to the Afghan jihad as compared with that of Hikmetyar. This perceived injustice turned him against Pakistan. Although his father was buried in Peshawar and his brothers were living there, he never liked coming to Pakistan.

The Taliban factor was, therefore, not the only cause for the rupture of relations between the government of Pakistan and the Rabbani regime. The rift began when Rabbani refused to step down after the expiry of his term of office on 28 June 1994 as per the Islamabad Declaration, of which he was a signatory. Sardar Aseff Ahmed Ali, Pakistan's Foreign

Minister at the time, is reported to have remarked that, 'Anything that happens in Afghanistan after 28 June will have no legitimacy.' This was not a very diplomatic statement to make—Rabbani was, after all, head of an independent state, the rulers of which were to be chosen by the Afghans themselves and not by an outside power.

The Foreign Office was thus constrained to tone down the statement of the Foreign Minister by issuing a clarification. 'The question of legitimacy of the government of Afghanistan after 28 June is an issue to be decided by the Afghan people themselves,'[122] said the Ministry of Foreign Affairs spokesman. But this did not quell the anger which had, in the meantime, been built up against Pakistan amongst the followers of Rabbani and Masood.

The very next day six Pakistanis were shot dead by Rabbani's forces and seven others were arrested on trumped-up charges. The Pakistan Embassy was rocketed and the Foreign Minister was attacked by some men from Masood's militia. The unprecedented love for Pakistanis, shown during and after the Afghan jihad, had suddenly vanished. Pakistani citizens in Kabul were being termed enemy agents and mercenaries. Rabbani began to flirt with India to spite Pakistan. The Pakistan Embassy in Kabul was closed down in July 1994.

The breach was widened when the Afghan hijackers of a school bus were shot dead by Pakistani commandos in February 1995 in the process of freeing the child hostages. Since the hijackers had taken sanctuary in the Afghan Embassy compound in Islamabad, Rabbani had expected that greater restraint would be exercised by Pakistan in dealing with the unfortunate incident. Amir Usman, Pakistan's Ambassador in Kabul at that time, opined that the killing of the hijackers was a major factor in the increasing quarrel between Rabbani and the Government of Pakistan.

The closure of the Pak-Afghan border soon after, created severe problems for the Afghans as many of them had families residing in Peshawar. Many others were engaged in commercial deals and had been moving freely across the Durand Line until then. Thousands of people were left stranded on both sides of the border. Trade was stopped and tension increased. This sudden reprisal by the Government of Pakistan was greatly resented by Rabbani.

By giving its moral support to Hikmetyar, who was trying to unseat Rabbani by military means, Pakistan turned Rabbani totally against his erstwhile benefactors.

Afghans of almost all shades are unanimous in their view that much of the trouble which their country faced was due to the fact that there had been outside interference in the internal affairs of their country. There is a great deal of justification in their contention. The Taliban factor too has drawn in the neighbours and some outside powers. 'Foreign governments are back with a vengeance in Afghanistan, feeding weapons to their proxies on a scale not seen since the mujahideen victory,' opines Ahmed Rashid.[123]

The Government of Pakistan has repeatedly stated that it is remaining strictly neutral in the present conflict raging in Afghanistan between the Taliban and the ousted Kabul regime and that it has no favourites in the power struggle in that war-torn country. The fact that several anti-Taliban elements have been allowed to open offices in Pakistan gives credence to their professed neutrality. Haji Qadeer, the ousted Governor of Nangarhar, was living comfortably in Peshawar; his 'tactical headquarters' were in Landi Kotal. Rabbani's Jamiat-e-Islami was functioning from Chamkani refugee camp near Peshawar. General Painda Khan, Dostum's representative in Pakistan, was operating from Islamabad. Karim Khalili's Hizb-e-Wahdat had their man in Peshawar. Hikmetyar, even when he had moved to Tehran, continued to remain in contact with his supporters in Peshawar with the full knowledge of the intelligence agencies. The Writers' Union of Free Afghanistan (WUFA), based in Peshawar, was permitted to publish its quarterly magazine even though it contained articles against the Taliban and blamed Pakistan for supporting them. The

Revolutionary Afghanistan Women's Association (RAWA) often took protest marches out onto the streets of Islamabad to voice their anti-Taliban feelings.

Pakistan Tilts Towards the Taliban

Despite these apparently democratic gestures, there was enough evidence to prove that Pakistan was not only providing moral and diplomatic support to the Taliban, but was also extending financial and technical assistance to them for the rehabilitation of the Chaman-Kandahar-Herat-Kushka highway. Rabbani was unhappy with this move as Pakistan had not obtained his government's approval to go through Afghanistan. It not only undermined his authority, but it was also going to give Pakistan an opportunity to establish commercial relations with Afghanistan's neighbours despite Rabbani's hold over Kabul.

Pakistan's friendly attitude towards the Taliban became more evident when General Babar welcomed and publicized the action taken by the religious students against the local warlords who had ambushed the Pakistani convoy near Kandahar. This was not appreciated by Rabbani and Masood, who began spreading the word that the Taliban were being supported by Pakistan.

General Ismail Khan, who was Rabbani's man in Herat, blamed Pakistan for his defeat. He went to the extent of saying that Pakistan carried out air strikes and sent in ground troops, which of course was not true. Some sources supportive of Rabbani wanted the people to believe that Pakistan had refurbished Kandahar airport and had supplied parts and armaments for the Taliban's war planes and helicopters. Pakistan's former Foreign Minister, Sardar Aseff Ahmed Ali, however, continued to state that all of these allegations were baseless.

Rabbani and Masood Turn Against Pakistan

Masood retaliated by sacking Pakistan's Embassy in Kabul. Two Pakistani employees were killed and the Ambassador manhandled. Islamabad all but broke off diplomatic relations with the Kabul regime; it shifted its embassy to Jalalabad when that city fell to the Taliban. It was perhaps the first time in diplomatic history that an embassy was functioning from a place other than the capital. Relations between the government in Kabul and Pakistan had reached their lowest point. Who could have imagined that the Afghan leaders would one day turn against their benefactors. Rabbani and Masood could not have such short memories that they could forget that Pakistan had given shelter to over three million Afghan refugees for seventeen long years, and that there were still a million and a half Afghans on Pakistani soil. It had been spending $400 million a year on their upkeep at the height of the struggle against the Soviet occupation. Moreover it was a Pakistani Prime Minister who had hammered out the formula which had enabled Rabbani to assume power in Kabul.

When the Taliban reached the gates of Kabul and a real threat to Rabbani developed, his regime made loud noises blaming Pakistan for providing military assistance to the student militia.

It is ironic that the very people who had enjoyed the hospitality of the Pakistan Government asked the United Nations Security Council to call on Pakistan to refrain from encouraging opposition groups bent on toppling the Kabul authorities. The Vice Foreign Minister of Afghanistan, Abdul Rahim Ghafoorzai, in a letter to the UN Secretary-General, asked him to bring to the notice of the members of the Security Council that, 'Pakistan has enabled some groups (Taliban) to undertake major ground and air attacks against the capital in the near future.' He urged the Security Council to call upon Pakistan to desist from pursuing this heinous plot.[124]

Pakistan paid no attention to the complaints of Rabbani and his team and went ahead with its objective of finding a safe route to Central Asia, despite the tirades.

According to an agreement, signed between Islamabad and Kandahar, Pakistan was allowed to open branches of the National Bank in areas under the control of the Taliban. Utility stores were put up in Afghanistan. The Pakistan Telecommunications Corporation installed satellite communications linking Kandahar, Herat, Mazar-e-Sharif, Kabul, and Jalalabad with important cities in Pakistan. The Al-Shifa Eye Hospital, Rawalpindi, sent teams to Herat to provide free treatment, and Afghans living in refugee camps in Pakistan received medical treatment and supplies. WAPDA sent lubricants to enable generators to function. Rs 15 crores were allotted for a feasibility study of a road and railway link between Quetta and Turkmenistan.[125]

Opening the Western Route

Pakistan was planning to send a high-powered delegation to south-western Afghanistan by the end of March 1996 to initiate repair work on the 800-kilometre Chaman-Torghundi road. The project, which was to be completed at a cost of Rs 150 million in two years, would reduce the travel time between Chaman on the Pak-Afghan border and Torghundi on the Afghan-Turkmenistan frontier from forty-two to thirteen hours. The road would pass through five provinces controlled by the Taliban, including Kandahar.

The fact that the Taliban would execute the repairs under the supervision of Pakistan's Afghan Trade Development Cell angered the Rabbani regime even further. Rabbani had earlier protested to the Pakistan Government when a high-level Pakistani delegation had gone to Kandahar to talk to the Taliban leaders and discussed with them the Islamabad-sponsored reconstruction and development activities in south-western Afghanistan.

A spokesman of the Kabul regime, before it fell to the Taliban, termed all this a blatant interference in the internal affairs of Afghanistan. Rabbani's Embassy in Islamabad formally handed over a protest note to the Foreign Office asking the Government of Pakistan to abandon the plan for upgrading the road.[126] The then Afghan Minister of State for Foreign Affairs, Najibullah Lafraie, warned Pakistan that it should not go ahead with the repair work on the road. 'It is better for Pakistan to halt the work immediately and not interfere in the internal affairs of Afghanistan,' said Lafraie.

Pakistan maintained that it was not violating any agreement as a plan to open this particular route had been agreed upon by the Pakistan, Afghanistan, and Turkmenistan governments in 1993. The Minister replied that this contention was 'ridiculous' as the accord had only been agreed in principle and more discussions were needed, between Islamabad and Kabul, before the work could begin. He went on to say that his government did not object to the reconstruction of the road in principle; 'In fact, it would be very good for the people of Afghanistan to have a transit route,' he said. What Rabbani did not appreciate was that the Pakistan Government was ignoring him totally. Lafraie in fact likened the Taliban-controlled area to a war zone into which outsiders should not tread.

On the other hand, Maulvi Wakil Ahmed, Secretary to the Taliban Islamic Movement, had stated that the Taliban would have no objection if a non-government organization was formed to undertake these road repairs. 'We have already allowed NGOs to work in Taliban-held areas. We can have another NGO to repair this important highway linking Pakistan with Turkmenistan through Afghanistan,' said Mullah Mohammad Omar, but he pointed out that a formal agreement between the governments of Pakistan and Afghanistan to undertake repairs of the Chaman-Torghundi road, and other projects, could not be concluded until there was a representative central authority.[127]

Pakistan was basing its initiative on an agreement-in-principle made when the Islamabad Declaration had been signed which stated, among other things, that Pakistan would assist in the reconstruction of Afghanistan. The Foreign Office, therefore, came up with a statement saying; 'Pakistan in line with its stated policy of helping their Afghan brethren will continue to do whatever it can, within its limited resources, to contribute to the process of rehabilitation and reconstruction of Afghanistan'. The Foreign Office spokesman went on to say: 'Pakistan cannot in deference to a junta, which does not represent the Afghan people, ignore the well-being and prosperity of more than eighty per cent population of a brotherly Muslim country which stands in urgent need of international support and assistance to rebuild their war torn country'. (sic)[128]

Abdul Kareem Ghareeb, Afghanistan's Ambassador to Turkmenistan, warned Pakistan that financing the Chaman-Torghundi Highway would create further tension and destabilization in the region. Professor Mohammad Asghar, head of the Milli Rastgar party in Afghanistan, went to the extent of asking the US and other western nations to punish Pakistan for aggression against Afghanistan, as Iraq had been when it attacked Kuwait.[129] The Kabul regime strongly criticized Pakistan for planning to repair the Chaman-Torghundi road. Asghar is reported to have said that no self-respecting Afghan would approve the Pakistan Government's decision. 'It appears that Pakistan considers the four south-western provinces of Afghanistan as part of Pakistan,' said Asghar.

Islamabad should have also taken note of the fact that other groups opposing the Rabbani-Masood duo at that time were also not very happy with the idea of upgrading the road, which passes through Taliban-controlled areas only. They would have liked their areas to have received the same kind of reconstruction assistance.

In the event, the money promised for the improvement of the Chaman-Torghundi road was not released as

Pakistan's Ministry of Finance could not spare the necessary funds.

Pakistan was supporting the Taliban in the hope that they would prove to have the military strength and the determination to control the major part of Afghanistan. Pakistan's policy of assisting the Taliban, however, was based more on the anger they felt against Rabbani, who was instrumental in the sacking of the Pakistan Embassy in Kabul, than a genuine love for the Taliban whose interpretation of the *shariah* Islamabad did not share.

Pakistan's humanitarian and economic assistance to the Taliban was based partly on a desire to promote its national interest—they occupied the areas through which the road to the landlocked Muslim republics led—and partly to put military pressure on Rabbani and Masood, who had bitten the hand that had fed them. However, by supporting the Taliban against Rabbani and Masood, Pakistan highlighted its policy of giving preference to the Pushtuns over other ethnic minorities. This was a negation of the declared statements of the Pakistan leadership that they had no favourites in Afghanistan. It was also not in keeping with ground realities, as the Tajiks were now strong enough to play a significant role in Afghan politics in the future. Alienating them was not a sound policy.

By overplaying its hand Pakistan lost the goodwill it had developed with Rabbani and Masood. Pakistan's earlier insistence that Rabbani must quit the presidency as his term of office had expired created bad blood between erstwhile allies.

Even the United Nations' Special Envoy directly accused Pakistan of interfering in Afghanistan. 'Foreign interference exists and Pakistan's interference is real and something big,' said Mestiri. He hoped, however, that Pakistan would take part in the peace talks which he was trying to organize between the more powerful warring factions. Pakistan, of course, continued to deny the charges that it supported the Taliban. A government spokesman maintained that Pakistan was only interested in promoting a stable settlement in

Afghanistan so that new trade and pipeline routes to Central Asia could be opened up. This objective itself meant that Pakistan had to befriend the Taliban, who controlled the western route to the Central Asian States.

Dr Goga A. Khidoyatov, adviser to the Foreign Minister of Uzbekistan, remarked during a press conference held in Peshawar in February 1996, that Pakistan's Afghan policy wasn't very passive, implying that Islamabad was involved in supplying arms to its favourites in Afghanistan.[130]

Ambassador Ahmed Kamal, Pakistan's permanent representative to the United Nations, while participating in the general debate on the situation in Afghanistan, hinted at the need to force Rabbani to step down. He is reported to have said that only a broad-based interim mechanism, in which all factions would participate, could pave the way to a democratic government in Afghanistan. He elaborated Pakistan's view by saying that: 'Durable peace in Afghanistan required abandoning the politics of domination and exclusion, and a genuine national reconciliation among all the political and ethnic segments of the Afghan society.' Kamal emphasized that the current issue was that of legitimacy. While not mentioning the Rabbani government by name, he did stress that legitimacy is not acquired by military means, but by gaining the confidence and support of the people. He said that Pakistan favoured a complete ban on weapons and arms supplies to the warring factions. He believed that the imposition of an arms embargo by the United Nations would send the right signals to the Afghan warlords. He proposed that the arms embargo could be carried out by UN personnel assisted by the OIC.

Apparently, the United States succeeded in convincing both Rabbani and the Pakistan Government to open direct talks, with each other, with a view to normalizing their relations. The negotiations began in Islamabad in May 1996. Rabbani's regime agreed to repair the Pakistan embassy building in Kabul, which had been partially destroyed by government troops on 6 September 1995, and

Pakistan decided to reopen its Embassy in Kabul when the situation in Kabul permitted them to do so. In the meantime, Rabbani was prepared to offer an alternative building in Kabul to house the Pakistan Embassy.

Now that the Taliban had become a reality, and controlled two-thirds of Afghanistan, Pakistan wanted to strengthen them further. Islamabad tried to form an anti-Rabbani alliance comprising the Taliban, Abdul Rashid Dostum, Gulbadin Hikmetyar, and Sibghatullah Mojeddedi.[131] However, when Hikmetyar broke away and joined Rabbani, Pakistan had to change track once again. The government began making overtures towards the Rabbani regime by sending food convoys to Kabul, which was still under Rabbani's control.

Pakistan Attempts to Broker a Peace Accord

Pakistan also offered to assist the various Afghan factions to establish a broad-based government in Kabul. Although no specific proposals were made, feelers were sent out to both Rabbani and the Taliban. Benazir formed a committee comprising the Interior Minister, Major-General Naseerullah Babar, the Adviser on Afghanistan, Ijlal Haider Zaidi, Governor of the NWFP, Major-General Khurshid Ali Khan, and the Additional Secretary, Foreign Office, Iftikhar Murshid. Representatives from GHQ and ISI were also members of the team.

After the Taliban were pushed back to the outskirts of Kabul, Pakistan realized that the Taliban might not be able to hold out against the combined forces of Dostum and Masood now that the Iranians openly supported them. Islamabad, therefore, decided to send their top negotiators to Mazar-e-Sharif and Kandahar to try and hammer out a cease-fire before Kabul was retaken by Rabbani. General Babar, accompanied by Ijlal Haider Zaidi, shuttled between the two towns during the last week of October 1996 and finally succeeded in persuading Dostum to agree to meet the leaders of the Taliban. Masood's representatives joined them later.

The issues which came under discussion were: an immediate cease-fire; return of prisoners taken by either side; return of dead bodies; control and demilitarization of Kabul. While the first three points were accepted by all three groups, the Taliban were unwilling to withdraw from the capital. Despite Babar's efforts, Dostum and Masood were unwilling to drop the condition of the demilitarization of Kabul before accepting a cease-fire, while the Taliban, on the other hand, were insisting that the cease-fire should precede and not follow the handing over of Kabul to a neutral body under UN control. Ahmed Shah Masood wanted UN troops to be stationed in Kabul to oversee the implementation of the agreement, but Norbert Holl, head of the UN Special Mission to Afghanistan, quite obviously could not make that kind of commitment. Babar was trying to persuade the two antagonists to accept a formula by which Bagram airport could come under the control of Masood and Kwaja Rwash airport in Kabul would remain in the hands of the Taliban, thus giving both an outlet to the outside world. If they had agreed to this formula, Babar maintains, an understanding could have been reached later to find a solution for Kabul itself. According to him he was trying to adopt a step-by-step approach to the complex problem of power-sharing in Afghanistan.

Babar had succeeded in obtaining the names of six representatives each from the Taliban and the anti-Taliban alliance, who would be responsible for the maintenance of law and order in Kabul, and for working out the composition of an interim administration. According to the former Interior Minister, Norbert Holl talked to New York from Mazar-e-Sharif but made no mention of the future control of Kabul, as a result of which Ahmed Shah Masood adopted a harder line, saying, 'If there is no de-militarization of Kabul the whole agreement will fall through', which is what happened.

A meeting was consequently held on 3 November at Islamabad with President Farooq Ahmed Leghari in the chair. General Babar, the Chief of the Army Staff, and the Director-General of the Inter Services Intelligence Directorate were present. It was decided to continue trying to bring about a reconciliation between the Taliban and the anti-Taliban alliance; to persuade them to agree to a cease-fire; and that Babar should continue his efforts towards making the three power groups accept a formula for ending the conflict. However, the second Benazir government was dismissed by the President on the night of 4/5 November 1996, and General Babar could no longer wield his baton.

The caretaker government of Malik Meraj Khalid preferred to play down the role of Pakistan and remained content with supporting the United Nations' efforts toward bringing about peace in Afghanistan. There were too many pressing domestic issues which the caretaker government had to deal with in the three months of their rule. Quite naturally, therefore, the Afghan problem was brushed under the carpet for the time being.

Pakistan renewed its interest in Afghan affairs when the new government of Nawaz Sharif was formed. The members of the OIC were persuaded to leave the Afghan seat vacant at the Special Session of the OIC Summit, which was held at Islamabad on 23 March 1997 to celebrate the fiftieth anniversary of the founding of Pakistan. No invitation was issued to the ousted Rabbani regime, and the Taliban were invited as observers.

A major change in Pakistan's Afghan policy was noticed after Nawaz Sharif took over the reigns of government. The responsibility of dealing with the Afghans was no longer shared between different ministries. The task of finding an amicable solution to the Afghanistan imbroglio was given solely to the Ministry of Foreign Affairs.

On the directions of Prime Minister Nawaz Sharif, Additional Secretary Iftikhar Murshid, a senior diplomat in the Ministry of

Foreign Affairs, met the leaders of the Northern Alliance in Dubai. He then shuttled between Kandahar and Mazar-e-Sharif to try and make the rival groups agree on a minimum agenda so that a dialogue between them could begin. He was assisted by Pakistan's Ambassador to Afghanistan, Aziz Khan, and Rustam Shah Mohammad, Chief Secretary of the NWFP, who as the former Chief Commissioner of Afghan Refugees was well known to all the Afghan leaders. Murshid also travelled to Moscow and Tehran and co-ordinated his activities with those of Norbert Holl.

The main emphasis was on an immediate cease-fire, the exchange of prisoners, and the setting up of a political commission to discuss the formation of a broad-based government. Enforcement of the *shariah* all over Afghanistan was a condition which every faction accepted; its interpretation by the Taliban and those opposed to them, however, differed widely.

Murshid carried the proposals back and forth but to no avail. While each party accepted the proposition *in toto*, the sequence in which the measures were to be implemented created another deadlock. The Taliban, as before, insisted on an exchange of prisoners immediately after the cease-fire went into effect, while the northern alliance demanded that the demilitarization of Kabul and the establishment of the political commission precede the exchange of prisoners. In fact Younus Qanooni, the Rabbani spokesman, maintained his earlier stand on the formation of a political commission being a pre-requisite for even a cease-fire. Consequently the fighting not only continued but even intensified. Innocent Afghan men, women, and children, who so far had been leading a relatively peaceful existence in areas not yet affected by the civil war, now found themselves caught in the cross-fire between their own co-citizens. Casualties mounted; many more bread-winners lost their lives, many more were maimed. The destruction of Afghanistan by its own people continued unabated. Murshid, despite all his sincere efforts, could not get the warring factions to sit round the negotiating table and settle their differences through a dialogue. The gap in their conditionalities remained as wide as ever.

Pakistan's proposal for a five-nation conference of regional powers on Afghanistan, to include Iran, Russia, Pakistan, China, and the United States, did not bear fruit; the leader of the Pakistan delegation did achieve a minor breakthrough by opening up a dialogue with Ahmed Shah Masood, who had declined to meet any Pakistani official for two years. Masood, who had been built up by the western press as the Lion of Panjsher during the Afghan jihad against the Soviets, had no love for Pakistan. He had firmly believed then, with some justification, that although he was doing most of the fighting, the Hizb-e-Islami (H) was receiving more arms and ammunition from the ISI than his own Jamiat-e-Islami.

Although Pakistan did not officially recognize the Taliban administration, its representative in Islamabad was permitted to function as a proper embassy, albeit without the required protocol. Anti-Taliban activities from Pakistani soil were banned—Haji Abdul Qadeer, who was allegedly supporting an uprising in the province of Kunarh, was told by the intelligence agencies to either stop anti-Taliban activities in the eastern province or leave the country.[132] He and his lieutenants decided to leave Pakistan, despite the fact that he had substantial assets in the country that had given him shelter. However, he was determined to continue his endeavour to oust the Taliban from the provinces he once controlled, so he started operating through Tashkent and Mazar-e-Sharif. The arrest of his son Mohammad Zair by the Taliban was one of the reasons why he had turned openly against the Taliban.

The Issue of Recognition

The Taliban had been urging the Government of Pakistan to give them official recognition ever since they had ousted President Rabbani from Kabul. The pressure increased when they occupied the entire area of Afghanistan south of the Hindu Kush, and were poised to move into the northern provinces as well.

Pakistan had already allowed the Taliban representative in Islamabad to function as the head of the Afghanistan mission after the eviction of Rabbani from the capital, so it was not surprising that Pakistan extended official recognition to the Taliban Government the very next day after the Taliban entered Mazar-e-Sharif.

The reverses suffered by the Taliban immediately thereafter raised doubts about the wisdom of recognizing them as the *de jure* rulers of Afghanistan so early in the day. Did the Taliban regime fulfil the criteria for the recognition of a new government when Pakistan formally recognized them?

Sir Ernest Satow, a British diplomat of the late nineteenth and early twentieth century, in his book *Satow's Guide to Diplomatic Practice*, the Bible for all English-speaking foreign ministries, laid down the following four criteria for the recognition of a new government: (i) the new political arrangement should have assumed a permanent character; (ii) the *de facto* government should have proved itself to be substantially in control of the country; (iii) it must have the support of the majority of the population; (iv) the new set-up must be in a position to abide by international agreements.

Pakistan based its decision on the fact that the new government was now in effective control of most of the territory of Afghanistan including the capital, and it was representative of all the country's ethnic groups. Was that the situation after the fall of Mazar-e-Sharif?

The Taliban had indeed occupied ninety per cent of the territory on 25 May, when Pakistan recognized the regime. On that day they appeared to have the support of the majority of the people of Afghanistan and they had also given a few posts in their administration to Tajiks and Uzbeks. But did the Foreign Ministry really believe that

the new political arrangement was there to stay? Surely
their advisers must have been aware that those who had
rebelled against Dostum and invited the Taliban to enter
Mazar-e-Sharif had done so, not because they loved the
Taliban, but because they hated Dostum. Clashes between them
should have been expected, given the sharp differences in their
approach to governance.

Pakistan's objectives ever since the power struggle
between the rival Afghan militia began have been: durable
peace in the war-ravaged land; a friendly government across
its western border; repatriation of Afghan refugees; access
to Central Asian markets; and a safe route for the oil and
gas pipeline from Turkmenistan to the Arabian Sea.

How many of these was Pakistan hoping to achieve by
recognizing the Taliban regime so early in the power game, and
what actually transpired. The expectation of peace and stability in
Afghanistan was shattered just three days after the Taliban
government was recognized. Islamabad had hoped that once it
had recognized the new political set-up, others would soon follow
suit, but only Saudi Arabia and the UAE did so. Pakistan wanted
to be the first country to oblige the Taliban and thereby earn their
good will. That they did. 'We heartily appreciate this move and
are thankful for it,' said the Taliban leadership. But so had
Mojeddedi, Rabbani, Hikmetyar, and Dostum, all of whom turned
against Pakistan when Islamabad's policies went against their
interests.

Over a million Afghan refugees stayed on in Pakistan,
although there had been peace in the areas they came from
for the last three years. The Afghan refugees in Akora
Khattak, who had come to Pakistan after the Taliban had
taken control of the capital, were indeed unanimous in their view
that Kabul was calm and quiet. On being asked why, in that case,
they had left, their answer was that there was no work to be
found for them in Taliban-controlled areas.

Mohammad Yunus, Deputy Director of Afghan Refugees
in Peshawar, put it very correctly when he said, 'They are
all economic migrants.' The return of the refugees,

therefore, depended upon the generation of economic activity within Afghanistan, among other factors, not just on peace returning to that country.

While the Taliban did indeed have the support of the majority of the population, their regime could not yet be considered to be broad-based. This was because neither had the second largest ethnic group, the Tajiks, nor had the Shias of central Afghanistan accepted the Pushtun-dominated Taliban when Pakistan recognized them.

In taking this initiative, Pakistan paid no heed to the reaction of its immediate neighbours. Iran had never been happy with the Taliban, and official recognition by Pakistan only widened the gap between the two countries on this particular issue. Although the Ministry of Foreign Affairs MFA did inform Tehran that it was going to recognize the Taliban regime before actually doing so, and also came up with an announcement that there was a positive response from Iran, the statement of Ali Akber Velayati, the Iranian Foreign Minister, belied the assurance given by the MFA. He reiterated his earlier statements to the effect that interference by certain other countries was causing bloodshed in Afghanistan. The implication being that Pakistan was meddling in Afghanistan's internal affairs, and he also went on to say that Iran would not remain indifferent to what was happening on its eastern border. He went to the extent of asking Kazakhstan, Kyrghistan, and India to do everything possible to stem the crisis in Afghanistan.

The Taliban reacted to these statements by closing the Iranian Embassy in Kabul and asking the staff to leave the capital within forty-eight hours. The Taliban were thus instrumental in further straining the ties between Iran and Pakistan.

Russia warned the Taliban not to attempt to cross the Amu Darya, threatening a riposte if they did so. President Islam Karimov of Uzbekistan bluntly told Nawaz Sharif at the ECO summit in May 1997 that Pakistan must desist from interfering in the internal affairs of Afghanistan. Turkey, which is busy trying to curb the Islamic resurgence in its own country, has no love for the Taliban's brand of Islam. Its historical ties with Pakistan notwithstanding, it has every reason to support a more liberal regime in Afghanistan.

Why, despite the unfavourable reaction of the neighbouring countries, did Pakistan go ahead with recognizing the Taliban regime so soon?

The primary reason seems to have been Islamabad's determination to gain access to the oil and gas reserves of Turkmenistan. Also, recognition of the Taliban regime might have helped to promote Pakistan's economic interest, but in the event it had a negative impact on its security because of the alignment of India with Iran and the Central Asian states and a further interaction with Russia on the issue of the Taliban. Furthermore, with Qazi Hussain Ahmed threatening to launch an Islamic revolution, and Maulana Fazalur Rahman and Samiul Haq wanting to introduce the Taliban phenomenon in Pakistan, too deep an involvement with the Taliban was fraught with internal security risks.

Pakistan should have also realized that keeping 'client' states in power is an expensive business. A great deal of financial and military assistance is needed to do so. With the economic crunch that it was facing at that time, Pakistan could ill afford to take on an additional liability.

The Foreign Office continued to defend its decision to recognize the Taliban government in Kabul by saying that in fact it was late in doing so.[133] That is true, for if the Taliban were to be accepted as the *de jure* rulers of Afghanistan at all, it should have been when they occupied the capital and formed a central *shoora* to run the administration of the country. Pakistan's recognition of the Taliban immediately after the fall of Mazar-e-Sharif became controversial because of the dramatic set-back suffered by the Taliban only three days after their finest hour.

Points in favour of Pakistan recognizing the Taliban Regime

- Pakistan had all along been providing political and moral support to the Taliban, and had been more or less drifting into recognizing them ever since they occupied the capital.
- The Taliban are predominantly Pushtuns and therefore have the sympathy of the Pushtuns living in Pakistan.
- The Taliban were strongest in areas adjacent to Pakistan and hence needed to be supported in the interests of better relations with Afghanistan in the future.
- Turkmenistan's Karakorum desert is believed to hold the third largest gas reserves in the world, some 3 trillion cubic metres, and has estimated oil reserves of 6 billion barrels.[134] The shortest route to the open sea from Turkmenistan is through Afghanistan and Pakistan. It is not surprising, therefore, that Pakistan supported the Taliban, who had total control over the route to Central Asia.
- The Taliban were in control of twenty-seven out of the thirty-two provinces of Afghanistan and were in complete control of the capital; as such they were the strongest claimants to the throne of Kabul.
- The Taliban had been able to maintain complete law and order in the areas they controlled.
- Support for the Taliban was appreciated by Saudi Arabia, with whom Pakistan has always had the best of relations. In recognizing the Taliban regime, Pakistan expected many other countries to follow suit.

Points against supporting the Taliban

- No country should try to impose its will on the fiercely independent Afghans, as various nations have learnt to their cost. Even the best of allies would resent any such attempt.

Map 7
Gas and Oil Pipeline Projects from Turkmenistan

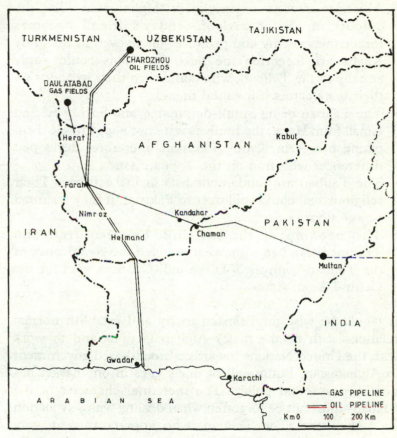

• The Afghans today are so divided that supporting one antagonizes all the others.

• Alliances change overnight in Afghanistan, like the colours of the chameleon—today's friend becomes tomorrow's enemy and promises made even in the Holy Kaaba are forgotten the next day. This could apply equally to the Taliban, who could turn their weapons on their benefactors if it suited them.

• The Taliban being Sunni-dominated and having evicted Ismail from Herat, the Iranians were not happy to see them taking power in Kabul. Pakistan, therefore, developed differences with Iran on the Taliban issue.

• The Taliban are fundamentalists in the extreme. Their religious zeal could spill over to Pakistan if they assumed power alone.

• The opening of the rail link between Iran and Turkmenistan had somewhat reduced the significance of the Taliban-controlled Torghundi-Chaman road for the Central Asian states.

It would be wise for Pakistan to try and establish normal relations with all the major Afghan factions and to work with the United Nations towards a broad-based government in Afghanistan. Putting all of one's eggs in one basket has not been a sound policy. The mercurial character of the Afghans must not be forgotten when dealing with any faction in Afghanistan. The Taliban, who apparently were very friendly with Pakistan, did not appreciate the closing of the Pak-Afghan border for three days prior to the general elections in Pakistan on 3 February 1997. The Taliban border guards resorted to aerial firing and closed the border at Torkham in retaliation for the action taken by Pakistan.[135]

Personnel of Pakistan's Anti-Narcotics Force (ANF) were arrested by the Taliban when they inadvertently crossed into Afghanistan while chasing drug traffickers, and it was only after some hectic negotiations that the *Shoora* agreed to release them. Despite the fact that Pakistan has given its

wholehearted support to the Taliban, there are those
amongst them who believe that their country has been
devastated because of the interference of Pakistan and Iran.

Since only Saudi Arabia and the UAE had recognized
the Taliban government, Pakistan found itself at odds with
the rest of the regional countries. The Foreign Minister,
Gohar Ayub Khan, decided to visit the Central Asian states
and Russia to explain to them the reasons for the
recognition of the new regime. His words fell on deaf ears,
however, and none of them was convinced. They continued to
recognize Rabbani as the *de jure* head of state of Afghanistan
despite the fact that he and his allies controlled only one-third
of the country.

CHAPTER 7

THE ROLES AND INTERESTS OF OTHER POWERS

Iran

Iran's interest in Afghanistan is rooted in its historical ties with its eastern neighbour. The area east of the Dasht-e-Lut in Iran, known as Khorasan, once included the cities of Meshed, Herat, Balkh (Mazar-e-Sharif), and Merv (Turkmenistan). The whole of this territory was part of Iran until it was conquered by the Gilzai Pushtuns in the early seventeenth century. In 1737 Nadir Shah of Iran overran Afghanistan and aligned it with his country once again. After his death Ahmed Shah Abdali took control of the area around Kandahar and gradually spread out towards Kabul and beyond. At that time the boundary between the Kingdom of Bokhara and Afghanistan was the Hindu Kush. It was the British and the Russians who decided to have the river Oxus as the dividing line during the Great Game being played between the two rivals on the political chessboard of Central Asia.

The present boundary between Iran and Afghanistan was delineated by the British in the eighteenth century. It cut through territory inhabited by people with similar cultural and linguistic backgrounds—the Persian influence in Herat in many ways remained very visible.

Besides historical ties and the Persian language widely spoken by the Afghans, support for the cause of the Shias was another factor which caused the Iranians to take a major interest in the future of Afghanistan. Tehran also stood to gain economically if it could convince the Central Asian states that the trade route through Iran would be more secure. Indeed, some political analysts in Pakistan are of the opinion that Iran would like Afghanistan to remain unstable so that the shorter route to the open sea is not developed. This view, however, is not supported by the majority of Afghan watchers. They believe that because of the presence of a million or so Afghan refugees still in Iran, its leaders would like stability to return to Afghanistan so that the burden of supporting the refugees is lessened.

Because of ideological differences between the Ayatollahs and the Taliban, however, Tehran-Islamabad relations came under great strain. The aloofness that Iran had maintained during the Geneva negotiations gave place to the Iranian leadership taking more direct role in the affairs of Afghanistan during the civil war that followed the withdrawal of the Soviet troops. In order to sustain the existing warm relations with Iran, it was necessary for Islamabad to keep in close touch with Tehran over developments in Afghanistan. Consequently, although Iran was not taking part in the Geneva negotiations on the withdrawal of Soviet troops from Afghanistan, the Foreign Office briefed its counterpart, the Iranian External Affairs Ministry, after every meeting in Geneva. In those days Iran was engaged in a war with Iraq, hence it could not devote much time to the situation on its north-eastern border. Iran was, therefore, grateful to Pakistan for looking after its interests as well.

Iran did feel that it was not in the driver's seat during the negotiations and was somewhat apprehensive that the Geneva talks were being influenced by the 'Great Satan' (USA). Foreign Minister Sahibzada Yaqub Khan, who was representing Pakistan at the UN-sponsored talks, maintains that he was able to reassure Iran and put their anxieties to rest.[136]

However, when Pakistan began playing a direct role in the formation of the transitional government in Afghanistan, the Iranians felt left out. They had no say in the establishment of the Afghan Interim Government (AIG) which was cobbled up in Rawalpindi. This created a distance between Islamabad and

Tehran on issues dealing with Afghanistan. The representation of the Shias in any future government in Afghanistan also became a bone of contention between the two Muslim neighbours. Iran was looking for a role for the Shias in Afghanistan far in excess of their population, something which the Sunni-dominated *Shoora* was not willing to accept. Pakistan was seen as supportive of those who were not prepared to accommodate Iran's demands in this respect. Iran felt that, being a next-door neighbour, it would be directly affected by the composition of the future government in Afghanistan. It therefore began taking a deeper interest in developments across its eastern frontier, especially when the civil war began taking on a sectarian and linguistic colour. Tehran supported the cause of the Shias in Afghanistan, who were represented by the Hizb-e-Wahdat (Brotherhood). The Hizb, however, was split into two factions, one led by Karim Khalili (pro-Iran) and the other by Akbari, who was pro-Hikmetyar.

The rise of the Taliban added to the differences between Iran and Pakistan which had begun to develop during the Afghan jihad. The Iranian leaders considered the Taliban, who had suddenly appeared from nowhere and overrun large tracts of territory without meeting any physical resistance, 'a strange phenomenon'. Another reason why the Iranian leadership was unhappy with the Taliban movement was because it consisted mainly of Pushtuns, who have ruled over the Hazaras and the Dari (modified Farsi)-speaking Tajiks for centuries. Iran's mistrust of the Taliban increased further when a prominent Hizb-e-Wahdat leader, Abdul Ali Mazari, was murdered while in Taliban custody. Their explanation was that Mazari had tried to grapple with the guards while in flight and a struggle had ensued in which Mazari was killed—an explanation which the Iranians did not accept.

The Ayatollahs of Iran have given the impression that it is their undeclared policy to support the rights of minority Shia populations in neighbouring countries. This is perceived to be so in Pakistan and Afghanistan in particular. Iran has been trying to ensure that the Shias in Afghanistan, who form around fourteen per cent of the population, get a share in the future set-up in their country, something which had been denied to them during the rule of the Durrani kings. They will, in all probability, continue supporting the Hazara Shias and the Tajik-dominated political parties in Afghanistan.

Initially, the Shia-dominated Hizb-e-Wahdat party of Afghanistan, headed by Karim Khalili, had serious differences with the Iranian leadership. When Deputy Foreign Minister Alauddin Borujerdi visited Yakolang (Bamian), Khalili refused to meet him, but when he visited the area again the causes of dissatisfaction were removed and the two met in December 1995.[137] Further talks were held between the two in April 1996 in an attempt to bring all the Afghan Shia factions together.

It is because Rabbani advocates giving the Shias a role in the future government of Afghanistan that the Iranian leaders favour him over the Taliban.

In spite of Hikmetyar's stance on not giving the Afghan Shias a special dispensation the Iranians succeeded in convincing him to join Rabbani's government so that he could get the support of more and more Afghan groups, thus giving the regime some much-needed legitimacy.

The Taliban believe that the Iranian clergy were supporting the Rabbani regime against them because of an inherent dislike of Sunnis. This reasoning carries no weight, however, as Rabbani and Masood are also Sunnis. Antipathy towards the Taliban, therefore, is not entirely because of sectarian differences but also on ethnic grounds. Iran hopes to get a better deal for the Shias from Rabbani and Masood as they are non-Pushtuns.

Iranian dissatisfaction with the Taliban deepened when the latter occupied Herat and forced Commander Ismail Khan to take shelter in Iran. The Iranians allegedly gave Ismail all the assistance he needed to enable him to carry out cross-border attacks into the Taliban-controlled provinces of Herat, Farah, and Nimroz and eventually, retake Herat. Tehran is reported to have established upto five training camps in eastern Iran for some 8,000 fighters,[138] including mercenaries from Kabul, ex-Heratis, disgruntled elements from Kandahar, and refugees from Persian-speaking northern provinces. This motley crowd was expected to fight alongside Ismail and his men when they launched their counter-offensive against the Taliban.

The Taliban reported that they had nabbed 166 Afghans who had infiltrated into the provinces of Herat and Farah from Iranian territory to prepare the ground for an assault on the Shindand airbase, which was under control of the Taliban. They displayed the Iranian arms and vehicles captured from these Afghans to the press. The report was confirmed by independent sources, but the Iranian authorities denied that they were in any way involved. The Iranian authorities said that these arms had been given by Iran to the Afghan mujahideen during their struggle against the Soviet forces.[139]

According to some foreign diplomats, the commander of Iran's elite Revolutionary Guards, General Mohsin Rezai, moved his base to Meshad, close to the Afghan border, to help Ismail prepare for the planned battle to retake Herat. Some kind of counter-offensive was indeed being planned by those who had fled to Iran when the Taliban overran their stronghold in Herat. Iran had no intention, however, of getting militarily involved in support of Ismail for fear of widening the conflict and enabling the USA to start another proxy war. The use of Iranian artillery deployed on its own side of the border could, however, assist Ismail in his attempt to retake Herat and restore some of his damaged reputation. Dostum, still supportive of the Taliban, vowed to meet force with force if they put their intentions into practice.

Maulvi Ihsanullah, Governor-General of the five Taliban-controlled provinces adjacent to Pakistan, addressed a gathering of Afghan refugees in Akora Khattak in Pakistan in February 1996. In his address he accused Iran of giving refuge to Ismail Khan, arming him and his men and interfering in the internal affairs of Afghanistan.

Maulvi Yar Mohammad, the Taliban Governor of Herat, is reported to have warned the Iranian Consul-General on 11 February 1996, that the Taliban would declare war against Iran and bomb Iranian cities if they dared to get militarily involved with the proposed counter-offensive against Herat from Iranian soil.[140] He is also reported to have said that the Taliban in India and Bangladesh would come to Afghanistan to fight alongside their brethren if Iran dared to attack them; he did not name Pakistan for some reason.

Armed patrols of Taliban and Iranian border guards are reported to have clashed occasionally in Islam Qila near Herat with casualties on both sides. Though this has not been substantiated, it is a fact that the Taliban have rocketed areas inside Iran territory. Luckily matters did not get out of hand, and both the Iranians and the Taliban kept their emotions in check.

Iran was also concerned about the Taliban advances beyond Herat because of the presence of large numbers of Sunnis in their areas close to Afghanistan.

Ambassador Dr Ali Khurram, former member of the Iranian Institute of Policy Studies (IIPS), Tehran, while speaking at a seminar organized by a local think tank in Islamabad, expressed the view that ever since the emergence of the Taliban, terrorism and drug trafficking had increased. General Mohammad Zaeri, the Iranian police chief and head of the joint law enforcement agency, accused the Taliban, of smuggling large quantities of morphine and heroin into Iran. According to the General, around 147 tonnes of drugs, which were being smuggled by the Taliban, had been siezed in the year ending March 1996. Zaeri asserted that the militia, which controlled the western provinces bordering Iran, were processing opium into heroin and morphine before shipping them into Iran.[141]

The alarm bells, which had sounded in Tehran after the capture of Herat by the Taliban, reached a crescendo when Kabul fell. The Iranians believed that this was the result of the encouragement the Taliban had received from Saudi Arabia and the United States—their perceived arch-enemies.

Iran repatriated 250,000 of the two million Afghan refugees who had taken shelter in Iran during the days of the Soviet occupation. They travelled through Turkmenistan under an agreement between Kabul, Tehran, and Ashkabad. Each refugee was given $25, a carpet, and 50 kilograms of wheat to help them in settling down. This gesture by the Iranians created a measure of goodwill amongst those Afghans returning to Afghanistan, and also helped in their efforts to create a shield against the Taliban tide, by creating a group of pro-Iran supporters amongst the returning Afghan refugees, who would (so Iran hoped) resist Taliban incursions into the territory that they belonged to.

After the sacking of the Pakistan Embassy in Kabul by Ahmed Shah Masood's men, Islamabad all but broke off diplomatic relations with the Rabbani-Masood duo. This gave Iran an opportunity to seize the initiative in Afghanistan. The Iranian Deputy Foreign Minister began to contact the various Afghan leaders in an attempt to find a political solution which would be in Iran's national interest.

Differences in Tehran's and Islamabad's approaches towards a permanent solution to the Afghan imbroglio became obvious from then on. While Islamabad was openly anti-Rabbani and Masood, and even hosted a meeting of all anti-Rabbani factions in Islamabad, Tehran was supporting the ousted regime. Rabbani paid an official visit to Iran in March 1996, much to the embarrassment of Pakistan, reinforcing the fact that Tehran considered the Rabbani regime the legal government in Afghanistan even though it was holed up in the northern province of Badakhshan. This brought Iran closer to India as New Delhi continued to recognize the ousted regime of Rabbani.

The Iranian Deputy Foreign Minister, Murtaza Sarmadi, during his visit to Pakistan, on 4 March 1996, reiterated the fact that, while the position of Iran and Pakistan might not be completely the same on the Afghan problem, the two had reached the conclusion that they should assist in the restoration of peace in the war-torn country.[142] He went on to say that war was no solution to the problem.

In February 1996 the Iranian Foreign Minister, Ali Akber Velayati, expressed the hope that the co-operation between Iran and Pakistan in working towards a reconciliation between the different factions in Afghanistan would lead to the restoration of peace and tranquillity in that country. On the question of the legitimacy of the Rabbani regime, however, he was quite clear that the government had not only been accepted by Iran but also by the UN, the OIC, and the NAM. He did not accept Pakistan's contention that, Rabbani's term of office having expired, his was not a legitimate regime.

Tehran had been wanting to divert the Central Asian trade route to the Arabian Sea through its territory so as to minimize the importance of the Taliban-held areas through which the Chaman-Torghundi road passes. The Iranian leadership succeeded in linking the railway system of the Central Asian republics to its own, thus providing access to the port of Bander Abbas on the Persian Gulf to its land-locked northern neighbours. Though not openly opposing the improvement of the Torghundi-Chaman highway, Tehran was keen to produce an alternative route to the open sea for them. Maulvi Wakil Ahmed, member of the Central Shoora, is reported to have stated that Iran was opposed to the repairs of the Chaman-Torghundi road as it wanted the Central Asian states to use the Bander Abbas route for trade.

Rabbani, along with the other heads of state of the member countries of the OIC, attended the inauguration ceremony of the railway line linking Iran with Turkmenistan and other Central Asian states. This visit was utilized to further reinforce the policy of keeping the Taliban at bay. Rabbani and his delegation reportedly also met Ismail Khan, who had been evicted from Herat by the Taliban in September 1995.

Tehran Parleys

Despite the animosity shown by the Taliban leadership towards Iran, Alauddin Borujerdi continued his efforts to iron out the differences between Rabbani and the opposition, including the Taliban. According to him, he had several rounds of talks with the militiamen in Pakistan, and the Taliban leadership agreed to send a delegation to Tehran for further talks.[143] Although the Taliban delegation did go to Tehran, they went there only to take up irritants with relation to Iran, i.e., 'material support, including supply of arms to the rivals of the Taliban which was an attempt to undermine Taliban control'.[144] They rejected Iran's self-appointed role as a mediator. Maulvi Masoom Afghani, the Taliban representative in Pakistan, ruled out any discussion on the question of mediation between the Taliban and the Rabbani regime.

The Iranians supported the idea of an international conference on Afghanistan, to be convened either in Pakistan or in Afghanistan itself; meanwhile, the Iranian Government tried again to get all the Afghan factions together in order to make them agree to a cease-fire and to the formation of a broad-based government in Kabul. The conference, which was held in Tehran on 25 January 1997, was attended by Professor Burhanuddin Rabbani, Engineer Gulbadin Hikmetyar, Karim Khalili of the Hizb-e-Wahdat and representatives of Abdul Rashid Dostum and Ahmed Shah Masood. Additional Secretary Iftikhar Murshid from the Pakistan Foreign Office also attended the meeting.

The Taliban leadership, however, did not accept the invitation as they continued to doubt Iran's stance in the ongoing conflict between them and the anti-Taliban forces. 'We have sent no delegation to Tehran as we consider Iran is not neutral', said Mullah Abdul Jalil, Deputy Foreign Minister of the Taliban *Shoora*.[145]

The Iranian Foreign Minister, Ali Akber Velayati, admitted that, because of the Taliban boycott, the conference could not come to a definite conclusion. In fact, it amounted to making no progress whatsoever, as without the presence of the Taliban no decisions could be binding.

Iran, according to its Ambassador in Islamabad, Mohammad Mehdi Akhundzadeh, was interested only in peace and stability in Afghanistan so that the Afghan refugees in Iran could be persuaded to go back to their country. He also emphasized that Tehran would like to see a negotiated settlement with the Hizb-e-Wahdat, not a conflict which would result in continuing casualties. He was also of the opinion that, despite the fact that Dostum and Rabbani had been forced to flee Afghanistan when Mazar-e-Sharif was occupied by the Taliban, they still retained some influence in Afghanistan, and, therefore, could not be ignored in any future political arrangement in that country.

Akhundzadeh also pointed out that the Taliban were pushing Afghanistan into the medieval age, and that Natiq Nuri had lost the presidential elections in Iran in May 1997 because there was a rumour that he would bring in a Taliban-style government in Iran.[146] Mohammad Khatemi, the newly-elected President of Iran, said in his first televised press conference that he was against all forms of terrorism and welcomed dialogue and negotiations to solve disputes. He emphasized, however, that unilateral and enforced peace was not acceptable. Though this was in the context of the Middle East peace process, it could very well be applied to his attitude towards the Taliban. His desire to give greater freedom to the women and youth in his country also indicated his preference for a more liberal regime in Afghanistan.

During his meeting with the Pakistani Prime Minister in Tehran in June 1997, Khatemi ruled out the policy of looking for a military solution to the Afghan imbroglio. He reiterated the stand of the Iranian Government that negotiation was the best way of ending the miserable situation in Afghanistan. President Khatemi made it known that he would take up the issue of Afghanistan at the OIC Summit scheduled to be held in Tehran in December 1997.

Iran maintains that it is not interfering in the internal affairs of Afghanistan and that it is providing only humanitarian assistance to that country. Its declared policy is non-interference;

prevention of war; formation of a broad-based government; welcoming the efforts of the United Nations in Afghanistan; and supporting the development and reconstruction of its war-torn neighbour. However, like all other nations, the policy actually followed is different to the one that is announced to the world. In keeping with its national interest, Iran continues to give moral, diplomatic, and military assistance to the anti-Taliban forces.

Velayati and Alauddin Borujerdi, head of the Afghan desk, remained very active throughout July. They visited Islamabad and met Pakistani officials and Sibghatullah Mojeddedi. Later they had meetings with General Malik and other anti-Taliban leaders in Tehran. They were in close contact with India, and continued to encourage the Central Asian Republics to use the Iranian route for their trade and commerce.

With Iran trying to move into the driving seat previously occupied by Pakistan, problems were bound to occur between them. While leaders on both sides continued to say that the Taliban factor would not have an 'adverse impact' on the time-tested relationship between the two countries, the fact remained that Islamabad and Tehran had drifted away from each other because of their different approaches to the Afghan problem.

Saudi Arabia

Saudi Arabia had given a great deal of financial support to the Afghan mujahideen during their struggle to oust the Soviets. The Saudi monarch had taken a direct interest in trying to resolve the differences between the Afghan leaders after the fall of Najibullah. Many Saudi welfare organizations continued to operate in Afghan refugee camps. It was, therefore, understandable for the Saudis to continue to take an interest in the developments in that country. Saudi money allegedly flows into Taliban hands. Riyadh's rivalry with Tehran has much to do with the Saudis keeping a toe-hold in Afghan affairs.

The Taliban, however, did not feel themselves indebted to Saudi Arabia to that extent that they would be obliged to accept all of their demands, even if it was against their immediate interest not to do so. Osama Bin Laden was a Saudi dissident temporarily residing in Taliban-held areas. He was critical of the monarchy in his country, accusing them of being subservient to American interests. A billionaire himself, he was supporting the Taliban financially, so when the Saudis asked Mullah Omar to extradite him they declined to do so, though they did indicate that he would not be allowed to use Afghan territory for anti-Saudi activities.

Pakistan, being friendly to both Saudi Arabia and Iran, found it difficult to accommodate the interests of both countries while formulating its policies towards Afghanistan. Putting one's foot in two different boats is not an easy task in the best of circumstances, more so in troubled waters.

Saudi Arabia's recognition of the Taliban regime a few days after Pakistan's was indicative of the fact that Islamabad and Riyadh were on the same wavelength as far as support to the Taliban was concerned. As a reciprocal gesture, the Taliban reiterated that Osama would not be permitted to make statements against the Saudi monarchy while in Afghanistan.

The United States

After backing the Afghan mujahideen for ten long years in their struggle to evict the Soviet Union from their country the United States withdrew from the scene, leaving the Afghan factions to fight amongst themselves. The US administration pulled out from the Afghan quagmire with no remorse for the fratricidal conflict it was leaving behind. It was a cheap victory for Uncle Sam for, although billions of dollars were spent in containing the southward flow of the communist tide, not a single American soldier lost his life in the Hindu Kush.

Anthony Lewis, writing in *The International Herald Tribune* admitted that the United States shared responsibility for what happened to Afghanistan after the Soviets left. 'In the unthinking zeal of the Cold War, we Americans, destroyed what was there in order to fight the Soviet Union. And then we walked away,'[147] he wrote.

The United States had achieved its objective of pushing the Soviet forces out from Afghanistan through a war by proxy. As soon as their aim was achieved the Afghan mujahideen were forgotten. No more military aid and no more economic assistance came from Washington. The Clinton administration did, however, continue to monitor events in Afghanistan, particularly because of the presence of Russian troops in the Central Asian Republics bordering Afghanistan. Adding insult to injury, an official of the State Department said after the job was done, 'We are not going to allow Afghanistan to become our problem now'.[148] US involvement was accordingly confined to statements by its leaders appealing to the warring parties to settle their differences through negotiations. The nonchalant attitude of the Americans towards Afghanistan was a stark reminder of the adage that nations act in pursuit of their national interests, and when they change, so does their policy.

Some Americans, however, began to acknowledge that they had a moral responsibility to take a greater interest in trying to resolve the ongoing conflict in Afghanistan. They simply could not walk away after having spent $3 billion arming the Afghans. 'Together with the Soviet Union we fed the civil war that still goes on seven years after Soviet forces left,' writes an American specialist on Afghanistan.[149] His concluding sentence should have been: 'We cannot just leave them in the lurch'.

The United States also had a strategic reason for keeping themselves abreast of the developments in the region. Although the US Ambassador to Pakistan, Thomas W. Simons, played down the Iranian, Russian, and Indian factors, he did emphasize the fact that his country would not want the Central Asian Republics to become client states of Russia. 'Washington would prefer that these newly independent states look towards other nations also for commercial benefits,' he said. To that extent the US administration did not wash their hands off Afghanistan completely after the withdrawal of Soviet troops, Simons admitted.[150]

Washington is generally believed to have initially encouraged the Pushtun-dominated Taliban to overrun large tracts of Afghanistan in order to keep the Iranians and the Russians out. Anthony Lewis blamed the United States along with its allies for backing the 'grotesquely repressive' Taliban.[151]

Those who are convinced of the theory that, after the collapse of communism, the Judaeo-Christian world is determined to crush the Islamic resurgence wherever it is occurring, felt that the emergence of the Taliban was a conspiracy by the United States against Islam and was intended to balkanize Afghanistan. When seen in the light of the fiercely independent character of the Afghans, and given the fact that Afghan factions had been fighting against each other since the Saur revolution of April 1978, this theory does not appear to be very feasible.

The pro-Iranian element in Pakistan sees in the rise of the Taliban movement an attempt by the Jewish-dominated US Congress to block the 'concentric effects of the Islamic revolution'.[152] It cannot be denied that Washington, and for that matter, all the western democracies, are fearful of the perceived Iranian policy of exporting their Islamic zeal, which has manifested itself in the form of terrorist attacks by the Iranian-backed militia. It is difficult to accept the contention, however, that the United States would create a Muslim extremist outfit that would in the long run prove to be more of a headache for them in Afghanistan than the Iranians.

Some political analysts and the religiously-oriented political parties in Pakistan sincerely believe that the Taliban had the backing and the full support of the United States. They quote several instances where Washington has supported fundamentalist regimes when it suited them. According to them, if the Taliban continue to control the western provinces they would be able to prevent the Iranian influence from permeating into that area, which, they believe to be the real aim of the United States.

Another reason for the initial encouragement allegedly given to the Taliban by the USA is that they could act as a shield against Russian intrusion into Afghanistan through the Central Asian Muslim republics, and by allowing the construction of an alternative trade route, those republics would become less dependent upon Russia.

Humayun Shah Asefi, expatriate based in Islamabad, while speaking at a seminar on the Taliban factor organized by the Foundation for Research on National Development and Security in May 1996 felt that the United States wants to keep the turmoil in Afghanistan brewing if only to show to the world that the result of so-called fundamentalism is chaos and instability. This view is not shared by Simons, who was justified in saying that continued infighting inside Afghanistan could spill over into neighbouring countries, thus threatening the security of the whole region, which would not be in US interests. 'Although these could be genuine reasons for the Americans to get involved in Afghan affairs again, I find it difficult to accept the view that the success of the Taliban will be in the short or long term interests of the United States in this region,' said the American Ambassador.[153] The fickle and mercurial character of the Afghans has disappointed many a supporter of their cause.

Murtaza Sarmadi, an Afghan national, speaking at a seminar organized by a local think tank, also did not see any truth in the speculation that the United States was trying to destabilize his country through the Taliban.

Simons denied the charge that the Taliban had ever had the backing of the United States. The US Ambassador felt that the rise of the Taliban was purely indigenous in character. 'It was a reaction to the degeneration of the Afghan jihad into a civil war. There is no shred of evidence that the US gave any encouragement or support to the Taliban,' said he. He did acknowledge, however, that Washington was not totally surprised by the sudden appearance of the Taliban on the Afghan scene, and also that it was not a negative development as the new arrivals could have provided a path to a solution of the Afghan problem.

'We do not support the Taliban or any other group. But neither do we put the blame on the Taliban for the ills of Afghanistan, for which all parties are responsible,' is how the US Deputy Representative to the United Nations, Edward Gneham, put it while speaking at an open debate on the situation in Afghanistan in the Security Council on 14 April 1997.[154]

When Pakistan and the Kabul regime fell out and Rabbani turned towards Iran, India, and Russia for assistance, the White House decided to get some first-hand information about the new developments in Afghanistan. The US Consul-General in Peshawar, Richard Smith, went to Kandahar and met the Taliban leaders; he later met Ahmed Shah Masood at Bagram airbase. This was followed by the visit of the influential Republican Senator Hank Brown to Afghanistan. In his thirty-six-hour stay he met various Afghan leaders and tried to gauge both the extent of the differences between them and their attitude towards Mahmoud Mestiri's plan of action. Hikmetyar enquired from Brown whether the United States was prepared to see Afghanistan divided, which appeared to him to be its objective as Dostum was meeting US officials in Washington at that time. The answer was in the negative.

Senator Hank Brown, Chairman of the Senate Foreign Relations Subcommittee on Near Eastern and South Asian Affairs invited all the Afghan factions to Washington in the last week of June 1996 in order to arrive at a consensus on the issues which divided the various Afghan groups. Gulbadin Hikmetyar and Yunus Khalis were not invited as the US administration was not willing to grant visas to them on the grounds that they were allegedly supportive of terrorist activities against the United States. The Taliban, though present in Washington, did not attend as they felt that they had not been formally invited. The conference was not regarded as a US government initiative, and no concrete results emerged from it.

While it is true that the legislative and the executive branches have well-defined roles in the United States, and that policies are made by the latter and not by the former, congressmen and senators do have an influence over the officials of the US administration. The interest Hank Brown showed in looking for a solution to the Afghan impasse did raise hopes of a US revival in the developments in that war-ravaged nation.

Brown's visit was followed by that of the Assistant Secretary of State for South Asia, Ms Robin Raphel, who also held the charge of Afghan affairs. In this capacity she was to advise the Secretary of State on the conduct of foreign relations with the countries of South Asia and offer suggestions to guide the operations of US diplomatic missions within the South Asian region. She made it a point to visit Kandahar and meet the Taliban leaders to assess their real intentions, and to try and convince them of the need to broaden their base. The Deputy Foreign Minister of Afghanistan, Abdul Rahim Ghafoorzai, appeared to be somewhat perturbed over the renewed interest that the US was taking in Afghan affairs. He is reported to have remarked rather sarcastically, 'We seem to be re-emerging on the US foreign policy map'.

While in Kandahar, Raphel was told by Mullah Muttaqi, the leader of the Taliban delegation, that the United States should use its influence in the United Nations to impose economic and military sanctions to force the Afghan President to step down as a precondition for an intra-Afghan peace dialogue. 'Unless there is international pressure and an end to foreign assistance to the region, Rabbani will not relinquish power,' said the Taliban representative. Since the US was interested in an end to the strife in Afghanistan, Raphel did try to persuade the Taliban to participate in an intra-Afghan peace moot in Jalalabad. Muttaqi, however, did not agree to meet Rabbani as he believed that Rabbani was not sincere and that such meetings would not bear fruit.

Raphel insisted that the US did not intend to get directly involved in Afghanistan. 'We do not see ourselves as inserting our government in the middle of Afghan affairs, but we consider ourselves as friends of Afghanistan,' said

Raphel. 'I am here to urge the Afghans themselves to get together and talk. The idea of an intra-Afghan dialogue is very important and I think everybody should participate in it.' The hint was at the Taliban not wanting to do so. She did agree with the Taliban's demand that a call for a halt to foreign interference in Afghanistan affairs must be supported. 'We have been saying for a long time that outside governments should stop military support to the Afghan factions,' she said. By this she presumably meant that Iran, Russia, and India should stop providing military hardware to their favourites showing no apparent concern at others who were allegedly doing the same.

Raphel also visited Uzbekistan, Tajikistan, and Kazakhstan in an attempt to persuade them not to give military assistance to their favourites in Afghanistan and to help the United Nations' Special Mission in its efforts to bring about peace in Afghanistan. The US Assistant Secretary also sought Russia's help in resolving the Afghan crisis.

Later, during her testimony on Afghanistan before the Senate Foreign Relations Subcommittee for Near East and South Asia, Raphel reiterated that the Clinton administration did not favour one faction over the other, nor was Washington giving support to any group or individual. She informed the Senate Subcommittee that the United States was trying to 'garner support for its proposal to impose an arms embargo on Afghanistan and for a regional conference that would advance the prospects of peace'. She was reporting on her recent visit to Afghanistan and some of the Central Asian Muslim republics, from which she had returned with the impression that Rabbani's government had the strongest military force and that it was receiving strong diplomatic backing from Russia, India, and Iran.[155]

Raphel's formula for peace in Afghanistan included: a cease-fire; a neutral security force; demilitarization of Kabul; agreement on an interim governing arrangement and planning for a permanent form of government. All of these proposals had been made before and were acceptable to all the Afghan factions including the Taliban. The major hurdle in the implementation of these ideas was that each group wanted to secure its own interest in the final deal and was not willing to compromise on any of its initial demands.

When asked by Raphel why girls' schools had been closed, Muttaqi evaded a straight answer by saying, 'There was no question of closing down schools which never existed'.

The Taliban did not accept the request made by President Clinton through Raphel that the seven-member Russian crew of a cargo plane which they had forced to land in Kandahar be released on humanitarian grounds. The anguish of the families of the detained Russian, Tatar, and Ukrainian personnel made no impact on the Taliban. They reminded Raphel that sixty thousand of their brethren were missing and unless something was done to discover their whereabouts, they could not be expected to release the Russian crew. In any case, said Muttaqi, 'These men are prisoners of the Afghan nation and only they can decide about their fate'.[156]

The United States soon realized that the Taliban were becoming too big for their boots and were creating more problems. Instability in Afghanistan was growing. The Taliban were not co-operating with Mahmoud Mestiri, the UNSG's Special Representative for Afghanistan. Their extreme religious views were also a matter of concern as this according to their view could lead to Taliban involvement in international terrorism against the United States and their allies in the Arab world. Karim Pakravan, an Afghan banker domiciled in Chicago, went to the extent of saying that the term Afghan had become synonymous with 'extreme, ruthless, and anti-western Islamic elements' because of the policies of the Taliban in the areas they controlled.[157]

It is true that Barker did try to bring Zahir Shah back to Afghanistan. Being liberal and accustomed to western ways, he would be preferred by the west, over the Taliban or, for that matter, over any of the present Afghan factions. But that did not work out as Sardar Wali, his son-in-law, could not enter Afghanistan when he visited Pakistan for that very purpose.

The United States was deeply concerned about the fact that

Afghanistan under the Taliban had become the world leader in heroin export.[158] While she was in Kandahar Robin Raphel had also tried to try to persuade the Taliban to reduce poppy cultivation in Taliban-controlled areas, and to check the flow of narcotics across the border. The Taliban representative retorted that they were not patronizing poppy cultivation but, on the contrary, they had destroyed large tracts of poppy and dismantled heroin laboratories in areas under their control.

Another factor that influenced the decision of the US to take a more direct interest in bringing about peace in Afghanistan was the involvement of the US firm Unocal in the construction of two pipelines from Turkmenistan, through Afghanistan and Pakistan, to the Arabian Sea. The US administration was keen to see oil and gas pipelines constructed through Afghanistan and on to open waters which would allow the oil to pass through a more secure route than through the Iran-dominated Persian Gulf. Unocal had put in a bid to construct the pipeline, but the $2 billion project could only come online if a broad-based government was established in Afghanistan, this naturally increased US interest in Afghanistan.[159] Soon, however, Unocal began looking for alternative business opportunities in the region as the prospects of peaceful conditions returning to Afghanistan in the near future were fading away. That being so, Ambassador Simons played down the view that US interest in Afghanistan was commercial in nature. However, despite the fact that the US Ambassador had given little importance to the economic factor, Unocal, along with Delta, a Saudi company, went ahead and signed an agreement with Turkmenistan and the Taliban for the construction of the proposed pipeline.

Washington was also interested in verifying the presence of training camps in Taliban-controlled areas as, according to US intelligence agencies, some of the Islamists who tried to blow up the World Trade Centre had been trained on Afghan soil.[160] The refusal of the Taliban to compel Osama Bin Laden, a known opposer of the Saudi monarchy, to leave Afghanistan irked Washington as it believed that he posed a threat to the United States as well. Laden had called upon the United States and other countries to pull their armies back from Arab lands without further delay. He even threatened to carry out attacks against military installations in Saudi Arabia targeting foreign troops and their protectors if his demands were not met.

The Taliban were reluctant to ask Osama to leave Afghanistan, although it meant annoying Riyadh and Washington, as he was believed to be their main financier. In fact, they had shifted him from Nangarhar to Kandahar as they felt that he would be safer there since parts of Nangarhar province had still not fully accepted the new regime.

Although the religious attitudes of the Taliban were unacceptable to the US administration, it could not just wish them away—the mullahs did control two-thirds of Afghanistan and seemed set to do so for quite a while. Though not acquainted with the art of running a modern state, they had been able to restore peace wherever their authority existed.

The United States, according to Ambassador Simons, was willing to do business with the Taliban. 'We have dealt with all of them before. We will keep in touch with them also, but the amount of business will be severely restricted because of our feelings on the issue of women and our concerns over drugs and terrorism,' said the Ambassador. He was critical of the Taliban for having what he termed a 'rug merchant mentality', i.e., if the US wanted these restrictions lifted, then they would have to pay for it through recognition.

Washington had been providing $50 million a year since 1990, although none of it was given directly; it was channelled through the UN relief agencies and through certain NGOs. This kind of financial assistance was likely to continue.

The United States would continue to support the UN mission's attempts to arrange dialogues and promote negotiations between all factions leading to a broad-based government in Afghanistan which would protect the interests of all ethnic communities and be committed to international obligations.

On 12 April 1997 Robin Raphel was replaced by Ambassador Karl F. Inderfurth, as the new Assistant Secretary of State for South Asian Affairs. It remains to be seen whether he will follow the footsteps of his predecessor or come up with new initiatives to protect the interests of the United States in Afghanistan which, though peripheral, can move the peace process further.

Central Asian Republics

Central Asia was the cradle of Islamic civilization for a thousand years. A large number of saints and mystics moved out of this region to Afghanistan and to the far corners of South Asia to spread the message of Islam. Khwaja Qutbuddin Kaki (1205–1235), Maulana Jalaluddin Rumi (1207–73), and Sheikh Usman bin Hasan Marandi, commonly known as Hazrat Lal Shabaz Qalandar, were amongst the luminaries from Central Asia who are still revered in all Muslim lands. Imam Bokhari from Uzbekistan and Sheikh Ahmed bin Ali Tirmidi were authorities on *hadith, tafsir,* and *fiqah.* Their works are a positive contribution to Islamic theology.

The decline of Islamic civilization in Central Asia began with the rise of the Tsarist and British empires in the eighteenth century. In the Great Game that followed, the Khanates, weakened by internecine conflicts, fell by the wayside. They soon lost their independent entities. After the 1917 Bolshevik Revolution in Russia, the godless creed of communism radiated out of Moscow and engulfed the whole of Central Asia. Having lost their freedom, they now had to give up their religious rituals as well. Though they remained Muslims they could not practise their faith in all its ramifications. For seventy long years they lived under the Soviets. Russian replaced the native languages, which were closely linked to Turkish and Persian. The Cyrillic script cut them off from their roots. Mosques were destroyed and religious gatherings forbidden. Political boundaries were created with no regard to ethnic and linguistic consideration.

After the collapse of the Soviet Union and the demise of communism, the Central Asian states became independent republics. Their strategic importance increased when several nations started to show an interest in benefiting from their mineral wealth. The fact that they are surrounded by Russia, China, and Iran, and lie close to several international flashpoints, put them on the world stage.

The revival of some Islamic practices began to be noticed. Religious schools were once again allowed to function. The regional languages slowly started to replace Russian. Voices were heard urging the adoption of the Roman or the Arabic script and doing away with Cyrillic. But despite these measures, strong linkages with Russia and a secular orientation remained. The economies of Central Asian Republics (CAR) continued to be integrated with Russia. The rouble remained the currency for commercial transactions, and former communists held sway in most of them. All of them joined the Russian-sponsored Commonwealth of Independent States (CIS).

The economic importance of these states can be judged from the fact that over $22 billion is being invested by six foreign companies for the extraction and transportation of their oil and gas reserves. The transition from a centralized economy to that of a free market will need financial expertise, managerial skills, and monetary aid. Pakistan, which is trying its best to reach out to the CAR, will not be alone in the field even when durable peace returns to Afghanistan.

The Muslims of Central Asia lived under a non-religious regime for seven decades. They have, therefore, become accustomed to a more liberal interpretation of Islam. All of them are concerned at the possibility of Afghanistan being ruled by a group of religious extremists. The presence of an ultra-orthodox regime in the neighbourhood will remain a source of worry for all of them. Though all six new Muslim republics were concerned about the rise of the

Taliban, the three directly affected were Turkmenistan, Uzbekistan, and Tajikistan as they all share a common border with Afghanistan.

Turkmenistan

Turkmenistan, with an area of 488,100 sq. km. and a population of around 3.5 million (1989), shares more than a thousand kilometres of border with both Afghanistan and Iran. It is rich in mineral resources and has proven reserves of 284 trillion cubic feet of natural gas. The biggest gas producers of the CIS are Russia and Turkmenistan; the latter supplies gas to all the Central Asian republics, Azerbaijan, Armenia, Georgia, Ukraine, and even to Russia. Its neighbours in the north, however, are not paying world prices for the gas they import from Turkmenistan and are also reluctant to pay in hard currency. President Saparmurad Niyazov is, therefore, looking for other outlets for his country's gas so that he can earn more from his country's natural resources.

Turkmenistan is connected to Pakistan by the Torghundi-Herat-Kandahar-Quetta highway, which is badly in need of repair. While the shortest route to the open sea remains through Afghanistan and Pakistan, the unstable situation in Afghanistan has prompted Niyazov to sign an agreement for the construction of a Turkmenistan-Iran-Turkey-Europe gas pipeline. The pipeline is going to cost around $5 billion, the bulk of which is presumably to be provided by Saudi Arabia.

Iran has taken the lead by joining its railway system with that of its northern neighbour. The Tagen-Serakhs-Meshad rail link was constructed by Iran in 1996. Tehran also opened up a number of international transit points on the Turkmen-Iran border. Despite these moves, the importance of the route through Afghanistan will remain. Turkmenistan would like to have as many routes out of its country as possible to avoid being dependent on one or two outlets alone.

Though the Turkmenistan government was keen to sell its natural gas to Pakistan through a pipeline to be laid in

Taliban-controlled areas of Afghanistan, it still considers Rabbani's regime to be the legitimate government and has no formal ties with the Taliban.[161]

Turkmenistan has a fairly large Russian (12.6 per cent) and Uzbek (8.5 per cent) population, but despite this it has remained neutral in the ongoing Afghan conflict and has friendly relations with Turkey, Iran, Pakistan, and the Taliban. Although there are a substantial number of Turkmen living on the north-western border of Afghanistan, Ashkabad has not interfered in the internal affairs of Afghanistan. A number of *madrassas* and mosques have indeed come up in Turkmenistan since the downfall of communism, but its outlook on religion is liberal. It would oppose any attempt by the Taliban to export their brand of Islam into their country.

Uzbekistan

Uzbekistan, along with Kazakhstan, Kyrghistan, and Sinkiang, forms the eastern branch of the former Turkistan republic and is, therefore, historically more closely linked to Turkey than to its southern neighbours. It has an area of 447,400 sq. km., and a population of 20.3 million (1989). In size it is as large as Turkmenistan, but its border with Afghanistan is relatively small. It is connected to Afghanistan by the Termez-Mazar-e-Sharif-Kabul-Jalalabad-Peshawar highway. The road, even when an agreement has been reached between the warring factions, will remain vulnerable to sporadic attacks by those presently opposed to the Taliban as it passes through Bamian, a Hizb-e-Wahdat stronghold, and very close to the Panjsher valley, from where Masood can disrupt commercial traffic at will. The strategic Salang Tunnel can easily be blocked if differences erupt between the coalition partners.

The Uzbeks are the third largest ethnic tribe in Afghanistan. Almost all of the one million Uzbeks in Afghanistan are concentrated in the area adjacent to Uzbekistan. The Uzbek leaders are, therefore, keen to see that their kith and kin across the border, along with their allies, remain in control of the area north of the Hindu Kush. They have reportedly been supplying fuel and armaments to Dostum to enable him to keep the Taliban at arms' length.

Dr Goga A. Khidoyatov, adviser to the Foreign Minister of Uzbekistan, during his visit to Pakistan in February 1996, stated that his country would try to host an international conference on Afghanistan to which the Taliban would also be invited. He believed that the *status quo* should be preserved and that each group should be permitted to continue controlling their respective areas while agreeing to establish a coalition interim government.

Tashkent, however, was angered when the Taliban continued to try to overthrow Dostum and showed their unwillingness to broaden the composition of the Kabul regime. President Farooq Ahmed Leghari's visit to Uzbekistan in 1996 highlighted the differences between the two countries on their respective assessments of the Taliban phenomenon. The Uzbek President, Islam Karimov, lashed out at Pakistan during the two-day ECO summit at Ashkabad in May 1997 for supporting the Taliban. He denounced external meddling. 'Nawaz Sharif ought to state that support for the Taliban must stop,' said Karimov bluntly to the nine heads of state at the meeting.[162] He went on to say that if the Taliban's aggressive designs and calls to war were supported, the war would not stop. It was apparent that his government would not hesitate in getting directly involved in the conflict. With 10 per cent of the population Russian, and several thousand Tajiks living in Samarkand, Tashkent's attitude towards the Taliban remained one of disdain.

Tajikistan

Tajikistan, like all other newly independent republics of Central Asia, is multi-lingual and poly-ethnic. Though Tajiks, consisting of 58.8 per cent of the total population, are in a majority, there are large Uzbek and Russian communities in that country. However, it is the Persian culture and language that prevails, linking them closely to the Afghan Tajiks.

Tajikistan unfortunately entered into a crisis soon after it gained its independence in 1991. Fighting broke out between two groups of Tajiks, the Garmis and the Kulyabis. It also took on a religio-political tone when the Islamic Rebirth Party headed by Said Nuri clashed with the pro-communist Democratic Party of President Rakhmon Nabiyev. Hundreds of thousands of Tajiks fled to neighbouring countries to avoid being caught in the crossfire. As many as 60,000 Tajik refugees sought shelter in Afghanistan.[163]

The civil unrest in Tajikistan was an invitation to the Russians to deploy Moscow-supported CIS troops along the borders of Tajikistan and Afghanistan to prevent the opposition activists from continuing the conflict while safely housed on Afghan soil. According to sources in the Tajik capital, Dushanbe, several military helicopters flew in from the Afghan side in April 1992.[164] Five years later the Taliban blamed Tajikistan for allowing its territory to be used by their arch enemy, Ahmed Shah Masood. Mullah Omar warned the Tajikistan government in no uncertain terms. 'Stop this blatant interference in Afghanistan from your soil or be ready for the consequences,' said the *Amirul Momineen*. According to him, the bombing of Taliban positions in the north by opposition jet fighters could only be from Kulyab airport in Tajikistan, as the airports of Mazar-e-Sharif and Shiberghan were in Taliban hands. The Tajik government denied this allegation.

Imam Ali Rakhmanov has no love for the Taliban. He supports the UN efforts to arrange a transitional government in which 'all Afghan ethnic groups and nationalities would be represented and the political situation in Afghanistan would be resolved peacefully, by means of consultations and negotiations'.[165]

As long as the Taliban stayed clear of the northern provinces, the CARs did not react to their presence elsewhere. But when Kunduz, bordering Tajikistan, came under the control of the Taliban and their local Pushtun supporters, alarm bells rang in Dushanbe, and when Mazar-e-Sharif and Hairatan fell to the

Taliban, Tashkent closed its borders with Afghanistan to prevent the spillover effect of the instability next door.

Even Kazakhstan, which was not directly affected by the Taliban factor, refused to accept the Taliban as the new leaders in Kabul. It continued to recognize the government of Rabbani even though he was barely in control of only five provinces.

Turkey, Pakistan's closest ally in the Middle East, also did not welcome the rise of the Taliban in Afghanistan because of its own secular orientation. It willingly gave shelter to General Abdul Rashid Dostum when he was forced to leave Mazar-e-Sharif after an uprising against him in May 1997. Later, Ankara backed his return to his native province, and even arranged for a reconciliation meeting between Dostum and General Malik. This placed Turkey also in the opposite camp, leaving Pakistan as the only country in the region to give its wholehearted support to the student militia.

Russia

The erstwhile Soviet leaders followed a deliberate policy of enlarging their perimeter of security by creating client states in their neighbourhood. It was with this aim in view that they moved southwards with a vengeance when they found that they were losing control of Afghanistan. The humiliating defeat they suffered at the hands of the fiercely-independent Afghan mujahideen made them realize, though too late, that they had made a mistake in getting involved in the internecine conflict in Afghanistan.

After the collapse of the Soviet empire, Russia was faced with numerous domestic problems which stopped it from reasserting itself in south-west Asia. When a new set of independent Muslim states came up between Russia and Afghanistan, Moscow began to be concerned about their ethnic and religious ties with a conservative Muslim nation across their borders. Central Asia, with its vast natural resources and having been part of the Soviet Union for seven decades, remained strategically and economically very important to Moscow. Soon after they gained independence, Russia formed the Commonwealth of Independent States (CIS) and took on the responsibility of their security and territorial integrity. When Tajikistan faced an internal uprising, President Boris Yeltsin stationed his soldiers along the Tajikistan-Afghanistan border to prevent a possible threat from extremist Muslim factions from that direction. He also made a deal with Rabbani's regime in Kabul, according to which the Afghan President promised not to support the dissidents who were operating from Afghanistan against the Russian-supported government in Tajikistan. In return, Russia agreed to provide military assistance and economic aid to Rabbani and Masood, who were struggling to keep the Taliban away from Kabul.

In order to assist the *de facto* government in boosting up Afghanistan's failing economy, Russia is believed to have been supplying $20 million worth of Afghan currency every month.[166] Though this resulted in galloping inflation, it did provide Rabbani with enough money to keep his forces paid and reasonably well-fed. Ten Russian technicians were reportedly upgrading facilities at Bagram airport, then under the control of Ahmed Shah Masood's forces. According to some reports, Russia was also providing some military hardware to Rabbani. Four ILL 76 transport airplanes arrived every day from Tajikistan, Russia, or Ukraine with Russian arms, ammunition, and fuel.[167]

One Ukranian aircraft flown by Russian pilots was forced down by the Taliban when it was flying over their territory on its way to deliver arms and ammunition to Rabbani's forces. Russian attempts to seek the release of the Russian crew did not succeed. Maulvi Muttaqqi insisted that Moscow was continuing to provide military support to Rabbani and Ahmed Shah Masood so that they could remain in power. It was perhaps for this reason, more than anything else, that he refused to release the Russian crew. (Incidently, the Russians escaped with the aircraft by bluffing the Taliban guards. They asked the unsuspecting militiamen to allow them to test the engines of the aircraft. Having been permitted to get into the cockpit, they opened the throttles and, under the very noses of the guards, took off for Dubai and safety.)

The fall of Kabul in September 1996 to the Taliban sent shock waves right up to Moscow. Russian policy makers, worried that the extremist ideology of the students of the religious seminaries would some day infiltrate into Russia's soft underbelly, called for a conference of the CIS which was held at Almaty, the capital of Kazakhstan, on 4 October 1996. Although Turkmenistan did not attend as it was interested in opening a southern route for its vast oil and gas resources, the remaining CIS states agreed to the further strengthening of Russian forces along the Afghan border in view of the perceived new threat from the Taliban. On 22 October Russia requested the United Nations Security Council to discuss the new situation that had developed in Afghanistan with the take-over of the capital by a group of religious extremists, and called another meeting on 28 April 1997 of Central Asian Republics in Dushanbe to review the advances the Taliban had made towards the Afghan border with the CIS.

Dr Rasul Baksh Rais, Director, Area Study Centre, Quaid-i-Azam University, maintains, with a certain amount of justification, that Russia still considers Afghanistan a strategic backyard of Central Asia which it wishes to retain under its sphere of influence.

During the visit of the Russian Deputy Foreign Minister to Islamabad in June 1997 he met the Taliban Ambassador and told him that a military solution to the Afghan problem would not bring about the desired results. Russia wanted the issue to be settled through dialogue and negotiations, and would expect the structure of the government to be broadened for it to be acceptable to them.

The Taliban, however, condemned Russia for allegedly supplying long-range Lunar rocket-launchers to Ahmed Shah Masood, which, according to them, were being used to bomb Kabul. They accused Moscow of airlifting the missiles by helicopter into the Panjsher valley. 'The Russian Federation intends to take its revenge for the humiliating defeat it suffered in Afghanistan,' opined the Taliban spokesman.[168] The Russians dismissed the allegations as false and totally untrue.

India

India had been interacting with Afghanistan even before the creation of Pakistan, for both security and economic reasons. The borders between British India and Afghanistan were porous, creating occasional security problems in the tribal areas which necessitated the adoption of the well-known 'forward policy'. Thousands of Sikh and Hindu traders were part of the Afghan population. Afghan moneylenders could be seen in Indian villages indulging in their exploitative business of usury. Contacts between India and Afghanistan continued after the partition of the subcontinent, but with a different motive.

India's interest in Afghanistan was now geared to preventing the two Muslim neighbours, Pakistan and Afghanistan, from having cordial relations with each other. It was at India's instigation that Kabul cast a negative vote at the United Nations when the question of Pakistan's membership of that august body came up in September 1947. Later, along with the Soviet Union, New Delhi continued to keep the issue of Pukhtunistan alive, as a result of which the two countries on either side of the Durand Line were unable to establish normal relations.

Although Afghanistan was swept under the Indian carpet during the occupation of that country by the Soviets, it went back onto their foreign policy agenda when Dr Najibullah was left alone to deal with the Afghan mujahideen. Besides giving him moral and diplomatic support, India invested in Afghanistan by providing a hundred-bed hospital staffed by Indian doctors and nurses, and by giving Najibullah's regime technical assistance.

According to Satish Chandra, India's High Commissioner in Islamabad, Najibullah was considered to be the best leader in Afghanistan, one who could ensure peace and stability in that country. 'He was acceptable to the royalists, communists, all ethnic groups, and the educated Afghans alike, and he was amenable to suggestions,' said Mr Chandra.[169] He was, however, being supported by New Delhi more because he had established very good relations with India where his family had settled due to the uncertain conditions of his country.

A major factor in India's support of their man in Kabul was the close relations between India and the Soviet Union. New Delhi and Moscow continued to co-ordinate their policies on Afghanistan even after the fall of Najibullah as both were unhappy about the possibility of the establishment of a fundamentalist regime so near to their borders. Since New Delhi had throughout supported the communist regime in Afghanistan, the mujahideen had no love for the Indians. However, when Rabbani felt threatened by the Pakistan-supported Taliban militia, he turned for help to India, which was looking for an opportunity to get back on the Afghan stage. 'India provided humanitarian assistance to Rabbani's government by way of food, medicines, and other consumer items,' confided Satish Chandra, but in fact they were trying to boost Rabbani's capability to withstand the pressure from the Taliban. The former Prime Minister of India, P. V. Narasimah Rao, flew in spare parts of weapons of Russian origin and sent technicians to maintain Soviet-made aircraft and other sophisticated weaponry, which boosted Ahmed Shah Masood's strength. Reports of daily flights from India to Bagram airbase near Kabul, bringing in military hardware along with humanitarian aid, were being received.

According to Pakistani intelligence sources, Indian cargo planes landed on 15, 16, 21, and 27 June 1995, with two or three aircraft landing on each occasion.[170] The Taliban claimed to have picked up messages from Indian pilots flying planes belonging to the government forces.[171] Rabbani, of course, denied this allegation, but it was later confirmed by Dostum. He is reported to have informed the then UN special emissary, Mahmoud Mestiri, that Ukraine had supplied thirty jet fighters to the forces of Ahmed Shah Masood, and that India was supplying military hardware and other assistance to the forces of President Burhanuddin Rabbani.

Delegations from India continued to visit Afghanistan, where they held meetings with Professor Rabbani and his Prime Minister, Ahmed Shah Ahmedzai. Rabbani's intelligence chief spent a week in New Delhi in December 1994. The aim of these visits was to strengthen the hand of the Kabul regime and ensure that it stayed in power for as long as possible.[172] India had also been refurbishing Afghanistan's Ariana airlines.[173]

India had been feeding the Iranian leadership false statements, trying to convince them that Pakistan had created the Taliban at the behest of the United States. They apparently told the Iranians that neither country wanted Iran to gain any influence in Afghanistan, and the statement by CIA officials that $ 20 million were to be allocated for destabilizing Iran encouraged Tehran believe the Indian assertions.

'There is a convergence of interest between Iran and India in preventing Afghanistan from becoming a base for extra-regional powers,' said J.N. Dixit, a former Indian External Affairs Secretary and a former Ambassador of India in Islamabad. He felt that Iran was playing a more effective role than the United Nations in bringing about peace in Afghanistan and should, therefore, be supported by India.[174]

New Delhi's main interest in Afghanistan and the Central Asian Republics is to prevent Pakistan from creating a solid block of Muslim countries which would give Islamabad the strategic depth it needs when confronted against an Indian attack.[175] 'South Block should aim for us to ensure that CAR do not go along with Pakistan within OIC or at any other international fora,' wrote the well-known Indian journalist K.P. Nayar.[176]

New Delhi also fears that if the Taliban consolidate their position in Afghanistan they would, because of their religious zeal, send their fighters to take part in the on-going insurgency in Indian held Kashmir. 'The Taliban are not only fundamentalists but also obscurantists,' remarked Satish Chandra in an interview with the author. A Taliban government would not be in India's interest; on the contrary, Rabbani and Masood, who have strained relations with Pakistan, would prevent Islamabad from reaping the fruits of their eleven-year support of the Afghan mujahideen.

India is short of energy resources and is keen to benefit from the vast gas reserves of the Central Asian Republics. It is monitoring the proposal by foreign firms to lay a gas pipeline from these countries to the Arabian Sea, and would like to work out an arrangement with them for extending the pipeline to the western states of India. New Delhi is concerned, however, that if the Taliban gain control of Afghanistan, they may not allow the pipeline to be extended to India as, besides being ultra-religious, they would be under the influence of Pakistan.

In matters of foreign policy Delhi has traditionally supported Russian interests in the region because of its dependence on Moscow for the supply of arms and spare parts, and the transfer of technology. Indian leaders have therefore co-ordinated their policies on the developments in Afghanistan with those of Russia. With Iran India has wide economic interests. Indian goods find their way to Afghanistan and Central Asia through Iranian ports. Indian engineers have been given contracts for the improvement of the infrastructure in Iran. An oil pipeline from Iran to India is contemplated. Political and economic interests have brought the two countries together on the issue of the Taliban.

India has also had very good relations with the Central Asian Republics since the days when they were part of the Soviet Union. Indian businessmen still retain their contacts with their counterparts in the CAR. High-level visits take place quite frequently between New Delhi and Central Asian capitals. They have a common interest in keeping Afghanistan out of the clutches of the ultra-religious

Taliban. P.V. Narasimah Rao visited Tashkent in October 1993. His visit was returned by the Uzbek President, Islam Karimov, within three months, which is not the usual diplomatic practice. Six agreements were signed between the two countries during Karimov's stay in India.

India continues to follow the dictum that your enemy's enemy should be your friend. When it found that Rabbani and Masood had developed serious differences with Islamabad because of the Taliban factor, New Delhi decided to lend its shoulder to Pakistan's adversary in the ongoing Afghan imbroglio.

The Organization of Islamic Conference (OIC)

The OIC Secretary-General, Dr Hamid Al Ghabid, took an active interest in trying to bring about a reconciliation between the various Afghan factions with a view to establishing a broad-based government in Afghanistan. He met all the Afghan leaders in Islamabad in June 1994 and discussed the plans for a transfer of power on the expiry of Rabbani's term of office, and to enable him to remain in constant touch with the Afghan leadership, he established an office of the OIC in Islamabad in July 1994. The lack of interest of the *ummah* in developments in Afghanistan can be judged from the fact that no Muslim country came forward with any concrete proposal for a solution to the Afghan impasse.

The OIC kept Afghanistan's seat vacant after the Taliban had taken control of Kabul, thereby indicating their willingness to accept the regime of the Taliban if they consolidated their position in Afghanistan. The Taliban were invited to attend the Special Session of the OIC which was held at Islamabad in March 1997 as observers.

The *Shoora-e-Ham-Ahangi* (Council of Understanding and National Unity) called upon the OIC to help the Afghans in setting up a friendly democratic government in Afghanistan which would refrain from exporting their fundamentalist ideas to neighbouring countries.

The Afghan seat was again left vacant at the OIC Summit meeting held at Tehran in December 1997. Rabbani was permitted to attend as an observer; the Taliban did not accept the invitation to attend the Summit because it was being held in Iran.

CHAPTER 8

THE UNITED NATIONS

The United Nations Secretary-General produced a five-point proposal which, he hoped, would form the basis for a solution of the Afghan problem. These were:

1. The necessity of preserving the sovereignty, territorial integrity, political independence, and non-aligned and Islamic character of Afghanistan.
2. The recognition of the right of the Afghan people to determine their own form of government and to choose their economic, political, and social system, free from outside intervention, subversion, coercion, or constraint of any kind whatsoever.
3. The need for a transition period, the details of which have to be worked out and agreed upon through an intra-Afghan dialogue, leading to the establishment of a broad-based government.
(a) The need during that period for transitional arrangements acceptable to the vast majority of the Afghan people, including the establishment of a credible and impartial transition mechanism with appropriate powers and authority that would enjoy the confidence of the Afghan people, and provide them with the necessary assurance to participate in free and fair elections, taking into account Afghan traditions for the establishment of a broad-based government.
(b) The need for cessation of hostilities during the transition period.

(c) The advisability of assistance, as appropriate, of the United Nations and of any other international organization, during the transition period and in the electoral process.

4. The necessity of an agreement—to be implemented together with all agreed traditional arrangements—to end all arms supplies to all Afghan sides, by all.

5. The recognition of the need for adequate financial and material resources to alleviate the hardship of the Afghan refugees and the creation of the necessary conditions for their voluntary repatriation as well as for the economic and social reconstruction of Afghanistan.

In September 1993 the United Nations General Assembly also passed a resolution in accordance with which a Special Mission for Afghanistan was established with the object of finding a peaceful settlement of the Afghanistan crisis (UN Resolution 48/308). The Special Mission was led by a number of prominent diplomats from different countries, all of whom were given the status of Under-Secretary-General for Political Affairs at the United Nations. It fell to the Tunisian former Foreign Minister, Mr Mahmoud Mestiri who was appointed the new personal representative of the UN Secretary-General in the early part of 1994, to deal with the Taliban.

In September 1994 the UN Secretary-General, Mr Boutros-Boutros Ghali, visited Pakistan, where he was briefed by Mestiri about the results of his extensive consultations with the Afghan leaders on the possibility of accepting a transitional arrangement which would lead to a cease-fire, and the convening of a *Loya Jirga* (Grand National Afghan Assembly). The UNS-G also met various representatives of various Afghan factions and some independents.[177]

Mestiri took the initiative of convening a meeting of an advisory group of recognized and respected independent personalities from within and outside Afghanistan; the nineteen-day meeting opened in Quetta on 29 September 1994. The purpose of the caucus was to advise the United Nations in its efforts to achieve progress towards finding a lasting solution to the Afghan problem. They came up with four recommendations: a country-wide cease-fire; early transfer of power to a fully representative Authoritative Council; a security force for Kabul; and the subsequent establishment of a transitional government.

This was endorsed by the Security Council in November and by the General Assembly in December 1994.[178] President Rabbani accepted the UN peace plan and the Afghan Ministry of Foreign Affairs gave its support in a written statement.[179] Rabbani had earlier, at a meeting at Jalalabad, made a conditional offer to transfer power on 23 October 1994. His eight-point proposal included: removal of all communists from the government; thirty representatives from each province to form a *jirga*; and the election of a new president by the *jirga* so formed.[180]

It was now left to Mestiri to get the approval of the other political party chiefs, including the head of the Taliban. Mestiri came back to Pakistan on 29 December 1994 and proceeded to Kabul to persuade Rabbani to set a date for the transfer of power. In the following month he also met all the other major leaders to get the names of those who would form the Authoritative Council. He even succeeded in obtaining the willingness of President Rabbani to step down on 20 February 1995.

Mestiri prepared a list of six Afghan personalities, any one of whom could be chosen to head the Authoritative Council. It included Dr Mohammad Yusaf, the former Prime Minister of Zahir Shah; Dr Abdus Samad Hamid, Deputy Prime Minster; Dr Abdus Sattar Seerat, Justice Minister; and General Ismail. The selection of persons who had held important positions in the government of the former king indicated the preference of the United Nations to bring back intellectuals who had fled the country after the communist take-over of Afghanistan.

In view of the military successes of the Taliban in early 1995, Mestiri realized that peace in Afghanistan could not be achieved without the willing co-operation of the student militia. He, therefore, tried to convince them to name some representatives who would join the others in the Authoritative Council. Unfortunately for him, the Taliban declined to participate in any process which would mean sitting with Rabbani or his nominees.

The convening of the Authoritative Council was therefore postponed to 21 March, and a committee of four personalities was formed to try and resolve the differences that had arisen over the proposals of the United Nations with special reference to the composition of the Authoritative Council. According to the Secretary-General's annual report to the UN on the situation in Afghanistan, the proposal that the Council be composed of two representatives from each of the twenty-nine provinces, plus fifteen or twenty representatives nominated by the United Nations to achieve the necessary ethnic and political balance, was accepted by some, but not all, of the Afghan factions.

Mahmoud Mestiri shuttled between Kabul and Islamabad, trying to arrange a transfer of power from Rabbani to an interim administration acceptable to all Afghan parties. After his talks with Rabbani, he announced a twenty-eight-member transitional Interim Council which would take over power. The broad-based interim government could then be charged with the responsibility of arranging the formation of a government acceptable to the majority of Afghans. He almost succeeded in getting the names approved.

The date and the modalities were about to be worked out when, on 6 March, fighting broke out between Hizb-e-Wahdat (Mazari) and Masood, and between Masood and the Taliban. The rapid advance of the Taliban towards Kabul had already angered Masood, who went back on his word and told the UN representative that there would be no transfer of power unless the Taliban also agreed to participate in the mechanism for the transfer of power. Since the latter rejected the proposals of Mahmoud Mestiri the efforts of the UN

once again failed. (Pakistan also felt that the list prepared by
Mahmoud Mestiri did not include the various power centres in
Afghanistan as they existed on the ground—a direct reference to
the omission of representatives of the Taliban in the list prepared
by the UN.)

Mestiri went back to New York for consultations with
Boutros Ghali who decided that the UN Special Mission
should resume its efforts towards peace in Afghanistan.
Mestiri consequently returned to Pakistan in July and once
again began contacting various Afghan leaders including
the Taliban. Mestiri was directed by the Secretary to move
his office inside Afghanistan. The Secretary-General also
enhanced the Special Mission and the Office of the
Secretary General for Afghanistan (OSGA) by stationing
additional political affairs officers in the country.

Mestiri's main concern at that moment was to prevent the
major outbreak of hostilities between the so-called 'mysterious
army' and Rabbani's forces which was likely to take place
when the weather improved. Rabbani is reported to have said
on 19 February 1995, that he did not consider Mestiri the
right person to act as a mediator as he seemed to be more
inclined towards a students' organization than a legal
government in Afghanistan. This was based on a reported
statement by Mestiri, who is alleged to have said, 'the Taliban
are the peacemakers,' which had annoyed Rabbani because
he believed that it was the force under his command which
could enforce peace and not a 'handful of newcomers'.

The Taliban, on the other hand, did not accept the list
of twenty-eight members of a transitional government
which Mestiri had prepared. The United Nations
representative had, therefore, to establish a rapport with
the Taliban so that they would co-operate with his efforts
towards a transfer of power in Afghanistan. They set three
conditions for their participation in any peace process: only
'good Muslims' were to be part of the interim
administration; all thirty-two provinces had to be represented in
the interim arrangement; and, according to Mullah Gulab Borjan,

a Taliban commander, 'the neutral force to ensure peace in Kabul (must) be taken from the Taliban only'.[181] The Taliban, who had set out to push aside all the older mujahideen leaders, were not willing to give any role to Rabbani nor to Hikmetyar. Neither would they agree to Zahir Shah's return.

While Mestiri did agree that the only way peace could be ensured in Afghanistan was by having a broad-based government in the country, he could not accept a list of 'good Muslims' from the Taliban only, nor could he allow only them to contribute to the neutral force to be placed in Kabul. Afghan watchers felt, however, that the United Nations was not doing enough nor was the international community taking adequate interest in the enforcement of peace in Afghanistan. Merely talking to all the parties and obtaining their views on the future political structure of their country was not getting them anywhere. What was needed was to convince the neighbouring powers to stop backing their favourites in the four year old fratricidal conflict in Afghanistan.

Mestiri at one stage announced that the Taliban were ready to talk to Rabbani in order to find a way out of the log-jam. His optimism about the peace talks was raised because Mullah Mohammad Rabbani, Deputy Leader of the Taliban, had assured him that the Taliban were ready for talks whenever the other side was willing. Although he had heard this from the mouth of an important Taliban leader, he should have been wise enough by now to know that anything an Afghan says can change overnight. He was aware of promises made and broken, alliances formed and reformed, allies becoming adversaries. It was naïve of him to have taken a Taliban leader at his word. He was naturally very disappointed when some elements in the Taliban hierarchy refused to meet Rabbani. Maulvi Wakil Ahmed, a spokesman of the Taliban militia, in an interview with the BBC, rejected Mestiri's statement that the Taliban were ready to hold direct talks with the Kabul regime. 'This is our principled stand that holding talks with the Kabul regime would be a waste of time and nothing else, therefore we shall not negotiate with them.' 'These conflicting views reflected a split between the

Taliban's religious and political leadership,' said a Kabul-based senior UN official in April 1996.

Unfortunately Mahmoud Mestiri could not get the Taliban to agree on a formula which would have helped in a *rapprochement* between the Taliban and the other factions in Afghanistan. His failure to do so prompted US Senator Hank Brown, chairman of the Senate Foreign Relations Subcommittee, to send a letter to President Clinton requesting him to support the removal of the UN special envoy as, 'He has little influence on the battling factions in that war-ravaged country.[182]

The US State Department, however, reposed its confidence in Mahmoud Mestiri. A statement released in Washington after Hank Brown's criticism of the UN Special Representative said, 'The United States actively supports and has confidence in the United Nation's Special Mission for Afghanistan, which is headed by Ambassador Mahmoud Mestiri. We believe that the best mechanism to further a peace process in Afghanistan is the UN Special Mission and have urged everyone to support it'.

Mestiri's failure to achieve any success was also criticized by a former Deputy Foreign Minister and tribal elder, Hamed Karzai. In Apirl 1996 he criticized Mestiri who, he felt did not focus his attention on one course of action but 'is moving in circles... he is unlikely to achieve anything the way he is going about his job'. A Western ambassador in Afghanistan also felt that Mestiri's credibility in Afghanistan had become zero and that nothing would move forward unless a new team was put in place.[183] Dr Elsadig Abu Nafeesa, senior political adviser to Mestiri, however, said that the 'UN special envoy will carry on until the political leaders say that they do not want negotiations with the government through the UN, at which point he may reassess'.

In order to carry out his mission with greater ease Mestiri on the advice of the UN Secretary General decided to move his headquarters from Islamabad to Jalalabad in Afghanistan, in order to be closer to Kabul and other Afghan cities. Jalalabad which was then under the control of the Nangarhar *Shoora*, was considered to be neutral turf by most Afghans. It was also comparatively stable and unaffected by the conflict raging elsewhere.

Mestiri's move to Afghanistan was welcomed by most Afghan factions as they felt that the United Nations representatives should operate from within the country rather than from a foreign land. Mestiri continued his efforts to find common grounds on which all Afghan parties could agree unconditionally. He held discussions with the Taliban at Kandahar; met General Dostum in Mazar-e-Sharif; talked to Rabbani in Kabul; briefed the Foreign Office in Islamabad; but the prospects of peace in the unfortunate land remained as elusive as ever, in spite of Francis Okelo, Director of the Office of the Secretary-General in Afghanistan and Pakistan (OSGAP), saying that the talks were fruitful.

The UN peace proposal included a cease-fire, handing Kabul over to an international peace-keeping force, an intra-Afghan dialogue, and the convening of a regional conference in or outside Afghanistan. An international conference to discuss these proposals was called by the United Nations on 18 November 1996. In addition to the five permanent members of the Security Council, Pakistan, Iran, and India were also included. None of the Afghan factions were invited, however.

Disappointed at not being able to make any headway towards finding an acceptable solution to the Afghan crisis, Mahmoud Mestiri resigned at the end of May 1996 for health reasons. The United Nations Secretary-General appointed Norbert Heinrich Holl, former German Foreign Minister, as head of the United Nations Special Mission to Afghanistan on 7 July 1996.

Norbert Holl's first visit to Kabul was welcomed by a hail of rockets fired by the Taliban. Quite naturally he was perturbed and angry at the Taliban for what he called 'spitting in his face'. Nevertheless, he continued with his peace mission and, like his predecessor, he made frequent trips to Kandahar and Mazar-e-Sharif and held talks with both the Taliban and those opposed to them. He also remained in touch with Islamabad and Tehran. He did manage to reduce the differences between the protagonists, and got them to agree to setting up a working group of rival factions who would try to seek a negotiated settlement. His efforts to arrange a cease-fire and to make the various factions agree to a broad-based government in Afghanistan did not, however, succeed. In fact, he was disappointed with the Taliban for renewing their offensive just when the UN-sponsored talks were moving towards a solution. He felt that because of their continued attacks against the anti-Taliban forces, the initiatives taken by the UN had received a set-back. He is reported to have told Mullah Mohammad Rabbani, chairman of the Taliban *Shoora* in Kabul, that starting a fresh offensive three hours after agreeing to set up a joint working group was a serious set-back.[184]

This did not deter Norbert Holl from continuing with his efforts to bring about a cease-fire in Afghanistan. He visited Kabul and Mazar-e-Sharif again in July 1997, but once again he felt that 'nobody was willing to compromise'. According to him, the Taliban were the more belligerent element because 'they consider themselves in a stronger position'.[185]

The uncertain situation in Afghanistan prompted the UN Secretary-General, Kofi Annan, to send Lakhdar Brahimi, an Algerian diplomat, as his special envoy to re-evaluate the UN role in Afghanistan and highlight the root cause of the conflict. In the meantime, the chief of the United Nations Development Programme (UNDP), Gustave Speth, warned the Taliban that donors would be hard to come by if the fighting continued and if the Taliban did not change their repressive attitude towards the female population. He also threatened that the UN agencies would pull out of Afghanistan and that UN projects in Afghanistan would be stopped if the war did not come to an end, and insisted that effective institutions had to be established to see that funds granted by aid-giving agencies were utilized for their intended purpose.

He stated that the world body was willing to set up some twenty foreign-funded schools for girls in Taliban controlled-areas, provided there was a visible change in the attitude of Mullah Omar in respect of education for women in Afghanistan.

The warning did have some effect, for the Taliban signed an agreement with the UNDP promising a review of the gender issue as far as the education of girls was concerned. They also agreed to see if women might be allowed to work in specific places where their presence was absolutely necessary.

The UN not only had differences with the Taliban, but their workers were harassed and their belongings looted by unsocial elements when fighting broke out in Mazar-e-Sharif in August. Norbert Holl had to appeal to the embattled groups to facilitate the evacuation of all those foreigners working with aid-giving agencies.

The UNHCR, however, found the situation in certain areas of Taliban-controlled Afghanistan quite normal. Consequently they were able to persuade sixty-five refugee families to return to Afghanistan in September. To encourage them the refugees were offered a package of incentives including Rs 500 per family, 300 kg of wheat, a plastic sheet, a tent, and free transportation from the refugee camp to their final destination. In Afghanistan they would be employed under the food-for-work programme to construct roads, schools, and dispensaries.

Arms Embargo

One of the reasons for the continuing conflict in Afghanistan was the supply of weapons to rival groups by outside powers. During a special debate on strife-torn Afghanistan at the Security Council, a US delegate pointed out that a number of countries supported the idea of an embargo as a means of halting the factional fighting. But Rabbani's regime, which was receiving military hardware from Russia, Iran, and India, was not in favour of such an action by the United Nations. 'The idea of an arms embargo alone, without the support of other UN peace measures, at the present time is not very practical,' said an Afghan Ministry of Defence official at Kabul in response to the delegate's statement.

He went on to say that, in his view, it could not be effective in the prevailing climate in Afghanistan as certain borders were so porous that arms flowed freely across them into Afghanistan.

While his statement contained a measure of truth, as movement of arms into Afghanistan could not be checked because of the mountainous nature of the terrain and the numerous mule tracks available to arms smugglers, the view expressed had a sinister motive behind it. What the Afghan official wanted to convey to the members of the Security Council was that it was Pakistan that was interfering in the internal affairs of Afghanistan, and that it was Islamabad which must be prevented from sending arms to the Taliban.

Mestiri had also opined that there was continued foreign interference in Afghanistan, and that it was a major hurdle in bringing about peace in Afghanistan.

Despite the fact that the Taliban had had an effective control of over two-thirds of Afghan territory since entering Kabul in September 1996, the United Nations continued to recognize the government of ousted President Burhanuddin Rabbani during the 1997 General Assembly Session. It was Abdullah, Vice-Minister of Foreign Affairs in the former Afghan government, who addressed the UNGA on 1 October 1997, not Abdul Hakeem Mujahid, the Taliban representative.

Aid to Afghanistan

Since there appeared to be no end in sight to the conflict that had been raging inside Afghanistan since 1979, donor fatigue began to set in. The UN decided to stop all aid to the Afghan refugees by September 1995, which hurt even those Afghans living in Taliban-controlled areas.[186]

Food Convoys: To alleviate the sufferings of the starving population in the Hizb-e-Wahdat stronghold of Bamian, UN officials arranged for food convoys to be despatched to them. The Taliban, however, did not permit the vehicles to move through areas controlled by them; consequently, in December 1997 food had to be airlifted to Bamian from Peshawar.

Mine Clearance: The UN mine clearance programme needed a sum of US$ 19,301,600 but was allotted only $ 14,548,808. Several thousand land-mines have been lifted, but many areas with concentrated clusters of mines still remain in Afghanistan. (*See,* Map 8).

Map 8

Location of Concentrated Clusters of Land-mines in Afghanistan
(High-priority mined areas, April 1996)

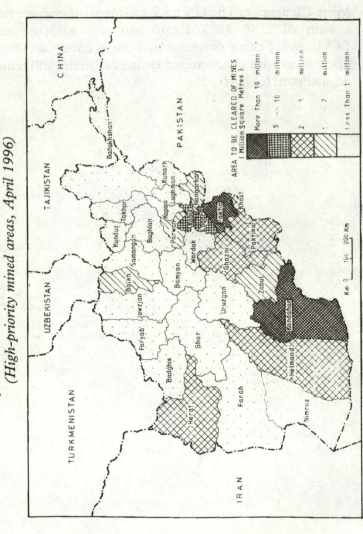

AREA TO BE CLEARED OF MINES
(Million Square Metres)

More Than 10 million

5 - 10 million

2 - 5 million

1 - 2 million

less Than 1 million

Km 0   100   200 Km

CHAPTER 9

MILITARY BALANCE

Before the rise of the Taliban, Rabbani's army under
Ahmed Shah Masood consisted of three corps headquarters, three armoured divisions, eight infantry divisions,
two mechanized divisions, and one National Guards
division. The total strength was around 25,000. These were
stationed as follows:

1 Corps Headquarters ...... Kabul
18 Armoured Division .. Khari Khanna
1 Infantry Division .... Kabul (Qarar Bagh)
2 Infantry Division .... Jabal-us-Siraj *
8 Infantry Division .... Kapisa
35 Infantry Division........ Salang Tunnel
40 Infantry Division........ Bagram airbase
70 Infantry Division........ Kabul
National Guards Division   Kabul

2 Corps Headquarters ...... Kandahar (Lt.-Gen. Naqib)*
7 Armoured Division ...... Kandahar *
15 Infantry Division. .... Kandahar (Maj.-Gen. Lale)*
7 Mechanized Division. ... Kandahar (Maj.-Gen. Alim)*

4 Corps Headquarters .... Herat (Lt.-Gen. Mohammad Ismail)*
4 Armoured Division ...... Herat (Maj.-Gen. Nasir)*
17 Infantry Division........ Herat (Alauddin Khan)*
21 Mechanized Division .. Shindand (M. Shah Ghazi)*

Abdul Rashid Dostum's Jumbish-e-Milli consisted of three infantry divisions and an armoured division. With a total strength of 50,000. These were deployed as under:

2 Infantry Division .... Yakka*
70 Infantry Division .... Hairatan*
80 Infantry Division .... Pul-e-Khumri*
Armoured Brigade, ex 53
Armoured Division .... Shiberghan*

* Source: *Reliable but withheld.*

Except for Ismail's corps in Herat and Dostum's in the northern provinces, which did maintain their units and formations after a fashion, the others vanished in the concept of the people's army.

The military situation on 1 December 1997 was as under:

Taliban regime	21	provinces
General Dostum/ Malik	4	"
Rabbani/ Masood	4	"
Hizb-e-Wahdat (Shia)	2	"
Being contested	1	"
	32	

The Taliban controlled Badghis, Kunduz, Herat, Farah, Nimroz, Helmand, Kandahar, Uruzgan, Ghor, Zabul, Ghazni, Khost, Paktia, Paktika, Wardak, Logar, Nangarhar, Laghman, Kunarh, Kabul, parts of Parwan, and Kabisa on 1 December 1997 with a force estimated around 50,000 fighters.

The second strongest element in terms of the extent of area controlled was the Jumbish-e-Milli of Abdul Rashid Dostum. After his ouster from Afghanistan, Jumbish-e-Milli came under the command of his rival, General Abdul Malik Pehalwan who was also forced to flee Afghanistan when Dostum returned. Weapon-wise and in matters of organizational ability and fighting qualities, his force was once the second strongest. However, he lost most of his forces at the hands of the Taliban. On 1 December Dostum controlled Samangan, Faryab, Jowzjan, and Balkh. His estimated strength was around 40,000 but later the force was badly depleted due to defections.

Rabbani remained the *de jure* ruler of Afghanistan in the eyes of the United Nations and all other countries except Pakistan, Saudi Arabia, and the UAE, even when forced to flee Afghanistan as a result of a defeat at the hands of the Taliban in May 1997. On 1 December only Badakhshan, Takhar Kapisa, and Parwan were under his control.

Rabbani's strength lay in his military commander, Ahmed Shah Masood, who had once been known, specially amongst western circles, as having the strongest force in Afghanistan during the Afghan jihad. He had blunted several attacks by the Soviets and retained his hold over the Panjsher valley throughout the eleven years of Soviet occupation of Afghanistan. He could not, however, withstand the onslaught from a rag-tag army of religious students of his own country, for the simple reason that he had come face to face with a determined group of fighters who had gained the confidence and the good will of those who surrendered to them. His 30,000-strong force was reduced to around 10,000 because of heavy casualties and defections amongst his followers. It had also lost much of its offensive spirit by retreating to the Panjsher valley.

He was able to make something of a comeback by advancing beyond the Salang Tunnel, by 20 July 1997, and entrenching himself twenty-five kilometres north of Kabul. Despite numerous counter-attacks by the Taliban in this sector, they had not been able to make any headway, and the frontlines until 31 December 1997 remained dangerously close to the capital.

The Hizb-e-Wahdat, under Karim Khalili, though present only in the province of Bamian and Baghlan, fought bravely against the Taliban and successfully resisted their attempts to overrun their stronghold. They allied themselves with General Malik in the defence of Mazar-e Sharif. They openly expressed their anger against Pakistan and the United States for supporting the Taliban.

After the loss of Spin Boldak, Charasyab, and Sarobi to the Taliban, Hikmetyar became a toothless tiger. He had lost his power base and had to be dependent on the military hardware of Masood and Dostum to recover some of his earlier prestige. His significance in the Afghan power equation after the fall of Kabul diminished substantially. Most of his followers joined the Taliban.

CHAPTER 10

IMPACT ON THE REGION

The Economic and Social Destruction of Afghanistan

Twenty years of continuous conflict have taken a very heavy toll of life and property in Afghanistan. Millions of people were killed, hundreds of thousands were disabled, untold numbers had to flee their country and seek shelter in neighbouring lands, while numerous families kept moving from one town to another within Afghanistan to escape being caught in the cross-fire.

Almost all major roads are full of potholes, their surfaces torn apart by the frequent movement of tracked vehicles. Bridges have been blown up, making crossing of obstacles slow and cumbersome. Houses have been razed to the ground by constant bombing and rocketing. Wells and water channels need major repairs before they can be used again. Fields have dried up. Electric installations and power lines have been damaged, in some case beyond repair. Telephone poles have been uprooted. The cultural heritage including the Kabul museum, which held some rare pieces of ancient times, has been destroyed or partially disfigured.

Much of the devastation was carried out during the Afghan jihad and the civil war that followed, well before the Taliban came on the scene. They too, however, have to take their share of the blame as, despite their pious intentions, they also contributed to the physical destruction of their country by using force to achieve their objective.

The problem of the reconstruction of Afghanistan is colossal. Billions of dollars will be needed. Nations which were instrumental in the destruction of Afghanistan must contribute the most. However, no one will come forward until durable peace returns to that unfortunate land and an effective government is installed in Kabul.

The biggest difficulty is the clearance of the land-mines which were laid during the conflict both by an outside power and by the Afghan factions themselves. 'Kabul has the dubious distinction of being the most mined capital in the world,' says a UN official responsible for the UN de-mining efforts in Afghanistan. Out of a total of 110 million mines lying in sixty-four countries of the world, around 10 million still lie buried in Afghanistan. These were planted not only by the Soviets and the pro-communist Afghans, but also by the various Islamic factions during the civil war. According to one UN report, over ten mine incidents occur every day in Afghanistan.

UNDCP annual estimates of the funds which will be required to clear the area of mines are as follows:

1997	US$ 4,697,000
1998	US$ 4,554,900
1999	US$ 3,667,600
2000	US$ 3,460,800
Total	US$16,380,300

The commitments made by different countries in 1997 were $ 3 million; Japan $ 1 million; Netherlands $ 1.5 million; Norway $ 675,000. The total support given by the United States since 1973 for mine clearance in Afghanistan comes to $17.2 million.

In addition to the physical destruction of Afghanistan, the twenty-year war has also torn the social fabric of the country. The Taliban factor has heightened the ethnic divide. It will not be easy for the Tajiks and the Uzbeks to forget the role played by the Pushtun communities living in their midst in northern Afghanistan, most of whom went over to the Taliban during the fighting.

Although the Taliban continue to maintain that they treat all Afghans alike regardless of which sect they belong to, the fact remains that the vast majority of Shias were in the opposite camp during the struggle for power. Hundreds of Shias lost their lives in the battles between the Hizb-e-Wahdat and the Taliban. With Iran taking an interest in seeing that the Shias in Afghanistan get due recognition in a Sunni-dominated Taliban regime, it is doubtful if a peaceful relationship between the two will prevail even when normalcy returns to Afghanistan.

A major upheaval in the social sector has taken place in the daily life of the Afghan women. Confined to their homes, deprived of education, prevented from going to work, they have felt the impact of the Taliban the most. It is true that the womenfolk in Afghanistan have always been kept secluded. There was, however, no law forbidding women from going to school or working or moving out of their homes without covering themselves from head to foot. They had the liberty to partake of whatever little freedom Afghan society permitted. This is no longer possible under the strict application of Islamic laws by the clerics.

The rise of the Taliban movement created a number of marriages of conveniences between erstwhile rival factions. Initially, forces loyal to Rabbani joined the Taliban in defeating Hikmetyar at Charasyab. A few months later, when the Taliban were at the gates of Kabul, Rabbani won Hikmetyar over to jointly defend the capital against what he believed to be an irregular force. Dostum, who was watching developments from his stronghold in the north, first decided to stay away from the infighting but, when the students clashed with his troops ahead of the Salang Pass, he formed an alliance with Rabbani and Masood, his former rivals, against the Taliban.

The Shia factions, which had split into two groups, one siding with Rabbani, the other with Hikmetyar, joined up again to become a force to be reckoned with in Afghanistan politics. Sectarian differences, so far not very significant in Afghanistan, were heightened because of the anti-Shia attitude of the Taliban.

Pockets of disgruntled elements remained within areas which came under the control of the Taliban. Some local warlords and smugglers were unhappy at being forced to surrender their weapons. Some others felt that life was too restricted because of the strict interpretation of the *shariah* by the Taliban administration. Though none of these elements posed a serious threat to Mullah Omar and his 'disciples', they did remain a source of instability.

The ethnic factor in Afghan politics considerably increased when the Taliban came on the scene, as the Taliban movement was centred on Pushtun dominance over the other ethnic minorities. The ethnic divide widened when the Taliban made the strategic error of taking over full control of the northern areas which had been handed to them on a plate by the Uzbek General, Malik Pehalwan.

Impact on Pakistan

With the Taliban and those opposed to them fighting it out in Afghanistan, the possibility of the struggle spilling over to Pakistan cannot be ruled out. When some elements of the ousted eastern *Shoora*, which had been commanded by Haji Abdul Qadeer, launched fresh attacks against the Taliban in Kunarh, there was a fear that the factional fighting might spread to Pakistan as Qadeer and his followers had taken refuge in Peshawar. The security agencies are reported to have warned both sides against any such developments.[187]

The Taliban factor had a profound effect on the historically strong ties between Iran and Pakistan. Their relations had never plummeted so low as during the Taliban movement. Iran was pushed into the arms of India, Russia, and China.

Continued instability in a neighbouring country has a potential spillover effect, particularly when the borders are very porous and there is a history of involvement in each other's internal affairs. If the struggle for power between the Taliban and their opponents continues in Afghanistan, sectarian, ethnic, and political factions in Pakistan could also get involved, with serious implications for peace and security in the border areas.

The Taliban's extremist views on the application of Islamic laws could encourage the mullahs in Pakistan to galvanize public opinion in favour of the imposition of the *shariah*, in its strictest form in Pakistan as well. The Tehrik-Nifaz-e-Shariat-Mohammedi, which was very active in the Malakand Agency on the borders of Afghanistan, cited the Taliban as a model for Pakistan and Maulana Samiul Haq of the Jamiat Ulema-e-Pakistan openly advocated that Pakistan needed a Taliban movement.

'Pakistan was created in the name of Islam, but Islam was not implemented here. In Afghanistan the Taliban movement is for Islam, if they succeed, then we in Pakistan will be happy. Many in Pakistan and Afghanistan will benefit,' said Abdul Hadi, a tribal elder.[188] Such feelings could one day sway the illiterate inhabitants living in the sensitive tribal areas against the government.

The religiously oriented parties have never fared well in elections in Pakistan, but what their influence in times to come might be cannot be assessed with certainty, specially if Afghanistan becomes a theocratic state under the Taliban. This could lead to internal disorder in Pakistan as it will be resisted by the more progressive sections in the government.

Though it was repeatedly denied by the Pakistani leadership, Rabbani and Masood firmly believed that the Taliban were Pakistan's baby. As the strength of the Taliban grew, bitterness against Pakistan increased, resulting in the sacking of the Pakistan Embassy in Kabul by Masood's men. The bitterness which the Taliban issue has created between Pakistan and Rabbani/Masood/ Karim Khalili is likely to linger for a long time.

As a result of the fighting between the Taliban and the other factions in Afghanistan, 150,734 Afghan refugees entered Pakistan between 1 November 1994 and 31 March 1997. However, the burden of maintaining this refugee influx did not increase because, during the same period, 153,520 Afghan refugees were repatriated. The Chief Commissioner for Afghan Refugees in Islamabad confirmed that no extra amount of foreign aid was received or promised for the refugees who came into Pakistan as a result of the Taliban phenomenon. (For a monthly breakdown of arrivals of new refugees after the Taliban entered Kabul, *see*, Table 7.)

UNHCR, WFP, and some NGOs did provide food and relief assistance to the new arrivals in the two special refugee camps set up in Nasir Bagh, near Peshawar and in Akora Khattak south of Nowshera.

Table 7

*Flow of Afghan Refugees into Pakistan
September 1996–March 1997*

September 1996	16,535
October 1996	21,515
November 1996	29,619
December 1996	21,989
January 1997	11,003
February 1997	4,752
March 1997	4,137

Source: *Office of the Chief Commissioner for Afghan Refugees, Islamabad.*

On India

The Taliban factor gave India an opening to re-establish a foothold in Afghanistan. Taking advantage of the strained relations between Rabbani and Islamabad, New Delhi did not waste any time in building up a close relationship with both Rabbani and Iran. The containment of the Taliban movement became the common goal of New Delhi, Tehran, and the ousted Rabbani regime. India's interests are also served by keeping the Afghan problem alive, thereby ensuring that Pakistan is involved on its western front. The Taliban provided that opportunity.

A new axis between Iran, India, and Russia developed to contain the influence of the USA, Saudi Arabia, and Pakistan in Afghanistan.

On Central Asia

The Central Asian Republics had been under communist rule for over seventy years. The Muslims of these newly-independent states have adopted modern ways, and are therefore concerned about the infiltration of conservative ideas into their countries. The extremist views of the Taliban are a matter of concern for all of them, but particularly for those republics whose borders meet Afghanistan.

Since Afghanistan has a fairly large Uzbek and Tajik population concentrated along the borders of Uzbekistan and Tajikistan, these two Central Asian Republics have ethnic affiliations with the northern areas of that country. They will not remain unconcerned if the Taliban disregard their political and social rights.

On Russia

Russia already has troops in Tajikistan to support the government in power. If the Taliban are able to occupy the northern provinces, they will come face to face with the Russian troops on the borders of Afghanistan and Tajikistan, which could lead to clashes and heightened tensions.

The Russo-Chinese 1997 Defence Pact is also an outcome of renewed American interest in Afghanistan and in the Central Asian States.

On Saudi Arabia

Relations between Saudi Arabia and Iran are likely to become even more strained as the two support different belligerents.

On the United States

The US is concerned about international terrorism as it feels that the Taliban could get involved with other Islamic organizations which believe in transnational activities. Another source of concern is drug trafficking, which the US believes will increase as the Taliban have not given a clear-cut policy on drug trafficking.

On China

In China's western-most province of Sinkiang, the Uighur Muslim community, possibly inspired by the Taliban movement in Afghanistan, has begun to demand an independent state.

Strengths of the Taliban

The Taliban's sincerity, honesty, and thorough devotion to their cause has been their main strength.

Their ability to disarm the various militia and to maintain law and order, with the minimum use of force, was their biggest achievement.

Rough and ready justice, in accordance with Koranic injunctions but mixed with Afghan traditions, and given out immediately without fear or favour, was appreciated by a people not accustomed to western laws.

No *talib* engaged in looting or forcible occupation of houses or doing anything for personal benefit. This endeared them to the people.

Their very simple lifestyle, with the *talibs* not even demanding any pay, and carrying out their designated duties from make-shift offices, was appreciated by the rest of the Afghans.

Until they reached Kabul they had avoided bloodshed as far as possible, giving the promise that peace was returning to Afghanistan. A war-weary nation was willing to support the Taliban because of this fact alone.

They have been able to acquire a good deal of sophisticated weapons and have plenty of ammunition, which has enabled them to continue with their objective of eventually controlling the whole of Afghanistan.

Their force increased from a mere handful in 1994 to over 30,000 by early 1997. Having adopted the 'people's army' concept, every adult *talib* is a willing fighter. Each one of them is prepared to lay down his life in the expectation of being rewarded by a place in heaven if he is martyred on the battlefield.

Since many soldiers and officers of the old Afghan armed forces have joined the Taliban, their effectiveness as a fighting force has increased. They have become battle-hardened and have, through trial and error, learnt how to hold ground or put in a deliberate attack against a well-entrenched enemy.

The Taliban have moral support and in some cases financial assistance from Saudi Arabia and, to a limited extent, from Pakistan.

The Taliban leadership had a large reservoir of *talibs* studying in Pakistan who were ready to move into Afghanistan whenever they received a call from the *Amirul Momineen*.

The Taliban initially had Dostum on their side, which strengthened their hands against those opposing their advance.

Their Weaknesses

The Taliban lack military expertise. They do have some well-trained ex-communists with them, but the majority are semi-trained fighters who have done well against light opposition but are finding it difficult to overcome a strong force.

As the conflict in Afghanistan continues and the casualties continue to mount with no end in sight, the people are gradually getting disillusioned with the Taliban.

An influential Afghan spiritual elder by the name of Syed Bahauddin Jan Agha was taken into custody by the Taliban in Kandahar province on suspicion of having been campaigning against the student militia. This reportedly was not the case.

Uprisings have taken place in Logar and some other provinces as not all Afghans living in Taliban-controlled areas have readily given up their weapons. The strict implementation of the *shariah* has also irked quite a few of the local *Maliks*.

The Taliban's rejection of the unilateral cease-fire announced by Rabbani during the holy month of Ramazan was not fully appreciated by the Kabulis, who were facing near-famine conditions.

The Taliban, the vast majority of whom are Sunnis, will have to accommodate the requirements of the Shias, who want a greater share in the government than before. This may not go down very well with the rest of the Pushtun elements in Afghanistan as it would mean a radical shift in the power equation in that country.

The brutal killing of former President Najibullah and his brother and the desecration of their bodies turned Dostum against the Taliban.

The warning given by the Taliban to Dostum to allow them to move beyond the Salang Pass, and the clash that ensued between the two militia, further changed Dostum's attitude towards the Taliban. He went to the extent of joining Rabbani and Masood to push back the Taliban.

Pressure from Russia and Uzbekistan probably also played a part in compelling Dostum to prevent the Taliban from overrunning areas close to the CAR. The Taliban, on the other hand, were determined to move into Dostum's stronghold and uproot him. They changed their original assessment of Dostum and now began to consider him to be an enemy of the people and a Russian hireling. Their failure to come to an understanding with Dostum pitched them against a formidable enemy, one who had the tacit support of Russia and Uzbekistan. But their tactics of obtaining the support of the local population, allied with the mercurial nature of the Afghans, helped the Taliban in weakening Dostum's hold over his own territory.

However, their attempt to control the whole of Afghanistan and administer it all by themselves is not likely to end in a durable peace in their country. They will have to accommodate the interests of all other factions in Afghanistan in order to achieve political stability. Their claim to be the sole party able to put an Islamic government in place will not be accepted by the other Islam-*pasand* political parties in Afghanistan, while their strict interpretation of the *shariah* will not be appreciated by the more liberal-minded Afghans, especially the educated women in Kabul, who would not like to see their country turned into a theocracy ruled by clerics and mullahs. The Taliban's decision to close girls' schools and prevent women from working or even carrying out domestic chores away from their houses has been criticized. Until such time as they change their attitude towards women, the liberal societies of the west are unlikely to recommence humanitarian aid to them.

The disarming of all rival factions has created bad blood amongst those who have come under their control— Afghans are very reluctant to give up their weapons, which they consider to be their birthright, and the fact that the Taliban are allowed to keep their arms only adds to the bitterness.

Their policies on drug trafficking and harbouring terrorists were appreciated, but exercising checks on these activities is not carried out as strictly as on their other *shariah* laws.

CHAPTER 11

FUTURE PROSPECTS

Afghanistan has virtually been divided into different power centres and is unlikely to be restored even to its original loose political structure in the near future. The extreme puritanism of the Taliban is not likely to be accepted by the rest of the Afghans. A struggle between them and more moderate elements will most probably continue for some time.

The United Nations' efforts are not likely to succeed in the near future as even the anti-Taliban factions have not agreed on the composition of an interim arrangement to take over power from the Taliban. The United Nations have to take a deeper interest in Afghanistan; only then can they hope to achieve a breakthrough. This could be in the shape of an international conference of those powers that have something at stake in Afghanistan, and their aim should be to place an embargo on the supply of weapons, and to station a peace-keeping force in Afghanistan.

Though predicting the results of the power struggle in Afghanistan is a hazardous game, because so many alliances and promises have been sacrificed at the altar of immediate gains, the likely scenarios could be as follows:

Hypothesis 1

The struggle for power continues in Afghanistan, with the Taliban trying to occupy the areas still out of their grasp and the anti-Taliban factions continuing to resist their attempts to do so, resulting in a stalemate. In such a situation peace will not return to the war-torn country, and the regional powers will continue to protect their interests by siding with those Afghan factions which would promote their objectives.

Casualties will mount and the infrastructure in Afghanistan will be further destroyed. The number of internal refugees will rise, and whenever the fighting intensifies along the borders, more and more refugees will pour into Pakistan and Iran. Those already present would be reluctant to return, thus the burden of the refugees along with the socio-economic pressures they have brought with them will intensify.

Relief agencies from foreign countries would gradually reduce their aid as they would not see any light at the end of the tunnel.

Hypothesis 2

The Taliban make a breakthrough and regain their hold over northern Afghanistan, either because of victories on the field, or through defections in the ranks of the Jumbish-e-Milli.

This would lead to Afghanistan being controlled by a single political party, one which has demonstrated its ability to enforce law and order. The danger of the disintegration of Afghanistan would fade away, but it is doubtful if durable peace would return as those opposed to the Taliban would continue to resist their interpretation of the Islamic code.

Hypothesis 3

The efforts of the United Nations and those of the neighbouring countries bear fruit and a cease-fire is agreed upon, prisoners-of-war are exchanged, and a broad-based interim administration is put in place. A neutral force under

UN supervision assumes responsibility for maintaining law and order.

A temporary respite would then be achieved, but the power-sharing formula is not likely to endure as there are serious differences over ideological concepts between the Taliban and the rest of the Afghan factions including expatriates.

Hypothesis 4

A coalition government is formed at the centre with limited powers, various ethnic regions being given maximum autonomy in their respective areas.

Dennis Kux, a retired US Foreign Service officer and George Tanham at the Woodrow Wilson Centre have suggested the Swiss model as a solution to the Afghan crisis.[189] If this were to come about, the Uzbeks, Tajiks, and Pushtuns might well affiliate themselves with similar ethnic communities in respective neighbouring countries.

Hypothesis 5

The possibility of an ethnic divide cannot be ruled out. If there is a stalemate in the military situation for an extended period of time, the country could break up, with the Hindu Kush becoming the new frontier. The danger of Afghanistan splitting up has not yet gone away as the ethnic divisions have widened since the new element of the Taliban came on the scene.

Afghanistan has never had a strong centre, even during the days of the monarchy. Except for the rule of Amir Abdur Rahman in the nineteenth century, the outlying provinces have always enjoyed a considerable amount of autonomy. It is also true that the Afghans owe allegiance to their own tribal elders first and the national government later. The three years of civil war have heightened the divide between the various ethnic factions and led to the possibility of the disintegration of Afghanistan.

The Hindu Kush remains a major hurdle in the way of achieving an integrated Afghan state. As soon as one crosses the massive barrier the terrain changes and the environment becames totally different. The northerners are generally more educated and are more liberal in their interpretation of Islam. They are socially and culturally closer to their northern neighbours, on whom they are economically dependent.

The most likely scenario in the immediate future is that of Hypothesis 1, i.e., the civil strife in Afghanistan continues with a see-saw effect.

The most damaging scenario would be the disintegration of Afghanistan along ethnic lines. This would have far-reaching strategic consequences for the entire region. Pakistan would be faced with the Pukhtunistan issue again, although it would not be supported to the extent that it was in the days of Zahir Shah and Daud by the Pushtuns on the Pakistani side of the Durand Line.

Major changes have taken place in the policies of the Awami National Party (ANP) since then. The ANP joined the mainstream of politics in Pakistan and for some time even became a partner of the Muslim League. Also for the first time it accepted a non-Pushtun Chief Minister of the Frontier Province. The people of Hazara Division are not Pushtuns and would not want to be part of an independent Pushtun state, while those in Dera Ismail Khan District are Saraiki-speaking and would certainly want to stay out of such a deal.

In any case, a land-locked Pushtun state with unfriendly relations with all its neighbours would not be a viable proposition. It is, therefore, most unlikely that the Pushtuns in Pakistan would even consider supporting such a move in the remote possibility of the disintegration of Afghanistan. However, one cannot rule out the pressure for a Pushtun state emerging on either side of the Durand Line if Afghanistan splits itself along ethnic lines.

The only answer to the present political impasse is a formula for power sharing. Future rulers cannot exclude any particular group. The government has to be broad-based and will have to give a greater share to the Shias than has been the case in the past. Only then will there be the legitimacy which is lacking today.

Reconstruction of Afghanistan

The Taliban will have to temper their religious extremism, particular in their attitude towards women, before they can hope to receive financial and technical aid from the world community to rebuild their battered and war-torn country. The United Nations Secretary-General in 1989 called for a sum of $1.116 billion for the reconstruction of Afghanistan.[190] The amount needed by the Taliban would be over $3 billion, if peace were to return in the near future, since the destruction of the infrastructure continued in the decade that followed the Soviet withdrawal. The rising cost of materials would further add to the funds required to rebuild the war-ravaged country.

Bringing about peace, though very important, will not be enough. Emergency food supplies will have to be obtained, agricultural activities revived, and business re-established; work will have to be found for both men and women; roads and bridges repaired and water sources have to be cleaned and resuscitated; schools and hospitals will have to be rebuilt, medicines supplied; trained doctors and nurses and engineers will be needed. Above all, ten million land-mines will need to be lifted. (*See*, Map 8 for the location of concentrated cluster of land-mines in Afghanistan).

The Taliban, with no visible source of funds and having little or no expertise in running a modern state, leave alone its reconstruction, cannot do without outside assistance. They, and their interpretation of Islam, will have to

accommodate universally-accepted human rights if they want
other nations to help them in their hour of need.

At best the Taliban are a transitional phenomenon to a
more stable political arrangement, at worst a nightmare to
the western world and a problem for their neighbours.

CONCLUSION

Pakistan's Afghan policy came under severe criticism after its failure to play a positive role in bringing about a lasting solution to the Afghan quagmire. There are those who believe that the civil war in Afghanistan would not have taken place if, along with the military assistance that was being provided to the Afghan factions, a political structure had also been set up which could have taken over when the military victory had been achieved. Failure to do so resulted in the internecine fighting.

Pakistan's Afghan policy has been based on wrong assumptions.

Initially it was thought that, as soon as the Soviet troops withdrew from Afghanistan, the Afghan factions would be able to oust Dr Najibullah, but not only did he stay in power, he remained there for three long years.

The second assumption was that the Afghans would be able to establish a stable government in Afghanistan after forcing Najibullah to quit. That too was unfounded—the rival Afghan groups continued to fight among themselves.

Thirdly, Islamabad was under the illusion that the Afghan leaders would be indebted to Pakistan for giving their people shelter for two decades, allowing them to move freely within the country, and permitting them to take up any occupation they liked. That was not to be. On the contrary, some of them felt no qualms in biting the hand that fed them when Pakistan's policies went against their personal interests.

The fourth assumption was that the Taliban would be able to capture power and Pakistan would be able to reach out to the Central Asian Republics if they were given all the support they needed to overthrow Rabbani. But that again was a false premise. The result was that Pakistan found itself on the wrong foot all the time.

In its attempts to place a friendly government in Afghanistan, Pakistan has lent its support first to one and then to another Afghan leader. It would be better if the decision-makers in Islamabad stuck to one objective only, i.e., bringing about peace in Afghanistan irrespective of who rules Kabul.

Pakistan has suffered the consequences of giving its wholehearted support to the Afghan mujahideen, for whom it became a conduit for arms and because of whom Pakistan carried out the biggest clandestine operation the world has ever known. Pakistan also gave shelter to over three million Afghan refugees, whose presence in the country led to a great many social ills. Over a million Afghan refugees still remain in Pakistan.

Pakistan, therefore, has a vital interest in the territorial integrity and political stability of Afghanistan. Having become victim to the Kalashnikov culture, drug trafficking, and smuggling of illegal arms due to the Afghan crisis, Islamabad cannot sit idle and let matters deteriorate further; its western border would become even more insecure. Pakistan should not, therefore, remain indifferent to developments across the Durand Line.

Policy-makers must not, however, place all their eggs in one basket. The approach that would pay the maximum dividend would be to try and bring about a *rapprochement* between the Taliban and those factions opposed to them.

It must be realized that durable peace in Afghanistan will not be achieved if a military solution is imposed on the Afghans. Even if the Taliban, with the alleged support of Pakistan, succeed in overrunning the whole of Afghanistan, peace is unlikely to return to that unfortunate land. The British tried to impose Sher Shah on the Afghans but he was overthrown in no time. The Soviets used force to impose their brand of communism but to no avail. One of the reasons why the two accords signed in Pakistan were not adhered to was that they were initiated by Pakistan. Officials in Islamabad should not try to be king-makers—many a leader in Afghanistan has come to grief merely because he was seen to be acting on behalf of a foreign government. Instead, Pakistan should join Iran and the UN in their attempts to broker peace. There appears to be no co-ordination between the various government departments in Pakistan which have something to do with the Afghanistan problem. The Ministry of Foreign Affairs, the ISI, the Ministry of Interior, and even SAFRON (States and Frontier Regions) often take independent decisions without consulting each other. Some well-meaning individuals in Pakistan even tried taking their own initiatives to find a solution to the Afghan imbroglio which they thought would be in the best interest of Pakistan, but which created problems for the government. The result has been a lack of a coherent Afghan policy, in the absence of which proper management of the Afghan crisis has suffered.

There were times when it appeared that the Foreign Office only reacted to events in Afghanistan. With every new development a new favourite was created or an old one resurrected. Pakistani officials should have realized that the Afghans' only concern is self-interest. They have no qualms about ditching their allies or even their benefactors if that is the need of the hour. To rely on any one group to achieve long-term objectives was, therefore, a wrong policy to follow in Afghanistan.

'It is better to work through the United Nations rather than get directly involved in bringing about a broad-based government in Afghanistan,' said Lt.-Gen. (retd.) Nishat Ahmed, President of the Institute of Regional Studies, Islamabad.[191] His view was that we must recognize and show an understanding of all the major factions in that unfortunate land. There is a great deal of wisdom in this approach.

Pakistan must not try to act alone in Afghanistan; it must take into account the interests of its neighbours, which should include not only Iran but also Uzbekistan,

Turkmenistan, and Tajikistan. Even those outside powers which contributed to the Afghan jihad and are likely to contribute to the reconstruction of Afghanistan must be kept in the picture.

Pakistan's position on Afghanistan should be based on the following three principles: support the territorial integrity of Afghanistan; insist on and implement the policy of non-interference in the internal affairs of Afghanistan; work towards a cease-fire and the establishment of a broad-based government in Afghanistan in co-ordination with the United Nations Special Representative for Afghanistan.

Pakistan should be content with having an independent, integrated, and friendly western neighbour, irrespective of which political faction or ethnic community is in power in Afghanistan.

AFTERWORD

A number of major developments took place in Afghanistan in the closing years of the century. Unfortunately, none of them helped in the final solution of the Afghan problem. In fact, in some respects, the situation was exacerbated even further.

The United Nations-supported six plus two[1] meeting held at Tashkent between 19 and 20 July 1998 was also attended by the Taliban and the anti-Taliban faction. But the meeting ended in a deadlock The UN called for a political settlement of the Afghan problem; the establishment of a broad based government in Kabul and an end to foreign interference. The Taliban, however, were not willing to share power with other factions as they felt that they had the military strength to over run the whole of Afghanistan, which as later events showed, was ill-founded.

Mazar-e-Sharif was re-captured by the Taliban on 8 August 1998, after a bitter struggle against the Hizb-e-Wahdat, whose militia was in control of the city. This brought the student militia once again to the borders of Turkmenistan. The success of the Taliban in northern Afghanistan was a matter of great concern to Tehran, as the Iran supported Hizb-e-Wahdat had been pushed out of their major stronghold in the north.

During the fighting some elements of the Taliban, acting on their own, attacked the Iranian Consul General's office in Mazar-e-Sharif. In the process nine Iranian diplomats and one Iranian journalist were killed. Around thirty-five Iranian drivers, who were also present in the town, managed to escape to Iran. The Ayatollahs reacted very sharply to this incident. They demanded that the bodies of the Iranians who had been martyred at Mazar-e-Sharif be returned immediately; the killers be arrested and tried and Iranian prisoners in Taliban hands be sent back. To put pressure on the Taliban, Iran amassed 70,000 troops along the Afghan-Iran border. In the meantime, the pro-Iranian Shiite stronghold of Bamian in central Afghanistan was attacked by the Taliban who succeeded in overrunning it in September 1998. This was a further blow to Iranian interests in the affairs of Afghanistan.

Since tempers were rising and the possibility of an all out war between Afghanistan and Iran was becoming a reality, Pakistan stepped up its efforts to bring about a reconciliation between the warring factions. A suggestion by Mulla Omar that an Ulema Commission be established formed the basis for the mediatory efforts of the Pakistan foreign office. The proposal, however, could not make any progress because the Taliban insisted that the *Ulema*, who were to be nominated by both sides, had to have a *sanad* (graduation certificate) from a Sunni religious seminary. The Taliban also wanted to have the right to cast a veto if the names given were not acceptable to them. The Ulema Commission, according to the Taliban, could only have the right to decide on a ceasefire and the return of prisoners in the on-going conflict. With such one sided conditions being placed by the Taliban the Ulema Commission did not even come into existence. Pakistan's efforts to find a peaceful solution to the Afghanistan imbroglio once again got bogged down.

In the closing months of 1998 the United States decided to take an active interest in Afghanistan once more. Several high-level US officials went into Afghanistan in the autumn of that year and met the Taliban leaders, ostensibly to talk about humanitarian rights but in all probability to locate Osama Bin Laden, an Arab exile, who had been living in Afghanistan since 1996. Washington claimed that the US had concrete evidence to prove that Osama was the mastermind behind the bombings of the US Embassy in Kenya and Tanzania, on 7 August 1998, which left more than 200 dead including a dozen US citizens. The Clinton administration was determined to get hold of Osama and try him for terrorist activities.

On 20 August 1998 the United States launched missile strikes on Sudan and Afghanistan. The suspected headquarters of Osama Bin Laden in Khost were struck by sixty cruise missiles from a US naval ship anchored in the north Arabian Sea. Except for some material damage the objective was not achieved as Osama was not present in Khost at the time and remained unhurt. The firing of missiles over Pakistan territory created a great deal of uproar in Pakistan, more so as a few of the cruise missiles landed on Pakistan territory.

India took advantage of the mood in the US Congress against the Taliban whom the US accused of harbouring terrorists. The Indian Foreign Ministry (South Block) sent Alok Prashad and Vivek Katju, joint secretaries, looking after America, Pakistan, Afghanistan and Iran in the Ministry of External Affairs, to Washington. They held discussions with Assistant Secretary of State, Karl Inderfurth and other US officials emphasizing the allegation that Osama Bin Laden was also sending militants into Indian–held Kashmir. New Delhi found common ground with Washington on this score and capitalized on it. The pro-Kashmir US Congressman, Dan Burton, had to withdraw his anti-India amendment as he realised that he did not have enough supporters.

On 9 December 1998 the United Nations Security Council adopted Resolution No. 1214 which called upon the Taliban to cease fighting, stop shielding terrorists and enter into peace talks with the opposition. Pakistan termed it as a one-sided resolution and not in keeping with the ground realities. In fact, Islamabad went one step further and asked the world community to recognize the Taliban regime, a plea that went unheeded. The anti-Taliban Alliance, on the other hand, were consolidating their position. They formed a United Islamic Front for the

Salvation of Afghanistan (UIFSA), to be commanded by Defence Minister Ahmed Shah Masood.

When Osama renewed his call for a *jihad* against the United States in January 1999, Washington sent Karl Inderfurth to Pakistan to try and pressurize the Taliban to evict Osama from Afghanistan. Inderfurth met Taliban officials in Islamabad in February 1999 and demanded that the Taliban should halt all support to Osama. In response, Mulla Omar announced that Osama had disappeared and his whereabouts were not known.

The UN-sponsored talks between the Taliban and the anti-Taliban Alliance were held at Ashkabad, the capital of Turkmenistan, from 10 March 1999 to 14 March 1999. The negotiations ended on a happy note as both sides agreed to share power with each other. Taliban's Foreign Minister, Wakil Ahmed Mutawakkil, announced at the end of the talks that the two sides had agreed to share executive, legislative and judicial responsibilities. Pakistan and Iran welcomed it as 'a positive development'. Andrew Tesoriere, acting head of the UN Special Mission for Afghanistan, described it as 'a major step forward on a fundamental issue'. It was too good to be true. On 10 April 1999 Mulla Omar suddenly declared that 'power could not be shared with those who have destroyed the country and looted the state treasury'. Efforts to find a peaceful solution had failed once more.

Fighting broke out once again between the Taliban and the opposing factions and Bamian was re-captured by the UIFSA in April 1999. To strengthen their position Tehran allegedly encouraged three Shiite Muslim parties to form a new coalition called The Supreme Council of Islamic Coalition of Afghanistan with the objective of putting up a joint opposition to the Taliban. Bamian was, however, overrun again by the Taliban in May 1999. The Taliban launched another major offensive in August 1999 and reached up to the mouth of the Panjsher Valley but were driven back to 30 kilometres north of Kabul a few weeks later by the militia of Ahmed Shah Masood. Once again this proved that neither of the protagonists had the military strength to achieve their objective with the use of force.

Washington succeeded in having UN Security Resolution 1267 passed unanimously on 15 October 1999. The UNSC demanded that the Taliban hand over Osama Bin Laden without further delay to appropriate authorities in a country where he has been indicted (USA) or to appropriate authorities in a country where he will be arrested and effectively brought to justice.

The Taliban, however, refused to oblige as they maintained that Osama was their guest and was to be treated as such, in keeping with Afghan traditions. In fact, more so because, according to them, the United States had not been able to prove that Osama was involved in terrorist activities. His movements were, however, restricted and he was categorically told not to indulge in terrorist activities. The Taliban then maintained that Osama has been deprived of all facilities with which he could be in contact with foreign elements.

Russia joined the United States in expressing serious concerns about the use of Taliban territory as a platform for international terrorism. The joint statement issued after the Russian Deputy Foreign Minister Grigoriy Karasin's meeting with Karl Inderfurth, called upon the Taliban to comply with the requirements of the UN Resolution 1267 of 15 October 1999[2]. It included the demand to turn over Osama Bin Laden to a jurisdiction where he can face trial. The Taliban were also to take steps to dismantle international terrorist organizations allegedly operating from their territory.

Since the Taliban did not oblige, economic sanctions were imposed by the UNSC on 14 November 1999 in accordance with UNSC Resolution 1267. Overseas assets of Ariana Airlines were frozen. All member nations were required to deny aircraft to take off from or land in their territory if owned by the Taliban. All funds controlled by the Taliban were to be frozen. Even Pakistan had to comply with these sanctions, which action was not appreciated by the rightist elements in the country who advocated full support to the Taliban. At this crucial time Iran won the appreciation of the Taliban by opening its borders with Afghanistan, which had been closed since September 1998. This action helped in reducing the impact of the UN sanctions. Much needed goods began to enter Taliban controlled areas bringing relief to the people of Afghanistan.

To soften their hardline approach, the United States joined international efforts to prevent a humanitarian catastrophe in Afghanistan by pledging $575,000 for the provision of food to the Afghans taking refuge in the Panjsher Valley as a result of the fighting between the Taliban and Ahmed Shah Masood[3].

At this time, when the Taliban were nearly completely cut off from the world community, an Indian Airline Flight IAC 814, with over 300 passengers on board, during its flight from Kathmandu to New Delhi, was hijacked and eventually forced to land at Kandahar by the hijackers on 24 December 1999. The role of the Taliban leadership throughout the eight days of their involvement in the unfortunate episode was appreciated by all concerned.

Contrary to what western nations and some people in Pakistan believed, the Taliban behaved in a dignified and mature manner. They did not act like uncivilized people; intolerant, trigger happy and unmindful of internationally accepted norms. The Taliban allowed the aircraft to land at Kandahar on humanitarian grounds just as Pakistan and UAE had done a day earlier. They condemned the hijacking and refused to give political asylum to the hijackers. They warned the hijackers not to harm any of the passengers or else they would storm the aircraft. The Taliban provided fuel to the aircraft to keep the passengers warm. The student militia guarded the aircraft night after night clad only in cotton *Shalwar* and shirts with the temperature falling to 10 degrees below zero. An Indian delegation was

permitted to come to Afghanistan despite the fact that New
Delhi had not recognized the Taliban regime and was, in
fact, supporting their opponents.

The Taliban were faced with a very difficult situation
which even developed nations find difficult to handle. It
goes to their credit that they avoided bloodshed and
facilitated the negotiations between the hijackers and the
Indians. They handled a very delicate issue with great
prudence and sagacity. They welcomed and cooperated
with the United Nations representatives and other foreign
nationals who descended on Kandahar to help in securing
the release of their citizens in the aircraft. The passengers
were eventually set free in return for the release of three
Kashmiri freedom fighters who had been languishing in
Indian jails. The hijackers were made to leave Afghanistan
within ten hours of their disembarking from the hijacked
plane. It is still not known where they went.

Towards the end of 1999 the Taliban continued to
control around nine tenths of Afghanistan. At the military
level there was a stalemate with neither the Taliban nor the
anti-Taliban Alliance having the strength to shift the battle
lines to their advantage. Limited successes and failures on
the battle field are likely to continue. At the political level,
the United Nations and all countries other than Pakistan,
UAE and Saudi Arabia still recognize the ousted regime of
Burhanuddin Rabbani. The Credentials Committee of the
United Nations rejected the claim of the Taliban to become
a member of the United Nations in September 1999. The
OIC have still kept the Afghan chair vacant. At the social
level, the Taliban have shown some flexibility. Rules have
been relaxed to enable lady doctors to work in hospitals.
Girls below ten years of age are being imparted education
in the countryside. The Taliban leadership are no longer
averse to being photographed.

Pakistan needs to modify its Afghan policy in the light of
the developments which have taken place since Islamabad
recognized the Taliban. Pakistan finds itself isolated as it is

being blamed by the United Nations and several other countries for its alleged support to the Taliban. Islamabad must work in concert with Iran and the United Nations in their efforts to resolve the Afghanistan problem. It must impress upon the Taliban that only a broad-based government would be able to bring about durable peace in Afghanistan. It must exercise greater influence on the Taliban to ensure that they do not act against Pakistan's national interests. It must persuade the Taliban to encourage the return of Afghan refugees. The Transit Trade Agreement between the two countries must take into consideration the interests of both nations. The Durand Line is a very porous border but efforts must be made to check free movement across it. Seminaries in Pakistan where Afghans are being imparted religious education must be screened to ensure that they do not become hot beds of terrorists.

NOTES

1. These included Afghanistan's neighbours (Iran, Uzbekistan, Turkmenistan, Tajikistan, China, Pakistan) Russia and the United States.

2. Joint statement issued on 29 October 1999 at Washington.

3. Office of Public Affairs, US Embassy, Islamabad, 23 November 1999.

APPENDIX I

Biographical Sketches of Important Personalities

Mullah Mohammad Omar Akhund

Mullah Omar is the founder and the head of the Taliban movement. He is a Gilzai Pushtun of the Hotak tribe. He was born in 1961 in Nauda village of Panjwai district in the province of Kandahar but later moved with his family to Dehrwut area in Tarin Kot (Oruzgan province). Soon after the Russian invasion of Afghanistan, he migrated back to Kandahar and settled in village Singesar of Maiwand District (Kandahar Province).

He fought against the Russians under Commander Mullah Faizullah Akhund (who was initially affiliated with the Harakat-e-Inqilab-e-Islami Afghanistan of Maulvi Mohammad Nabi Mohammedi and later joined the Jamiat-e-Islami Afghanistan of Burhanuddin Rabbani). Mullah Omar later fought against the occupation forces under Commander Nek Mohammad of the Hizb-e-Islami of Yunus Khalis. His followers claim that he is a crack marksman who destroyed a number of Soviet tanks during the Afghan jihad. He was injured four times during the Afghan jihad and lost an eye in combat. He does not want to have an artificial eye implanted as he is proud of having offered this sacrifice to God Almighty for the sake of Islam. His decision to fight against the militia to which he once belonged was because he found them to be corrupt and immoral.

A tall (6 feet 6 inches), well-built individual, he sports a flowing black beard. Omar comes from a poor farmer's family which had to leave its ancestral village to find employment in the neighbouring province of Uruzgan. He leads a simple life, preferring to sit on the ground along with those who come to meet him. He normally avoids meeting foreigners, leaving that task to his deputies.

He received his early education in the mosque schools of Jowzjan but regrets having left his studies when he was only in the seventh 'grade'. Strictly speaking, therefore, he is not entitled to be called a mullah as this title is given to those who have completed twelve years of formal religious education at different religious seminaries. Before launching the Taliban movement he was running a small mud-built *madrassa* in Singesar village, where he had thirty or forty students under him.

He is soft-spoken and speaks very little. He is, however, in full command of the *Shoora* and, while he listens to all very attentively, his decisions are the final word which all around him willingly accept. He is married and has one son.

He was declared *Amirul Momineen* at a congregation of around 1,500 mullahs in Kandahar in April 1996. All present took the oath of allegiance by kissing his hands. His followers are reported to have given him a Land Cruiser from the *maal-e-ghanimat* (war booty), since then he has moved about in his newly-acquired vehicle with tinted glass, followed by a stream of other cars.[192]

Many of the mullahs who on this occasion accepted Mullah Omar as the *Amir* had earlier given the same status to Rabbani when he held his *Shoora-Hal-o-Aqd* in Herat. Professor Sibghatullah Mojeddedi reacted angrily by saying, 'the nomination of Mullah Omar to such a high status is improper'.

Mullah Mohammad Rabbani

Rabbani, who is commonly known as *Moawin*, is a Pushtun of the Kakar tribe. He hails from the Pashmul area of Panjwai district of Kandahar. He is about thirty-eight years old. He has participated in a number of operations during the Red Army's occupation of Afghanistan. Later he joined

Commander Abdul Raziq of Hizb-e-Islami (Khalis group) and was appointed his Deputy Commander. He defected from the party when he found that they had deviated from their original aim of establishing peace in Afghanistan and were indulging in anti-social activities.

Those who have met him rate him as very intelligent and mature.

In spite of being the number two man in the Taliban *Shoora* and the head of the provisional government in Kabul, he leads a simple life, similar to that of the rest of the Taliban.

His decision to hang Dr Najibullah immediately after the Taliban captured Kabul drew adverse comments from several world capitals. He is alleged to have taken this step to avenge the killing of his brother by Dr Najibullah. His summary disposal of Najibullah was not appreciated by Omar; consequently Mullah Rabbani had to leave Afghanistan. He was, however, reinstated, and returned to become the senior member of the Taliban *Shoora*. He led the Taliban delegation to the Special Session of the Organization of Islamic Conference held in Islamabad in March 1997 which was attended by the Taliban as observers, as the Afghan seat had been left vacant.

Mullah Mohammad Hassan

Hassan is a Pushtun who comes from the village of Suzani in the Shahiwali Kot district of Kandahar. He was the sub-commander to Commander Mullah Haji Mohammad of Hizb-e-Islami (Khalis group). He was appointed Governor of Kandahar after it fell to the Taliban, and later became a member of the Central *Shoora* in Kabul. Like other Taliban leaders, he has no pretensions and follows the Islamic principle of equality in letter and spirit.

Mullah Mohammad Ghaus

Mullah Mohammad Ghaus is a Pushtun of the Noorani tribe. He hails from Oruzgan province. He was affiliated with Commander

Abdul Raziq of Hizb-e-Islami (Khalis group) during the Afghan jihad. He was injured during an encounter with the communists, due to which his eyesight was affected.

He had some formal education before he joined the Taliban movement, because of which he looks after the foreign affairs aspect of the Taliban administration. As Acting Foreign Minister he represented his government in talks with Pakistan and Iran and has travelled to the United States and several European countries.

Mullah Syed Ghayasuddin Agha

Ghayasuddin is a Persian-speaking Tajik from the northern province of Badakhshan. Though from the same area as Professor Rabbani, he decided to fight against him. He holds a post in the Central *Shoora* in Kabul.

Mullah Fazil Mohammad

Fazil was born in the central province of Uruzgan. Like most of the other Taliban leadership, he is a Pushtun. He is the Minister of Interior in the provisional *Shoora* in Kabul.

Mullah Abdul Razzaq

Razzaq was a member of the Hizb-e-Islami (Khalis) before defecting to the side of the Taliban. He was second-in-command to Mullah Borjan, the military commander of the Taliban.

Mullah Mohammad Akhunzada

Akhunzada is a Pushtun of the Barakzai tribe. He comes from the district of Arghandab in the province of Kandahar. He participated in the Afghan jihad under Akber Agha of the Hizb-e-Islami (Khalis). He was appointed as Commander 2 Corps in Kandahar.

A very bold person, he was injured in the fighting around Shindand.

Mullah Mohammad Abbas

Abbas is an Achakzai Pushtun from Tarin Kot of Oruzgan province. He was a subcommander of Mullah Rai Mohammad of Oruzgan. He was appointed as the Mayor of Kandahar.

General Abdul Rashid Dostum

Dostum was born in 1955 into a farmer's family. He left school at the age of fourteen to become an unskilled worker in a Soviet-built, state-owned gas company. He soon rose to become the leader of the labour union of the gas field.

He was the leader of an Uzbek militia which sided with the Soviet forces at the time of the Soviet invasion of Afghanistan. He commanded an armoured division in the Afghan army and took part in a number of campaigns against the mujahideen during the jihad. His defection in April 1992 brought about the downfall of Najibullah.

He commands a force of around 50,000 Uzbeks who are well armed, well trained, and organized on the lines of a regular army.[193] With a six-foot frame, he is stocky and well built, with a bullish countenance. Aggressive in his behaviour but liberal in his views, he allows women to study in the university and move around as they wish, with or without the veil. The shops in his domain are full of imported goods from Dubai. Local cinemas show Indian films, and Russian vodka and German beer are available.

He holds complete sway over the six northern provinces of Afghanistan, with a population of around five million. He is not as popular as is made out by his followers. Although every shop carries his photograph and every official building displays his portrait, behind the scenes he is being accused of corruption, nepotism, and leading a lifestyle far beyond what even the northern provinces could afford.

His area is believed to have gas deposits of around 100 billion cubic metres.

Though the majority of those who inhabit the area he controls are Uzbeks; Tajiks, Hazaras, and Pushtuns also live there. The Taliban have managed to infiltrate their ideas into his territory, which has weakened his power base somewhat.

Dostum rules over his domain as if it was an autonomous region. He has his own airline (Balkh Air) and his own currency. He visits foreign lands, signs treaties with them, and trades freely with the Central Asian Republics. He has thus been able to provide all the comforts of life. Because of his liberal views he is not willing to welcome the Taliban. His headquarters are at Mazar-e-Sharif, a city of around two million people.

Dostum entered into an anti-Taliban alliance with Masood and Khalili. The agreement was signed at Khinjan in the Hindu Kush mountains in October 1996. He is friendly with Russia and Uzbekistan and, as long as he can have maximum autonomy in the provinces he controls, he is not interested in who occupies Kabul.

Professor Burhanuddin Rabbani

Rabbani is a Tajik whose mother tongue is Dari. He was born in 1947 in Faizabad, the capital of the northern province of Badakhshan on the Afghan-Tajikistan border. He first studied in local schools in his area and later moved to Kabul, where he was enrolled in the Abu Hanifa Madrassa. In 1960 he joined the College of Theology at Kabul University. After graduating with honours he was appointed as a lecturer in the same institution. In 1966 he proceeded to Cairo for higher studies at Al Azhar, where he worked on his Ph.D. thesis on the life of Abdur Rahman Jami (the Afghan mystic poet). He founded the Jamiat-e-Islami Afghanistan in 1967 and was elected its leader in 1972.

To escape from the persecution of President Mohammad Daud he left for Pakistan in 1974. Four years later, from his base in Peshawar, he reorganized his party and turned it into an effective resistance group. His military commander was Ahmed Shah Masood, who reigned supreme in the Panjsher valley.

Jamiat was the only party which had offices both in Peshawar and in Iran. Rabbani has been advocating giving the Shias a role in the future government in Afghanistan and hence has had close relations with the clergy in Iran.

He took over as President of Afghanistan from Sibghatullah Mojeddedi in June 1992 for a two-year period, but failed to hand over power to an interim government after the expiry of his term in October 1994, because of which he fell foul of the government of Pakistan. When he was evicted from Kabul by the Taliban in September 1996, he formed an anti-Taliban alliance with Dostum and Hizb-e-Wahdat.

Ahmed Shah Masood

Masood was born in 1956, the son of an army officer. He is a Tajik from the Panjsher valley. A practising Muslim, he does not hold extremist religious views.

After his early education in a French school in Kabul, he went on to study engineering at a Russian-run polytechnic college in the capital but did not wait to get a degree. He chose politics instead, and began taking part in political activities against the government of President Mohammad Daud. Fearing persecution, he fled to Pakistan in 1973. Two years later he went back into Afghanistan and joined the resistance movement.

He returned to Pakistan in 1977 and spent some time studying guerrilla tactics employed by famous commanders. He went back to Panjsher in 1978 and since then has rarely visited Pakistan. His main complaint against the ISI was that they did not give him as much military hardware as was given to Hikmetyar—a grudge that he continues to bear and which has been heightened because he believes that the successes of the Taliban are due to the support they are receiving from Pakistan's premier security agency.

After his defeat at the hands of the Taliban he retreated to his hideout in the village of Jangalak (population 200) in the Panjsher valley, 100 kilometres north-east of Kabul, where he lives in a very modest mud-brick house built by his grandfather. There is a sizeable library in the house which contains about 3000 books.

His Shoora-e-Nazar militia, which during the Afghan jihad was the strongest force in Afghanistan, dwindled to around 7,000 after being pushed out of Kabul by the Taliban.

Masood has no love for Gulbadin Hikmetyar, against whom he has been engaged in occasional fighting, but later had no difficulty in breaking bread with him when both joined the anti-Taliban Supreme Council for the Defence of Afghanistan.

He is married and has four children.

Gulbadin Hikmetyar

Hikmetyar was born in 1947 in Imam Saheb in the northern province of Kunduz. He is a Kharuti Pushtun of the Gilzai Tribe. His parents came from a middle-class family from Ghazni but later moved to Kunduz, where they apparently settled. Hikmeytar received his early education in one of the local schools. Later he entered the Kabul military cadet school of Mahtabqila. While there he joined politics and was rusticated from the college for his anti-government activities. He went back to Kunduz and joined Shirkhan High School. After graduation he entered the Engineering College of Kabul University.

In 1968 Hikmetyar, along with ten other students, formed the Islamic movement then called the Muslim Youth Organization of Afghanistan. He was imprisoned in 1971 on charges of killing a communist student, Saidal, but was released in 1973. During the Daud Presidency, Hikmetyar went underground and spent about one year in the forests of Paktia.

He moved to Pakistan in 1974, from where he clandestinely organized a resistance movement against his country's pro-Soviet regime.

Haji Abdul Qadeer

Qadeer is a Gilzai Pushtun of the Ahmedzai tribe and hails from Jalalabad. He came to Pakistan in 1973, when Daud was courting the Soviets but went back to Nangarhar during the jihad against the Soviet occupation of his country. He took part in the ill-fated offensive on Jalalabad during the Najibullah regime.

After the fall of Najib he became the Governor of Nangarhar province, where he was able to form a *shoora* comprising eight Afghan factions, including almost all of those who had taken part in the jihad against the communists. During his four and a half year 'rule' he did succeed in maintaining a semblance of peace in the area under his control. He is not an extremist in his religious views and favours the education of girls. He claims to have opened a university in Jalalabad in which female students are also admitted.

Qadeer is in his late forties and has a pleasant personality. He can understand and speak both English and Urdu but is not very fluent in either of these languages. His lifestyle during his temporary residence in Peshawar is indicative of an assured source of income from his business deals.

He was deported from Pakistan for allegedly carrying out anti-Taliban activies from Pakistani soil.

Professor A. Rasul Amin

Professor Amin is the President of the Writers Union of Free Afghanistan (WUFA), an academic institution dedicated to producing papers on developments in Afghanistan.

Amin was born in 1948 in the northern province of Kunduz. At the age of eight he came to Pakistan and studied in the Islamia College in Peshawar, from where he obtained his masters degree in political science. He went back to Afghanistan in 1966 but, in 1980, after the entry of the Soviet troops, he moved to Peshawar, where he began working with Syed Bahauddin Majrooh as the chairman of the Refugee Department.

He established the WUFA in 1985 and continues to be its President. He led a delegation to Afghanistan in 1996 and met the Taliban leaders. Later he travelled to Mazar-e-Sharif and discussed the situation in Afghanistan with Abdul Rashid Dostum.

He maintains that the problem of Afghanistan has become complicated because of outside interference. He does not believe that the Taliban have the expertise or the wisdom to run a modern state. He is also not in favour of the Tanzeemat leaders, who have been quarrelling amongst themselves. He is more inclined towards the return of Zahir Shah, who he feels is still popular in Afghanistan. He wants the militia to be replaced by a UN peace-keeping force.

General Abdul Malik
(Chief of Jumbish-e-Milli)

Malik, an ethnic Uzbek, started to drift away from Dostum when his elder brother Rasool Pehalwan was assassinated in 1996, most probably at Dostum's instigation. Differences between Malik's family and Dostum multiplied when a pro-Malik commander was also murdered on 15 May 1997. Fearing a similar fate, Gen.

Malik staged a *coup* on 19 May 1997 and joined hands with the Taliban. This proved instrumental in the defeat of Dostum, who fled to Turkey on 24 May 1997. He was named as Deputy Foreign Minister by Taliban leadership. However, due to intriguing by Hizb-e-Wahdat and a dispute over disarming, Gen. Malik turned against the Taliban and forced them to vacate the north, including Mazar-e-Sharif, on 28 May 1997. He promptly joined hands with anti-Taliban forces, i.e., Hizb-e-Wahdat and Shoora-e-Nazar, and became part of the anti-Taliban alliance. However, with the arrival of Dostum in the north on 11 September 1997, Malik's position has again weakened and he has reportedly fled to Iran to find refuge.

Abdul Karim Khalili
(Hizb-e-Wahdat Khalili)

Khalili was a close associate of Mazari and, after the latter's death, assumed leadership of Hizb-e-Wahdat (Mazari). He has also acted as a minister when Hizb-e-Wahdat was part of the Rabbani government. Later Hizb-e-Wahdat (Mazari) joined the Shoora-e-Ham-Ahangi against Rabbani's regime. He took over the party when Mazari was killed while attempting to escape from the Taliban's custody and his party was expelled from Kabul (Karata Seh). Badly beaten in March 1995 by Ahmed Shah Masood, he reorganized his party, overcame Hizb-e-Wahdat (Mazari), and took control of the whole of Bamian province. After the fall of Kabul to the Taliban he joined the anti-Taliban alliance on 10 October 1996. His party is still in control of Bamian province. He is allegedly being massively supported by the Iranian authorities.

Osama Bin Laden

Osama Bin Muhammad Bin Awad Bin Laden was born in

1955. His father Sheikh Mohammad Bin Laden came from Yemen and had migrated to Saudi Arabia. Osama was one of over four dozen children his father had from four of his wives. Osama's mother was a Syrian. Sheikh Mohammad owned the largest construction company in the Kingdom which helped him to become a billionaire many times over.

Osama's father died in a helicopter crash in 1968. Osama inherited $80 million at the age of thirteen. He, however, continued his studies and graduated as a civil engineer from King Abdul Aziz University at Jeddah in 1979.

When the Soviets invaded Afghanistan, Osama decided to support the Afghan Jihad. He came to Peshawar in 1984 and initially confined his activities to raising funds for the Afghan Mujahideen. Later he also took part in the fighting against the occupying forces. When the Soviets withdrew their military contingents from Afghanistan, Osama returned to Saudi Arabia. He became disillusioned with the Saudi Royalty whom he believed had become corrupt. He also did not approve of the presence of US troops in Saudi Arabia. When he was expelled from Saudi Arabia in 1991 and stripped of his Saudi nationality he moved to Sudan where he stayed for five years. While in Sudan he is alleged to have given millions of dollars to various militant organization who were fighting against the United States. He reportedly supports an organization called *Al Qaida*. In May 1996 the Sudanese government asked him to leave Sudan. He then moved to Afghanistan where he is reportedly supporting the Taliban with money.

Osama is tall, slim and soft spoken. He has four wives and ten children and has become Mulla Omar's father in law as his daughter is married to him.

APPENDIX II
The Peshawar Accord

بسم الله الرحمن الرحيم

الحمد لله والصلاة والسلام على سيدنا رسول الله وعلى آله وأصحابه ومن يتبعه

بعدى ... أمّا بعد

د افغانستان د اسلامي دولت د موقت د دربار د تشکيل په باره

لاندى په دې لاندى حجره کښې شوه

– لومړۍ دسره، چه د حضرت مجتنی الله المهدي د برمشرۍ لاندى
دى يو پنځوس کسيزه هیئت داخل افغانستان ته ولاړ شي
ترڅو د دولت مشرتابه د مودني دکامل د مسؤولیت واکداري د نوې
قدرت په پوره ډول پیدا او د رسره ترلاسه کړي. دغه هیئت مشر
به د هیئت د دولت د سترگو دیپلماسي تشکیل کړي هم د دې
دغه هیئت که د دنۍ مودنی ته د ریاسته د عبوري دولت ترتيب
د اسلامي مشورې په حیث پاتې کیدو ته د ریاسته مه د محافظت ته
په اغاز د دغه شورې مودنه بحم خلور میاشتو دي

۱ – لومړی: دسره هم استاد ربانی دی د خلورو میاشتو د باره
د افغانستان د اسلامي موقت دولت د رئیس او د هغه
د شورای د مشر حیث د دې ته جبل کار رسماً د ملت شریک
کوي که د قدرت د استقلال د درو میاشتو پوره شورای دی

۲ – دا پوره ته تعیین شوی موده د کباره د څلور هم د میدرجومی

[signatures]

٤ ــ د صدارت مقام او دکابینی دورعربي به د تنظیم ومشرالو ؟

ـم د دعوتیلو دبهم دم غزرو قوت تا لپ لپری

٥ ــ د صدارت ستام د افغانستان اسلامي حرب ته درکریپر

٦ ــ د صدارت معاونیت او داخلو وزارت دافغانستان اسلام اباد ؟

٧ ــ د صدارت معاونیت او د معارف وزارت دداس هب حاله

٨ ــ د صدارت معاونیت او خارجو د وزارت دمعا د ملی اسلام

درکریپند

٩ ــ د دفاع وزارت د افغانستان اسلامي جمعیت ته

١٠ ــ ستره مکر د حرکت الثوره اسلامي تنظیم ته

او دابریکمته هم رشو و هه شورای رهرک به علاوه مرتبه

ارتیبات دوړو وراړتو د حرب رهرت ارشورای است

ادموله هت مصور او سره روسو دارد وراړه تقنیه

ددی ته لی پروش حریس میاشت دسم ارلای ترخ کس

انتبا حکر مته دناره اسلامي متفق پیلو شورو دییم سیس دهم

به درپ کاورو

صوم الحریب

حسان

سروای محرسته لرم

The Peshawar Accord

(Official Translation of Originial Dari Text)

Salutation and peace be upon the Great Messenger of Allah and his Progeny and Companions. And after that:

The structure and process for the provisional period of the Islamic State of Afghanistan, was formed as under:

1. It was decided that a 51 persons body, headed by Hazrat Sahib Sibghatullah Mojeddedi, would go inside Afghanistan so that they could take over power from the present rulers of Kabul, completely and without any terms and conditions during the two months period. The head of this body will also represent the Presidentship of the State during these two months. After this period, this body will remain as an Interim Islamic Council, along with the Transitional State and its Chairmanship will be held by Hazrat Sahib. The period of this Council, will also be for four (4) months.

2. It was decided that Professor Rabbani will remain as the President of the Transitional Islamic State of Afghanistan and the head of the Leadership Council for four (4) months. He will commence his work officially at the time when the two months of the transfer of power will have elapsed.

3. The above mentioned period will not be extended even by a day.

4. The Prime Minister and other members of the Cabinet will be appointed from the second grade members of the Tanzeemat, at the discretion of the heads of the Tanzeemat.

5. The Prime Ministership was assigned to the Hizb-e-Islami, Afghanistan.

6. The Deputy Prime Ministership and the Ministry of Interior, to Ittehad-e-Islami, Afghanistan.

7. The Deputy Prime Ministership and the Ministry of Education, to Hizb-e-Islami of Maulvi Khalis.

8. The Prime Ministership and Ministry of Foreign Affairs, were assigned to the National Islamic Front.

9. The Ministry of Defence to Jamiat-e-Islami, Afghanistan.

10. The Supreme Court to Harkat-e-Inqilab-e-Islami Organization.

11. It was also decided that the Leadership Council, in addition to making the division of appointments in the Ministries, will also determine Ministries for Hizb-e-Wahdat, Shoora-e-Etelaf (Council of Coalition) Maulvi Mansoor and other brothers.

12. The total period of this process will be six months. As regards the Transitional Government, the Islamic Council will make a unanimous decision. The period of this Transitional Government will be two (2) years.

APPENDIX III

The Islamabad Declaration

<u>AFGHAN PEACE ACCORD</u>

<u>Given</u> our submission to the will of Allah Almighty and commitment to seeking guidance from the Holy Quran and Sunnah;

<u>Recalling</u> the glorious success of the epic Jehad waged by the valiant Afghan people against foreign occupation;

<u>Desirous</u> of ensuring that the fruits of this glorious Jehad bring peace, progress and prosperity for the Afghan people;

<u>Having agreed</u> to bringing armed hostilities to an end;

<u>Recognising</u> the need for a broad-based Islamic government in which all parties and groups representing all segments of Muslim Afghan society are represented so that the process of political transition can be advanced in an atmosphere of peace, harmony and stability;

<u>Committed</u> to the preservation of unity, sovereignty and territorial integrity of Afghanistan;

<u>Recognising</u> the urgency of rehabilitation and reconstruction of Afghanistan and of facilitating the

return of all Afghan refugees;

Committed to promoting peace and security in the
region;

Responding to the call of Khadim Al-Harmain Al-
Sharifain His Majesty King Fahd Bin Abdul Aziz to resolve
the differences among Afghan brothers through a peaceful
dialogue;

Appreciating the constructive role of good offices
of Mr. Muhammad Nawaz Sharif, Prime Minister of Islamic
Republic of Pakistan and his sincere efforts to promote
peace and conciliation in Afghanistan;

Recognising the positive support for these efforts
extended by the governments of the Kingdom of Saudi
Arabia and the Islamic Republic of Iran who have sent
their Special Envoys for the conciliation talks in
Islamabad;

Having undertaken intensive intra-Afghan
consultations separately and jointly to consolidate the
gains of the glorious Jehad;

All the Parties and Groups concerned have agreed as
follows:

    i)   Formation of a Government for a period of 18
           months in which President Burhanuddin Rabbani

would remain President and Eng. Gulbadin
Hikmatyar or his nominee would assume the
office of Prime Minister. The powers of the
President and Prime Minister and his Cabinet
which have been formulated through mutual
consultations will form part of this Accord
and is annexed;

ii) The Cabinet shall be formed by the Prime
Minister in consultations with the President,
and leaders of Mujahideen Parties within two
weeks of the signing of this Accord.

iii) The following electoral process is agreed for
implementation in a period of not more than 18
months with effect from December 29, 1992:

a) The immediate formation of an independent
Election Commission by all parties with
full powers;

b) The Election Commission shall be mandated
to hold elections for a Grand Constituent
Assembly within 8 months from the date of
signature of this Accord;

c) The duly elected Grand Constituent
Assembly shall formulate a Constitution
under which general elections for the
President and the Parliament shall be

held within the prescribed period of 18
months mentioned above.

iv) A Defence Council comprising two members from
     each party will be set up to, inter alia,

     a)   enable the formation of a national Army;

     b)   take possession of heavy weapons from all
          parties and sources which may be removed
          from Kabul and other cities and kept out
          of range to ensure the security of the
          Capital;

     c)   ensure that all roads in Afghanistan are
          kept open for normal use.

     d)   ensure that State funds shall not be used
          to finance private armies or armed
          retainers.

     e)   ensure that operational control of the
          armed forces shall be with the Defence
          Council.

v)   There shall be immediate and unconditional
     release of all Afghan detainees held by the
     Government and different parties during the
     armed hostilities.

vi) All public and private buildings, residential
     areas and properties occupied by different
     armed groups during the hostilities shall be
     returned to their original owners. Effective
     steps shall be taken to facilitate the return
     of displaced persons to their respective homes
     and locations.

vii) An All Party Committee shall be constituted to
     supervise control over the monetary system and
     currency regulations to keep it in conformity
     with existing Afghan banking laws and
     regulations.

viii) A ceasefire shall come into force with
     immediate effect. After the formation of the
     Cabinet, there shall be permanent cessation of
     hostilities.

xi) A Joint Commission comprising representatives
     of the OIC and of all Afghan Parties shall be
     formed to monitor the ceasefire and cessation
     of hostilities.

In confirmation of the above accord, the following
have affixed their signatures hereunder, on Sunday the 7
March 1993 in Islamabad, Pakistan.

Prof. Burhan-ud-Din Rabbani
Jamiat-e-Islami
President of the
Islamic State of Afghanistan

Engr Gulbadin Hikmatyar
Hizb-e-Islami

*with my reservation
to the president time.*

**Prof. Sibghatullah
Mujjadidi**
Jabha-e-Nijat-e-Milli

Moulvi Muhammad Nabi Muhammadi
Harkat-e-Inqilab-e-Islami

*with my reservation to the
president time I sighen it.*

**Engineer Ahmed Shah
Ahmadzai**
Ittehad-e-Islami

Pir Syed Ahmed Gaillani
Mahaz-e-Milli

Sheikh Asif Mohseni
Harkat-e-Islami

Ayatullah Fazil
Hizb-e-Wahdat-e-Islami

DIVISION OF POWERS

PREAMBLE

The President of the Islamic State of Afghanistan is the Head of the State and symbol of unity and solidarity of the country and shall guide the affairs of the state in accordance with Islamic laws and the principles laid down in the Holy Quran and Sunnah.

I.   The Prime Minister shall form the Cabinet in consultation with the President and present the same to the President who shall formally announce the Cabinet and take its oath. The Cabinet shall operate as a team under the leadership of the Prime Minister and shall work on the principle of collective responsibility.

II.   The Prime Minister and the Cabinet shall regularly act in close consultation with the President on all important issues.

III. The President and the Prime Minister shall act in consultation with each other and shall try to resolve differences, if any, through mutual discussion. In case any issue remains unresolved it should be decided by a reference to a joint meeting of the President and the Cabinet.

IV.   All major policy decisions shall be made in the Cabinet, to be presided over by the Prime Minister. Ministers, Deputy Ministers and Ministers of State would be individually and collectively responsible for the decisions of the government.

The formal appointment of the Chiefs of the Armed Forces shall be made in accordance with the existing practice and after mutual consultation.

POWERS OF THE PRESIDENT

V.   The President shall have the following powers and duties:
a)   Appointment of the Vice-President of Islamic State of Afghanistan.

b)   Appointment and retirement of judges of the Supreme Court, the Chief Justices, in consultation with the Prime Minister and in accordance with the provisions of the laws.

c)   Supreme Command of the Armed Forces of the country in the light of the Objectives and structure of the Armed Forces of Afghanistan.

d)   Declaring war and peace on the advice of the Cabinet or the Parliament.

e)   Convening and inaugurating the Parliament according to Rules.

f)   Consolidating national unity and upholding the independence, neutrality and the Islamic character of Afghanistan and the interests of all its citizens.

g)   Commuting and pardoning of sentences according to the Shariah and the provisions of law.

h)   Accrediting heads of Afghanistan's diplomatic missions in foreign states, appointing Afghanistan's permanent representatives to international organizations according to the normal diplomatic procedures and accepting the letters   of   credence   of   foreign   diplomatic representatives.

i)   Signing laws and ordinances, and granting credentials for the conclusion and signing of international treaties in accordance with the provisions of the law.

j)   The President may at his discretion, delegate any of his powers to the Vice President, or to the Prime Minister.

k)   In the event of the death or resignation of the President, the presidential functions shall be automatically entrusted to the Vice President, who shall deputize till the new President is elected under the Constitution.

l)   Granting formal permission to print money.

m)   The President may call an extraordinary meeting of the Cabinet on issues of vital national significance which do not fall in the routine governance of the country.

POWERS OF THE PRIME MINISTER

VI.   The Prime Minister and his Cabinet shall have the following duties and powers:

a)   Formulation and implementation of the country's domestic and foreign policies in accordance with the provisions and spirit of this Accord and the provisions of law.

b)   Administering, coordinating and supervising the affairs of the ministries, and other departments and public bodies and institutions.

c)   Rendering executive and administrative decisions in
     accordance with laws and supervising their
     implementation.

d)   Drafting of laws and formulating rules and regulations.

e)   Preparing and controlling the state budget and adopting
     measures to mobilise resources to reconstruct the economy
     and establish a viable and stable monetary, financial and
     fiscal system.

f)   Drafting and supervising implementation of the socio-
     economic and educational plans of the country with a view
     to establishing a self-reliant Islamic welfare state.

g)   Protecting and promoting the objectives and interests of
     Afghanistan in the world community and discussing and
     negotiating foreign treaties, protocols, international
     agreements and financial arrangements.

h)   Adopting measures to ensure public order, peace, security
     and Islamic morality and to ensure administration of
     justice through an independent and impartial judiciary.

In confirmation of the above Accord, the following have affixed their signatures hereunder, on Sunday the 7 March 1993 in Islamabad, Pakistan.

Prof. Burhan-ud-Din Rabbani
Jamiat-e-Islami
President of the
Islamic State of Afghanistan

Engr Gulbadin Hikmatyar
Hizb-e-Islami

With my reservation about the President time

ulvi Muhammad Nabi Muhammadi
arkat-e-Inqilab-e-Islami

Prof. Sibghatullah Mujjadidi
Jabha-e-Nijat-e-Milli

Pir Syed Ahmed Gailani
Mahaz-e-Milli

Engineer Ahmed Shah Ahmadzai
Ittehad-e-Islami

Sheikh Asif Mohseni
arkat-e-Islami

Ayatullah Fazil
Hizb-e-Wahdat-e-Islami

APPENDIX IV

Text of the Agreement on Narcotics Control

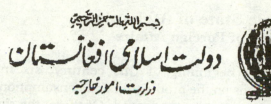

بسم الله الرحمن الرحیم

دولت اسلامی افغانستان

وزارت امور خارجیه

ISLAMIC STATE OF AFGHANISTAN
MINISTRY OF FOREIGN AFFAIRS

— ۱ —

جهانیه از شروع قرن حاضر تا کنون (۶) کنوانسیون عمده بین المللی درباره منسع
تولید مواد مخدر و اعتیاد به ان درسطح جهانی منعقد شده است که اتفاق کنوانسیون
بین المللی علیه تجارت غیر قانونی مواد مخدر و سایکو ترابیک (ویانا ۱۹۸۸) بمنظور
یک زمینه محسوب میشود . این کنوانسیون که افغانستان از امضا کنندگان ان بود
وسایل و ایکانات جدید به و بازار روا فزون اجهادکنترول موثر مبارزه با ترافیک غیرقانونی
مواد مخدره را فراهم نموده است .

مردم مسلمان افغانستان مخالف تولید و ترافیک مواد مخدر میباشند . حتی درجامعه
ما با وجود ید استمرار به صدمات و رسوم یمند به مردم و ارزشهای دین مبین اسلام
استفاده از مواد مخدر را به عمل زشت و قبیح تشبیه میکرده .

مبارزه برعلیه مواد مخدر با اعتیاد به مواد مخدر که هستی انسان و جامعه را تهدید
مینماید درسرحای توجه دولت اسلامی افغانستان قرار داشته و دریک اقدام کامل با روحیه
و مقررات منشور سازمان ملل متحد تد ابیر لازمه را جهت تحمیل همه کنوانسیونهای بمناسبا
اهمیت اداره مبارزه با مواد مخدر سازمان ملل متحد اتخاذ نمایند .

دولت دوباره اسلامی افغانستان را عقیده و خواست مبارزه موثر و عدلفند علیه تولید
بیوسید ترافیک مواد مخدر رسماً درنتیجه همکاری منطقوی و بین المللی
امکان پذیر میباشد . البته بر نسبیب ها و موازین حقوق بین الدول ام از برحسب عدم
مداخله در امور داخلی کشورها و جلوگیری استفاده از میثاله ترافیان مواد مخدر
جهت اهداف سیاسی و ستراتیژیک باید جداً مراعات کردد

وزارت امور خارجه یه ۱۰ افغانستان با اغتنام از فرصت به تجدید احترامات فایقه میپردازد .

Text of the Agreement on Narcotics Control

(Unofficial Translation of the Dari Text)

Islamic State of Afghanistan
Ministry of Foreign Affairs

Since the beginning of this century, six international conventions on the production and consumption of narcotic substances have been adopted. Of these, the signing of the international convention on the illegal trafficking of narcotics and psychotropic substances (1988, Vienna) is considered the most important achievement.

This convention, to which Afghanistan was the first signatory provides for valuable means and ways for the establishment of an effective system for the struggle against illegal trafficking.

Afghanistan's Muslim people are against production and trafficking of narcotics. Even in our society due to the existence and respect for our revered values and traditions and Islamic principles, abuse of narcotic substances is considered repugnant and an evil deed.

Struggle against the abuse of narcotics, which threatens the existence of man and society, forms the focal point of the Islamic Government of Afghanistan, and with the full compliance of the United Nations Charter, it will take the necessary measures for the implementation of the UNDCP conventions.

The newly established Islamic government of Afghanistan is of the opinion that an effective and purposeful struggle against the production, processing and trafficking of narcotic substances is only possible through concerted regional and international cooperation. Of course, principles and provisions of international law including the principle of non-interference in the internal affairs of states, rejection and use of narcotics trafficking for political or strategic purposes, should be observed.

The Ministry of Foreign Affairs of the Islamic Government of Afghanistan avails itself of the opportunity to extend its highest considerations.

APPENDIX V

This is an extract from the Report of the UN Secretary-General on the Situation in Afghanistan and its Implications for International Peace dated 14 November 1997.

Observations and Conclusions

36. Afghanistan, which was once a flashpoint of super-Power rivalry, has since become a typical post-cold war regional and ethnic conflict, where the major Powers no longer see a strategic incentive to get involved. It has also become a place where even responsible local political authorities, let alone a central government, have virtually ceased to exist. Herein lies much of the explanation why repeated international attempts to bring peace to the country have not borne fruit.

37. Since the early 1990s, the Afghan factions and warlords have failed to show the will to rise above their narrow factional interests and to start working together for national reconciliation. The United Nations successfully mediated the withdrawal of foreign forces from Afghanistan in the late 1980s. But, although the Najibullah regime was ready to hand over power to a broad-based transition mechanism, the Mujahideen parties were unable to agree among themselves on how to form such a mechanism. Their disagreements escalated to the point where Kabul was plunged into chaos and bloodshed once the Najibullah regime collapsed in April 1992. Since that time, the situation has only become worse.

38. Even today, the Afghan parties seem determined to go on fighting, while outside Powers continue to provide material, financial and other support to their respective clients inside Afghanistan. Meanwhile, although those major Powers that have potential influence in Afghanistan have recently started to show interest, they have yet to demonstrate the necessary degree of determination to move the situation forward.

39. In these circumstances, it is illusory to think that peace can be achieved. How can peace be imposed on faction leaders who are determined to fight it out to the finish and who receive seemingly unlimited supplies of arms from outside sponsors? It is this continued support from some outside Powers—combined with the apathy of the others who are not directly involved—which has strengthened the belief among the warlords and parties in Afghanistan that they can achieve their political, religious and social goals by force.

Responsibility of the Afghans

40. The Afghans, perhaps, understandably, are reluctant to accept responsibility for the repeated failures to put an end to their conflict. Nevertheless, the Afghan people cannot just simply shift all responsibilities for the tragedy that has befallen their country onto others. Even if they receive help from outside, it is the Afghans themselves who are fighting one another. Peace will become possible when—and only when—they truly desire it and start to work seriously for it.

41. Much to my regret, the Afghan factions have so far failed to prove that they are willing to lay down their arms, and cooperate with the United Nations for peace. To be sure, every side proclaims its readiness to work with the United Nations and accuses the other party or parties of bearing alone the responsibility for the continued fighting.

However, at any given time there has always been at least one party that has thought it could achieve military victory over its opponents and that, consequently, has rebuffed efforts to negotiate a cease-fire and only shown a willingness to compromise once the military situation has been reversed and it feels under threat. At the same time, there always exist spoilers inside and outside the country who are much better off with the continuation of the problem than they would be with the solution, a classic situation in failed States where warlords, smugglers, terrorists, drug dealers and others thrive amid the conflict and would only lose out with the return of peace, law and order.

Foreign interference

42. A similar situation prevails with the main foreign providers of support to the Afghan warring parties. They all enthusiastically proclaim their support to the United Nations peacemaking efforts but at the same time continue to fan the conflict by pouring in arms, money and other supplies to their preferred Afghan factions. These countries unanimously denounce 'foreign interference', but are quick to add that arms are delivered only to 'the other side'.

43. These external players may have their own reasons for continuing to support their respective Afghan clients, but they must be held responsible for exacerbating the bloody conflict in Afghanistan. They must also be held accountable for building a fire which, they should be aware, is unlikely to remain indefinitely confined to Afghanistan. Indeed, that fire is already spreading beyond the borders of Afghanistan, posing a serious threat to the region and beyond in the shape of terrorism, banditry, narcotics trafficking, refugee flows, and increasing ethnic and sectarian tension.

44. The supply of arms and other materials from outside provides the essential wherewithal for the continued fighting in Afghanistan. It is apparent, in the light of the evidence

collected so far, that large quantities of war-making materials are entering Afghanistan. It is hard to accept the argument that the Afghan warring factions are able to sustain the current level of fighting using only 'those weapons and ammunition left by the Soviet troops'. Neither is it credible that, with their limited financial capacity, those Afghan factions could afford to procure massive amounts of weapons on the black market and smuggle them into Afghanistan on their own.

International framework for settlement of the conflict

45. The unabated supply of arms, and the divergence of ways in which the countries concerned seem to be dealing with the conflict, lead me to believe that a solid international framework must be established in order to address the external aspects of the Afghan question. Such a framework would provide the neighbours of Afghanistan and other countries with an opportunity to discuss the question of foreign interference in a coherent manner. The main objective would be to debate how those countries could help the United Nations bring the Afghan parties to the negotiating table, including effective and fair ways to curb the flow of arms and other war-making materials into Afghanistan. Such countries should also find a way to speak unanimously by coordinating their individual peace initiatives through the United Nations. Only in this way would they send a message to the Afghans that the international community meant to achieve peace in Afghanistan and that the warring factions could no longer count on outside support.

46. One of the ways to curb the flow of arms into Afghanistan would be the imposition of an effective arms embargo. Although such an embargo should not become an end in itself, it is necessary for the United Nations and Member States to undertake preliminary studies on how a mandatory arms embargo could be implemented in a fair and

verifiable manner. If the cost estimates for such an embargo proved to be too high, other ways would need to be found to end, or at least significantly reduce, the supply of arms and other materials to the warring factions. One possibility would be for the countries concerned to take voluntary, unilateral but concerted actions by themselves to stop, to the degree possible, the supply of a designated list of goods to Afghanistan. This, of course, would also need to be done in a manner that did not provide advantage to any group.

47. The meetings held in New York of countries with influence in Afghanistan ('the Group of 21'), as well as those of the immediate neighbours and other counties ('the Group of Eight'), are part of my efforts in this direction. With the participation of my Special Envoy, I shall continue to convene informal meetings involving representatives of the neighbours of Afghanistan and other countries with influence in Afghanistan. The composition and the number of such groupings will remain flexible.

48. Furthermore, I am looking forward to attending the OIC summit, which will be held in Tehran from 9 to 11 December. I very much hope that OIC and its members will use this opportunity to adopt unanimously a strong decision in favour of peace in Afghanistan.

Intra-Afghan talks

49. Parallel to this, I intend to maintain through UNSMA and at United Nations Headquarters close contact with the warring parties, as well as with other influential Afghan individuals and organizations, with a view to preparing the ground for an intra-Afghan dialogue. Such a dialogue, if realized, should focus at first on a cease-fire, to be followed by political negotiations leading to the establishment of a broad-based representative government. It goes without saying that, for such a government to be acceptable, it should reflect the interests of all the major social, political and religious segments

of the country, I take note in this context that several Member States have offered to host such a dialogue.

50. It is hoped that a ceasefire and the beginning of a dialogue—or even the mere prospects for one—would serve to create its own momentum and, after some time, make it difficult for anyone to resume fighting. It is also hoped that the ceasefire and talks would give a boost to the efforts of some Afghan groups and individuals to mobilize Afghan public opinion in favour of peace.

Activities of UNSMA

51. UNSMA will continue to play the primary role in conducting the United Nations peacemaking activities in Afghanistan. I believe that the current structure, composition and strength of UNSMA should be maintained for the time being. This does not exclude the possibility that, should a cease-fire and other measures be agreed, additional personnel might be required. Nor does it prejudge the issue referred to in paragraph 56 below.

52. The Special Mission will maintain its temporary headquarters in Islamabad, until conditions permit it to return to Kabul. Meanwhile, I intend to explore the possible opening of a small office in Turkmenistan in order to enhance the Special Mission's information-gathering and liaison capabilities, especially with those parties for whom the location of the Mission's temporary headquarters in Islamabad presents difficulties.

Conclusions

53. As described in the preceding sections of the present report, a peaceful settlement in Afghanistan remains elusive notwithstanding the untiring efforts of the United Nations to broker peace among the country's warring factions. In the meantime, Afghanistan's civil war has continued to exact a

staggering toll in terms of human lives and suffering as well as material destruction. What we are witnessing is a seemingly endless tragedy of epic proportions in which the Afghan people's yearning for peace is being systematically and continually betrayed by leaders and warlords driven by selfish ambitions and thirst for power.

54. In earlier reports I have observed that the Afghan parties and their external supporters, while continuing to pursue military solutions, often also profess support for resolutions of the General Assembly and the Security Council calling for a peaceful settlement. Regrettably, their actions seldom seem to be motivated, however, by a desire to contribute to the implementation of those resolutions. Similarly, it is discouraging that with few exceptions, the international community as a whole has shown only limited interest in adopting tangible measures to discourage the Afghan parties and their outside supporters from pursuing their bellicose aims and objectives.

55. There is no doubt that a number of Governments both inside and outside the region would be in a favourable position, should they so decide, to encourage the Afghan parties to overcome their differences and seek a peaceful settlement. It is also clear, however, that as long as those Governments choose not to exercise their influence with the parties in a positive and constructive manner, the efforts made by my representatives, however dedicated and skilled, will not suffice to bring peace to Afghanistan. Sadly, it could be argued that in these circumstances the role of the United Nations in Afghanistan is little more than that of an alibi to provide cover for the inaction—or worse—of the international community at large.

56. Over the past several years, it has become increasingly difficult to justify the continuation of United Nations peace efforts and the attendant costs in the absence of any positive signs suggesting a fundamental change of attitude on the part of those Governments that are capable of contributing

decisively to a peaceful solution of the conflict. Recently, I have been somewhat encouraged, however, by the increased level of attention to the situation in Afghanistan now being manifested by a number of countries that have begun to discuss among themselves the adoption of practical measures to persuade the Afghan parties to embark on serious negotiations. But much more needs to be done by Governments with a greater sense of unity in order for the peace efforts spearheaded by the United Nations to stand a realistic chance of success.

57. I shall continue to keep the General Assembly and the Security Council informed about developments relevant to the search for a cease-fire and, ultimately, a negotiated solution in Afghanistan, including any actions taken by Member States with a bearing on the situation, whether positive or negative. In conclusion, I should like to express my special thanks to Mr. Lakhdar Brahimi, whose findings and suggestions form the basis for the present report, as well as to Mr. Norbert Holl, the Head of UNSMA, and his staff who continue to carry out their difficult tasks with the highest degree of dedication and professionalism.

APPENDIX VI

Chronology of Events

September 1994: Taliban capture arms and ammunition depot belonging to Hizb-e-Islami (H) at Spin Boldak, close to the Pakistani town of Chaman.

Late October 1994: Fighting between Rabbani's forces and Hikmetyar's Hizb-e-Islami intensifies, resulting in heavy casualties to both sides and untold miseries to the civilian population.

2 November 1994: Pakistani convoy heading for Central Asia is stopped by the local warlords near Kandahar. The Taliban have the convoy released and succeed in removing all the barriers between Chaman and Kandahar.

5 November 1994: Control of Kandahar city passes into the hands of the Taliban after three days of fighting.

December 1994: Provinces of Helmand and Zabul occupied by the Taliban.

14 January 1995: Charles Santos, member of the United Nations Special Mission to Afghanistan meets the Taliban leaders and discusses the prevailing situation in the light of the advances made by the Taliban.

20 January 1995: The Taliban overrun Ghazni, 145 kilometres south of Kabul.

21 January 1995: Hikmetyar launches an unsuccessful counter-attack on Ghazni. Rabbani/Masood support the Taliban to repel Hikmetyar's counter-attack on Ghazni.

31 January 1995: Taliban seize the eastern provinces of Paktia and Paktika on the borders of Pakistan.

10 February 1995: Taliban overrun the town of Maidan Sheher, thirty kilometres from Kabul, previously occupied by Hikmetyar's men.

11 February 1995: Taliban enter the province of Logar.

14 February 1995: Hikmetyar's headquarters at Charasyab, twenty-five kilometres from Kabul, falls to the Taliban along with plenty of arms and ammunition. Hikmetyar flees to Sarobi.

15 February 1995: Khost, on the Pakistan border, occupied by the Taliban.

6 March 1995: Rabbani/ Masood's forces attack the Hizb-e-Wahdat (Shia faction) occupying the southern portion of the capital. They go over to the Taliban, giving them a foothold in Kabul.

13 March 1995: Abdul Ali Mazari, leader of the Hizb-e Wahdat, who had been captured by the Taliban, killed while trying to escape.

28 March 1995: Shindand airbase captured by the Taliban.

April 1995: Unsuccessful attempt by the Taliban to capture Herat.

6 August 1995: A Russian cargo plane belonging to Tataristan forced to land in Kandahar by the Taliban. The plane was allegedly carrying arms and ammunition.

5 September 1995: Herat falls to the Taliban. Rabbani's Governor in Herat, General Mohammad Ismail Khan, flees to Iran.

6 September 1995: Pakistan's Embassy in Kabul ransacked by Masood's men in retaliation for the capture of Herat by the Taliban, who Rabbani and Masood felt did so with the direct help of the Pakistan army.

11 September 1995: Taliban enter Jalalabad.

May 1996: Mahmoud Mestiri, head of the UN Special Mission to Afghanistan, resigns for health reasons.

7 July 1996: UN Secretary-General appoints Norbert Heinrich Holl, former German Foreign Minister, as head of the UN Special Mission to Afghanistan.

27 September 1996: Taliban enter Kabul.

27 September 1996: Dr Najibullah, former President of Afghanistan, his younger brother, Shapur Ahmedzai, and their bodyguard Jansheer, who had all taken refuge in the United Nations Compound in 1992, are executed by the Taliban and their bodies hung in the Ariana Square.

28 September 1996: Taliban move beyond Kabul and capture Charikar, the capital of the province of Parwan, sixty-five kilometres north of the capital.

30 September 1996: Taliban exploit their success: surge forward behind the retreating militia and reach Gulbahar, Jabal-us-Siraj, and Charikar at the mouth of the Panjsher valley, and the Salang Tunnel. They come in direct contact with Abdul Rashid Dostum's Jozjani militia.

30 September 1996: Bodies of Dr Najibullah, his brother, and the bodyguard are handed over to the Ahmedzai tribe in Kabul for burial.

3 October 1996: Taliban move into the north-eastern province of Laghman.

4 October 1996: Member countries of the Council of Independent States (CIS) meet at Almaty (Kazakhstan) to co-ordinate their response to the growing strength of the Taliban.

22 October 1996: United Nations Security Council meeting on developments in Afghanistan after the fall of Kabul to the Taliban, at the request of the Russians.

29 October 1996: Iran convenes a conference of all Afghan factions to try and reconcile the differences between them. Russia and India also participate. The Taliban and Pakistan stay away.

October 1996: Taliban are pushed back to the outskirts of Kabul by the combined forces of Dostum and Masood.

January 1997: Bagram airport recaptured by the Taliban

January 1997: Taliban launch another offensive and retake all territories lost to Dostum and Masood. Once again they pose a threat to Masood in Panjsher and Dostum in the north.

February 1997: Clashes in Kunarh between the Taliban and the local timber smugglers.

26 February 1997: Russian, Uzbek, Tajik, and Kyrgyz leaders meet in the Uzbek capital, Tashkent, to plan a joint response to the Taliban threat.

18 March 1997: Explosion in a major arms and ammunition dump in Jalalabad which left 30 dead and 191 injured.

21 March 1997: Lt.-Col. Javaid Iqbal of the Anti-narcotics Force (ANF), along with seven others, arrested by the Taliban security agencies for entering Afghanistan without proper authority.

23 March 1997: Mullah Mohammad Rabbani, Chairman of the Caretaker Council, requests the OIC members present at the Extraordinary Session of the OIC held at Islamabad on 23 March 1997 to extend maximum possible help to the Afghan people.

19 May 1997: General Abdul Malik Pehalwan revolts against Abdul Rashid Dostum, triggering his downfall.

24 May 1997: Taliban forces, along with troops loyal to General Malik, enter Mazar-e-Sharif and Shiberghan, headquarters of Abdul Rashid Dostum, who flees to Turkey with his family. Rabbani joins Hikmetyar in Tehran.

25 May 1997: Pakistan accords formal recognition to the Taliban government.

28 May 1997: Fighting erupts between Taliban and Shi'ite Hizb-e-Wahdat and supporters of General Abdul Malik. Taliban troops pushed out of Mazar-e-Sharif by General Malik's forces. Mullah Abdul Razzaq, Governor of Herat, Foreign Minister Mullah Mohammad Ghaus, and Afghanistan's State Bank Governor, Maulvi Ihsanullah, along with hundreds of Taliban fighters, captured by General Malik.

29 May 1997: Fighting spreads north of Kabul as Ahmed Shah Masood battles with the Taliban for control of the strategic town of Jabal-us-Siraj at the mouth of the Salang Pass. Rabbani returns to Afghanistan. About 3,000 Taliban are besieged in Kunduz on the northern side of the Salang Tunnel.

31 May 1997: General Humayun Fauzi claims to be holding 10,000 Taliban prisoners.

15 June 1997: Anti-Taliban allies form a parallel government in northern Afghanistan comprising Burhanuddin Rabbani (Tajik), the Uzbek General Abdul Malik, and a faction of the Shia Hizb-e-Wahdat.

18 June 1997: Taliban troops, who were surrounded by Malik's forces in Kunduz and compelled to lay down their arms, occupy the city and raise their white flags with the help of the local Pushtun population in an Uzbek-dominated province.

18 June 1997: Pakistan embarks on yet another attempt to bring about a broad-based government in Afghanistan.

3 July 1997: Taliban elements in Kunduz, supported by local Pushtuns, attack Taloqan (Takhar).

5 July 1997: Pakistan recalls its staff from Mazar-e-Sharif when General Malik cannot guarantee their safety.

15 July 1997: Isolated pockets of Taliban in Kunduz continue probing forward. Chardara attacked and taken.

15 July 1997: General Abdul Malik declares Mazar-e-Sharif the capital of northern Afghanistan.

20 July 1997: Anti-Taliban leaders visit Iran.

20 July 1997: Anti-Taliban forces recapture Charikar and Bagram airbase and reach to within twenty kilometres of Kabul.

28 July 1997: Agreement signed in Islamabad between Government of Pakistan and the US firm Unocal for construction of a gas pipeline from Turkmenistan to Pakistan through Afghanistan.

31 July 1997: UN Secretary-General appoints Algerian diplomat Lakhdar Brahimi to report on the situation in Afghanistan.

10 August 1997: Fierce fighting north of Kabul breaks eighteen days of deadlock.

16 August 1997: Shadow government formed by the Northern Alliance.

21 August 1997: Malik and Dostum's forces clash in Mazar-e-Sharif.

23 August 1997: Abdul Rahim Ghafoorzai, the newly-appointed Prime Minister of the Northern Alliance, dies in a plane crash.

27 August 1997: Opposition forces claim gains in Nangarhar.

2 September 1997: Taliban sign an agreement with head of the UNDP, James Speth, designed to improve relations between the Islamic militia and the international aid organizations.

5 September 1997: Mullah Mohammad Rabbani, Chief of the Taliban Interim Council, visits Saudi Arabia.

8 September 1997: Taliban capture Tashkurgan, twenty-five kilometres from Mazar-e-Sharif, with the help of local supporters who switched sides to join the student militia.

9 September 1997: Taliban overrun Mazar-e-Sharif airport and enter the outskirts of the city.

11 September 1997: Three planes belonging to the anti-Taliban forces land in Herat after their pilots decide to defect.
Taliban forces are pushed back to Tashkurgan.
General Abdul Rashid Dostum arrives back in Mazar-e-Sharif and begins to regain control.

17 September 1997: Taliban capture the strategic town of Hairatan, a river port on the Amu Darya, opposite the Uzbek city of Termez.

September-October 1997: Fierce fighting rages on the outskirts of Mazar-e-Sharif.

7 October 1997: Anti-Taliban forces succeed in recapturing Hairatan and Mazar-e-Sharif.

11 October 1997: Taliban compelled to withdraw from Tashkurgan (Samangan) and fall back to their pocket in Kunduz.

8 August 1998: Mazar-e-Sharif over run by the Taliban

20 August 1998: US launch a missile strike on Khost in an effort to eliminate Osama Bin Laden.

September 1998: Bamian falls to the Taliban.

September 1998: Iran closes its borders with the Taliban held areas

9 December 1998: UN adopts Resolution No 1214 calling on the Taliban to cease fire, stop shielding terrorists and enter into peace talks with the opposition factions.

10-14 March 1999: Ashkabad talks between the Taliban and the anti-Taliban Alliance, which began well, ended in a fiasco.

April 1999: Bamian re-captured by the anti-Taliban Alliance.

May 1999: Taliban re-take Bamian

15 October 1999: UN Resolution No 1267 adopted demanding that the Taliban hand over Osama Bin Laden.

14 November 1999: UN imposes economic sanctions on the Taliban for refusing to evict Osama Bin Laden.

November 1999: Iran opens its borders with the Taliban held areas.

December 1999: Taliban assist the Indian delegation in getting the release of the passengers and crew of a hijacked Indian Airlines plane, which had been forced to land at Kandahar by the hijackers.

NOTES

1. Ahmed Khan, a Saddozai Pushtun of the Abdali tribe, was elected Shah of Afghanistan after the assassination of the Persian ruler Nadir Shah whose rule extended right up to the Indus. Ahmed Khan was crowned in Kandahar in 1747 and assumed the title of Durr-i-Durran (pearl of pearls). Since then the Abdalis began to be known as Durranis.
2. K. Matinuddin, *Power Struggle in the Hindu Kush*, Wajidalis, Lahore, 1990.
3. Olaf Caroe, *The Pathans*, Oxford University Press, Karachi, 1958, p. 252.
4. K. Matinuddin, op. cit., p. 14.
5. Kamal Matinuddin, *The News*, 9 February 1994.
6. For details, *see*, K. Matinuddin, *Power Struggle in the Hindu Kush*, pp. 266-301.
7. *The News*, 11 December 1992.
8. Ibid.
9. *The News*, 9 February 1994.
10. *The Frontier Post*, 19 June 1994.
11. Interview, Mullah Shahabuddin, Consul-General of the Islamic Republic of Afghanistan in Peshawar.
12. *The Frontier Post*, 1 June 1994
13. Interview, Col. Imam, an official of the Government of Pakistan with considerable expertise on Afghan affairs.
14. Interview, Haji Abdul Qadeer, former Governor of Nangarhar province.
15. Interview, General Mirza Aslam Beg, former Chief of Army Staff, Pakistan.
16. *The Nation*, 28 February 1995.
17. Interview, Lt.-Gen. (retd.) Hamid Gul, former Director General, Inter Services Intelligence Directorate, Pakistan.
18. Interview, Haji Abdul Qadeer.
19. Interview, Mullah Shahabuddin, Consul-General of the Taliban regime in Peshawar.
20. Interview, Mufti Mohammad Masoom Afghani, Ambassador-Designate of the Taliban regime in Islamabad.
21. Interview, Haji Abdul Qadeer, Governor of Nangarhar province during the Rabbani regime.

22. Interview, Mullah Shahabuddin.
23. *The News*, 27 April 1995.
24. *The Nation*, 20 February 1995.
25. Interview, Anwarul Haq, Deputy Administrator, Darul Uloom Haqqania, Akora Khattak, NWFP, Pakistan.
26. Interview, Anwarul Haq.
27. Interview, Anwarul Haq.
28. Abu Daud, *Tafsir ul Quran*, Vol. 3, p. 384, as quoted by Justice Aftab Hussain, 'Status of Women in Islam', Law Publishing Company, Lahore, 1987, p. 155.
29. Eqbal Ahmed, *Dawn*, 23 July 1995.
30. *The News*, 11 May 1997.
31. Interview, Mufti Mohammad Masoom Afghani, representative of the Taliban controlled areas of Afghanistan in Islamabad.
32. Interview, Ijlal Haider Zaidi, adviser to Prime Minister Bhutto in her second government.
33. *The Muslim*, 21 February 1995.
34. *The Frontier Post*, 20 June 1994.
35. Ijlal Haider Zaidi.
36. Rahimullah Yusafzai, *The News*, 4 October 1996.
37. The Daily *Zarb-e-Momin*, Karachi, 11-17 February 1997. A pro-Taliban weekly newspaper.
38. Interview, Colonel Imam, Head of the Pakistani Mission in Herat.
39. Interview, Mufti Mahmood Masoom Afghani.
40. Interview, Mullah Shahabuddin, Consul-General of the Taliban in Peshawar.
41. List compiled by Dr Syed Sher Ali Shah, in Arabic, at Khadima al Hadith al Nabavi, Miran Shah (NWFP), p. 10
42. Interview, Syed Hamid Gailani.
43. Interview, Haji Abdul Qadeer, Governor of Nangarhar.
44. L. Dupree, *Afghanistan*, Princeton University, New Jersey, 1973, pp. 59-64.
45. Konishi Masatoshi, *Afghanistan*, Kodansha International Ltd., Tokyo, 1963, p. 15.
46. The Pushtun heartland areas are Zabul, Paktia, and Paktika.
47. Kamal Siddiqui, *Friday Times*, 30 May-5 June, 1997.
48. *The News*, 16 March 1996.
49. Interview, Lt.-Gen. (retd.) Hamid Gul, former Director-General, Inter Services Intelligence Directorate, Islamabad.
50. Interview, Haji Qadeer Khan.
51. Interview, Mullah Shahabuddin, Consul-General of the Islamic Government of Afghanistan in Peshawar.
52. Interview, Ijlal Haider Zaidi, adviser on Afghanistan to the second Benazir government and member of the Pakistan negotiating team in 1996.

53. Interview, Lt.-Gen. (retd.) Hamid Gul.
54. Directive of the *Amirul Momineen*, published in the daily *Zarb-e-Momin*, 28 March-4 April 1997.
55. *The News*, 10 December 1996.
56. Eqbal Ahmed.
57. *International Herald Tribune*, London, 20 February 1996.
58. *International Herald Tribune*, London, 20 February 1996.
59. Afghan refugees interviewed at the Akora Khattak refugee camp established primarily for those who had moved into Pakistan after the Taliban had taken over their areas.
60. *International Herald Tribune*, February 1996.
61. Interview, Anwarul Haq, at Akora Khattak.
62. *The News*, 4 March 1997.
63. *The News*, 24 March 1997.
64. Interview, Qazi Hussain Ahmed, head of the Jamaat-i-Islami, Pakistan, and one who was very close to some of the ultra-conservative Afghan leaders.
65. Mark L. Urban, *War in Afghanistan*, St. Martin's Press, New York, 1988, p. 226.
66. *The News*, 27 April 1995.
67. M.L. Urban, op. cit., p. 230.
68. Interview, Ijlal Haider Zaidi.
69. Interview, Percy Abole, UN representative on Afghanistan.
70. *The News*, 20 April 1995.
71. *The Far Eastern Economic Review*, 1 February 1996.
72. Afrasiab Khattak, *The Frontier Post*, 28 February 1995.
73. Rahimullah Yusafzai, *The News*, 15 November 1996.
74. Interview, Haji Abdul Qadeer, former Governor of Nangarhar
75. Interview, Maj.-Gen. (retd.) Naseerullah Khan Babar.
76. *Washington Post*, 30 October 1996
77. Interview, Mullah Shahabuddin, Consul-General of Afghanistan in Peshawar.
78. *The Frontier Post*, 18 July 1994.
79. Interview, Col. Imam.
80. Interview, Amir Usman, Ambassador of Pakistan in Afghanistan (1992-5).
81. Interview, Col. Imam.
82. *The Frontier Post*, 4 November 1994.
83. Interview, Maj.-Gen. (retd.) Naseerullah Khan Babar.
84. *The Frontier Post*, 4 November 1994.
85. *The Frontier Post*, 6 November 1994.
86. *The News*, 5 January 1995.
87. *Herald*, February 1995, p. 55.
88. Ibid., p. 56.

89. *The Nation*, 20 February 1995.
90. *The News*, 15 February 1995.
91. *Time* Magazine, 27 February 1995, p. 15.
92. K. Matinuddin, op. cit., p. 156.
93. Rahimullah Yusufzai, *The News*, 15 November 1996.
94. Interview Haji Qadeer Khan, former Governor of Nangarhar.
95. Report of the UN Secretary-General, A/51/698, S/1996/988 dated 26 November 1996, to the 51st Session of the General Assembly, agenda item 39, p. 4.
96. *The Economist*, 28 October 1996.
97. Briefing by Professor Raja Ahsan Aziz, International Affairs Department , Quaid-i-Azam University, Islamabad, who claimed to have ventured 3,000 kilometres inside Taliban-controlled Afghanistan.
98. *Washington Post*, 30 October 1996.
99. *The News*, 27 January 1997.
100. *The News*, 1 February 1997.
101. *The News*, 12 February 1997.
102. *The News*, 25 May 1997.
103. *The News*, 25 May 1997.
104. *Defence Journal*, Golden Jubilee issue, August 1947, p. 111
105. Interview, Masoom Afghani.
106. *Dawn*, 29 June 1997.
107. *The News*, 19 June 1997.
108. *The News*, 20 March 1996.
109. *The News*, 12 February 1996.
110. *The News*, 29 March 1996.
111. *The News*, 20 March 1996.
112. UNDCP Update, 2 January 1997, p. 3.
113. Ibid.
114. *The News*, 11 March 1997.
115. *Washington Post*, 21 November 1996.
116. Afghan Opium Poppy Survey, 1995, pp. 17&18, UNDCP.
117. UNDCP Report, September 1996, p. 12.
118. *The News*, 28 October 1996.
119. *The News*, 27 January 1997.
120. *Herald*, Karachi, February 1995, p, 56.
121. *Washington Post*, 11 May 1997.
122. *The Nation*, 3 July 1994.
123. *Far Eastern Economic Review*, 1 February 1996.
124. *The News*, 6 March 1996.
125. Interview, Maj.-Gen. (retd.) Naseerullah Khan Babar.
126. *The News*, 14 March 1996.

127. *The News*, 16 March 1996.
128. *The News*, 14 March 1996.
129. BBC News.
130. *The News*, 9 February 1996.
131. Interview, Ijlal Haider Zaidi.
132. *The News*, 12 May 1997.
133. Discussion with Shamshad Ahmed, Foreign Secretary of Pakistan.
134. *The News*, June 1997.
135. *The News*, 31 January 1997.
136. Interview, Lt.-Gen. Sahibzada Yaqub Khan, former Foreign Minister of Pakistan.
137. *Writers Union of Free Afghanistan* (WUFA), Peshawar, issue No. 6, December 1995.
138. *Far Eastern Economic Review*, 1 February 1996.
139. *The News*, 13 February 1996.
140. *The News*, 12 February 1996.
141. *The News*, 19 May 1996.
142. *The News*, 5 March 1996.
143. *The News*, 17 April 1996.
144. *The News*, 18 April 1996.
145. *The News*, 27 January 1997.
146. Interview, Mohammad Mehdi Akhundzadeh, Ambassador of the Islamic Republic of Iran in Islamabad.
147. *The International Herald Tribune*, 20 February 1996.
148. According to a statement made by former US Ambassador Dennis Kux, at a seminar held in Islamabad.
149. *The International Herald Tribune*, 20 February 1996.
150. Interview, Thomas W. Simons, Ambassador of the United States to Pakistan.
151. *The International Herald Tribune*, 20 February 1996.
152. Agha Murtaza Poya, Chairman of the Institute of Strategic Studies, Islamabad.
153. Interview, Ambassador W. Simons.
154. United States Information Service, Islamabad, Official Text of Ambassador Gneham's Remarks.
155. *The News*, 11 May 1996.
156. *The News*, 21 April 1996.
157. *The Globe*, 27 February 1997.
158. *Washington Post*, 21 November 1996.
159. *Washington Post*, 21 November 1996.
160. *Washington Post*, 21 November 1996.
161. *The News*, 6 March 1996.
162. *The News*, 15 May 1997.

163. Gufran, Nasreen, *International Seminar on Central Asia*, Area Study Centre Central Asia, University of Peshawar, 1996, p. 146.

164. *Central Asian Significants/Political News*, Number 51, June 1992, p. 9.

165. Ibid.

166. *The Nation*, 2 February 1995.

167. *The Far Eastern Economic Review*, 1 February 1996.

168. *The News*, 16 September 1997.

169. Interview, His Excellency, Satish Chandra, High Commissioner for the Republic of India to Pakistan.

170. *The Frontier Post*, 16 July 1994.

171. *The Muslim*, 20 March 1995.

172. *The Frontier Post*, 22 December 1994.

173. *Far Eastern Economic Review*, 1 February 1997.

174. *Indian Express*, 23 January 1996.

175. *Economic Times*, New Delhi, 9 January 1994.

176. Ibid.

177. Boutros-Boutros Ghali, *Confronting New Challenges*, Annual Report of the Work of the United Nations, 1995, p. 230.

178. Ibid., pp. 230&231.

179. Ibid.

180. Boutros-Boutros Ghali, Secretary-General of the United Nations, Confronting New Challenges, Annual Report of the Working of the Organization, 1995 p. 231, para 615.

181. *The Nation*, 20 February 1995.

182. *The News*, 20 April 1996.

183. *The Far Eastern Economic Review*, 2 May 1996.

184. *The News*, 30 January 1997.

185. *The Frontier Post*, 16 July 1997.

186. *The Frontier Post*, 8 December 1994.

187. *The News*, 23 April 1997.

188. *Baltimore Sun*, 19 March 1997.

189. *Washington Post*, 18 June 1997.

190. K. Matinuddin, op. cit., p. 328.

191. Interview, Lt.-Gen. (retd.) Nishat Ahmed, formerly Commandant National Defence College, Islamabad.

192. Eyewitness account by Ms Megan Reif, a Fulbright scholar, who came across him during her visit to Kandahar in April 1997.

193. *New York Times*, 14 October 1996.

GLOSSARY

Amir	Leader
Amirul Momineen	Leader of the Faithful
Badla	Revenge
Bad-e-Naseem	Fresh breeze
Bad-e-Simoom	Hot desert wind
Burqa	Veil worn by Muslim women from head to toe
Deeni madaris	Religious schools
Deobandi	One who follows the teachings of the Deoband school of Muslim theology
Durrani	A branch of the Pushtun tribe in Afghanistan
Fatwa	A religious edict given by a learned mullah
Fiqah	The Islamic Penal Code
Gilzai	A branch of the Pushtun tribe in Afghanistan
Imam	A person who leads the prayers
Islam pasand	A party or a person oriented towards Islam
Jabha	A group of people, generally refers to a political party
Jadeedi	Modern
Jihad	Religious war
Jirga	A collection of notables and tribal elders chosen to give decisions on important issues
Jizya	Compulsory tax on non-Muslims living in an Islamic state in lieu of protection provided to them; they

	are exempt from other religious taxes imposed on Muslims
Jumbish-e-Milli	Abdul Rashid Dostum's political party
Haji	A Muslim who has performed the pilgrimage to Mecca
Kalima	Holy verses proclaiming that there is no other God but Allah
Khatib	A person who delivers an address before the commencement of Friday prayers
Khulafa-e-Rashideen	The first four Caliphs of Islam
Madrassa	Religious school, plural *madaris*
Maslak	A school of thought in Islam
Mujahid	One who fights for the cause of Islam
Mufti	Head of an Islamic court
Mullah	A person who has completed his studies at a religious institution
Naib	Second-in-Command
Nau Roz	Iranian New Year celebrating the advent of spring
Pawanda	A gypsy
Pir	A revered leader
Qadeemi	Ancient
Qari	One who recites the Holy Koran on designated occasions
Qayadi shoora	Leadership Council
Qazi	A Muslim judge who gives his verdict in accordance with the Islamic code
Shariah	The Muslim code of religious law
Shoora	A body of people nominated or elected for the purpose of running the affairs of the state
Shoora-e-Hal-o-Aqd	A handpicked gathering of persons loyal to President Burhanuddin Rabbani

Shoora-e-Ham-Ahangi	Supreme Co-ordinating Council of the Islamic Revolution of Afghanistan
Shoora Nazar	Ahmed Shah Masood's fighters
Silsila	Followers of a line of religious teachers
Talib	Student. In Pushto *talib* generally denotes a student of a religious institution
Taliban	Plural of *talib*
Tanzeemat	A collection of the original seven political factions
Tawaif-ul-Maluki	Free-for-all

BIBLIOGRAPHY

Interviews

Afghan Personalities

Haji Abdul Qadeer Khan, former Governor of Nangarhar.

Hamed Karzai, a western-educated Afghan who was present in Kandahar when the Taliban movement started.

Humayun Shah Asefi, former Afghan diplomat in the Daud government.

Mufti Mohammad Masoom Afghani, Ambassador-Designate of the Taliban-controlled areas of the Islamic Republic of Afghanistan.

Mohammad Sharif, Afghan national, Daulatzai Pushtun, resident of Kabul, farmer, stayed about a month under the Taliban administration.

Mohammad Yusuf, Tajik, mechanic in the Afghan transport system, was a *talib* in Darul Uloom Hanafia, Kabul, and migrated to Pakistan after the fall of Kabul.

Naseer Mohammad, Afghan national, Pushtun, resident of Laghman province, cloth shopkeeper in Kabul, migrated to Pakistan in March 1997.

Nisar Ahmed, Afghan national, Tajik, assistant police sub-inspector in Rabbani's regime who remained in Kabul for four months after it fell to the Taliban.

Painda Khan, Afghan national, Tajik, resident of Charikar, Parwan, labourer, came to Pakistan in February 1997.

Rasul Amin, Director, Writers Union of Free Afghanistan.

Mullah Shahabuddin, Consul-General of the Tailban regime in Peshawar.

Sharif Mohammad, Kata Khel Pushtun, resident of Kabul, working in the Ministry of Finance under the Rabbani regime, migrated to Pakistan in February 1997.

Syed Hamid Gailani, National Islamic Front of Afghanistan (NIFA).

Zalme Khalilzad, American-Afghan, Rand Corporation, USA.

Pakistani Personalities

Lt.-Gen. Sahibzada Yaqub Khan, former Foreign Minister, Government of Pakistan.

Ijlal Haider Zaidi, adviser to the second Benazir government on Afghanistan.

Maj.-Gen. (retd.) Naseerullah Khan Babar, Interior Minister in the second Benazir government and directly involved in negotiations with the Taliban and anti-Taliban factions.

Ambassador Abdus Sattar, former Foreign Secretary, Government of Pakistan.

Ambassador Amir Usman, Ambassador of Pakistan in Afghanistan from 1992-5

Ambassador Iftikhar Murshid, Additional Secretary, Afghanistan and Central Asia, Ministry of Foreign Affairs, Government of Pakistan.

Mohammad Abdul Naeem, Director, Afghanistan and Central Asia, Ministry of Foreign Affairs, Government of Pakistan.

Colonel Imam, Consul-General of Pakistan in Herat.

General Mirza Aslam Beg, former Chief of Army Staff, Pakistan Army, and Chairman, Foundation for Research on National Development and Security (FRIENDS).

Lt.-Gen. Arif Bangash, Governor of the North-West Frontier Province. (1997-)

Lt.-Gen. (retd.) Hamid Gul, former Director-General, Inter Services Intelligence Directorate (ISI), Pakistan.

Lt.-Gen. (retd.) Nishat Ahmed, President, Institute of Regional Studies, Islamabad, and former Commandant of the National Defence College, Islamabad.

Brigadier Bashir Ahmed, senior research fellow, Institute of Regional Studies, Islamabad.

Agha Murtaza Poya, Chairman of the Institute of Strategic Studies, Islamabad.

Fazalur Rahman, senior research fellow, Institute of Strategic Studies, Islamabad.

Brigadier Ibrahim Qureishi, former Ambassador of Pakistan and author of *Muslim Minorities*.

Dr Azmat Hayat Khan, Director, Area Study Centre, Central Asia, University of Peshawar.

Rahimullah Yusafzai, journalist who, until 1997, was the only Pakistani to have interviewed Mullah Omar.

Brigadier (retd.) Jamshed Ali Khan, Chief Commissioner for Afghan Refugees, Islamabad.

Mohammad Yunus Khan, District Administrator, Afghan Refugees, Peshawar.

Dr Ahmed Hasan Dani, internationally-known archaeologist and historian, an expert on Central Asia including Afghanistan.

Dr Ejaz Shafi Gilani, Director, Asia Study Centre, Islamabad, and a former co-author of the monthly *Afghanistan Report*.

Qazi Hussain Ahmed, Chief of the Jamaat-e-Islami Pakistan

Anwarul Haq, Chief of the Jamiat-Ulema-e-Islam (JUI), head of the Darul Uloom Haqqania, Akora Khattak, NWFP, where Afghan *talibs* are studying, and brother of Senator Samiul Haq.

Professor Raja Ehsan Aziz, Independent Bureau for Humanitarian Issues, Islamabad.

Foreign Personalities

Thomas W. Simons, Ambassador of the United States in Pakistan.

Satish Chandra, High Commissioner for India in Islamabad.

Mohammad Mehdi Akhundzadeh, Ambassador of the Islamic Republic of Iran in Pakistan.

Sita Moss, German lady who stayed in Afghanistan for twenty-six days in connection with her book on the Taliban.

Percy Abole, Canadian national on the staff of Mahmoud Mestiri, UNS-G's Special Representative on Afghanistan.

Mrs Megan Reif, an American Fulbright scholar, who went to Afghanistan and interviewed important Taliban and anti-Taliban personalities.

Books, Periodicals and Newspapers Consulted

Books

1. Matinuddin, K., *Power Struggle in the Hindu Kush, (Afghanistan 1978-91)*, Wajidalis, Lahore.

2. Yousaf, Brig. M. and Adkin, M., (1995) *The Bear Trap*, Jang Publishers, Lahore, pp. 84-7.

3. Caroe, O., (1983), *The Pathans*, Oxford University Press, Karachi.

4. Rais, R.B., (1994), *War Without Winners*, Oxford University Press, Karachi.

5. Dupree, L., (1973), *Afghanistan*, Princeton University Press, Princeton, New Jersey.

Magazines

Herald, Karachi.

Newsline, Karachi.

Globe, Karachi.

Times

Newsweek

Newspapers

The News, Dawn, The Nation, Washington Post, The New York Times, International Herald Tribune, Daily Telegraph.

INDEX